Everywhere and Nowhere

Everywhere and Nowhere

Contemporary Feminism in the United States

JO REGER

New York Oxford

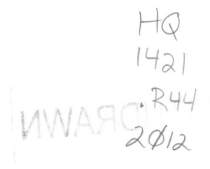

OXFORD
UNIVERSITY PRESS

OXFORD
UNIVERSITY PRESS

Oxford University Press, Inc., publishes works that further
Oxford University's objective of excellence
in research, scholarship, and education.

Oxford   New York
Auckland   Cape Town   Dar es Salaam   Hong Kong   Karachi
Kuala Lumpur   Madrid   Melbourne   Mexico City   Nairobi
New Delhi   Shanghai   Taipei   Toronto

With offices in
Argentina   Austria   Brazil   Chile   Czech Republic   France   Greece
Guatemala   Hungary   Italy   Japan   Poland   Portugal   Singapore
South Korea   Switzerland   Thailand   Turkey   Ukraine   Vietnam

Published by Oxford University Press, Inc.
198 Madison Avenue, New York, New York 10016

www.oup.com

Oxford is a registered trademark of Oxford University Press

Library of Congress Cataloging-in-Publication Data
Reger, Jo, 1962–
Everywhere and nowhere : contemporary feminism in the United States / Jo Reger.
    p.   cm.
Includes bibliographical references and index.
ISBN 978-0-19-986199-6 (cloth : alk. paper) — ISBN 978-0-19-986198-9 (pbk. : alk. paper)
1. Feminism—United States. 2. Feminists—United States. I. Title.
HQ1421.R44   2011
305.420973—dc23   2011026164

Printed in the United States of America
on acid-free paper

To my family who taught me how you can be small but mighty, fight cancerous foes, always be ready to rescue and make beauty out of life's driftwood. I thank you for all your lessons.

Table of Contents

Acknowledgments

ONE OF THE nice things about finishing a book is having a moment to reflect upon the incredible journey of researching, thinking, writing, and revising, revising, revising. I have had the extraordinarily good fortune to be surrounded by a community of scholars, friends and family who have supported and encouraged me during this entire decade-long project. Some have been constants in my life and others are newly discovered but each is equally treasured.

I began this project in earnest at Oakland University when my then-chair Professor David Maines got all incoming junior faculty a "start-up" research fund. Dave, in his brilliance, realized that social scientists, like those in other fields, need support and so I began my time at Oakland with money to use for travel, transcribing, conferences and other expenses. Oakland University also granted me two summer fellowships, which allowed me to dedicate my time to focusing on my research and writing. The brilliance of one chair was replaced by another, Professor Jay Meehan. Jay listened to my (almost constant) complaints about finding time to write and research and found travel money to allow me to collaborate with colleagues who helped me think through this project. I thank both of these men.

From the start I drew on the scholarly foundation provided by my graduate school advisor Professor Verta Taylor. Because of Verta, and her work with Leila Rupp, I had a breadth and depth of knowledge that was invaluable in puzzling out the direction of contemporary feminism. I also have depended on (as with all my work) my colleague and friend Nancy Whittier for her wise work and words. In other places, I have called her my touchstone and I again invoke this description—thank you, Nancy.

And then there are the colleagues who read my work and offered insightful comments. Thank you to Rachel Einwohner, Stephanie Gilmore, Laura Landolt and Judy Taylor, who all read some version of the work that appears in this book. My pal and colleague, retired Dean Julie Voelck, read every single word of this manuscript as my proofreader and offered encouragement along with the edit-ing. I cannot thank her enough. I would also like to thank the undergraduate research assistants who participated in this work: Lacey Story, Ashley McGhee, Heather Brewer and Amanda Deschamps, who edited this volume as I prepared it for publication. I also drew upon colleagues such as Dave Maines, Julie Wal-ters, Laura Landolt and Karen Markel to help me over the sticky intellectual (or emotional) spots. Sometimes it was just Karen or Laura asking how it was going that helped me stay on track. I also thank my "new" friends, Laurie Fortlage and Susan Webb, for their ongoing interest in this project. (I always appreciate a chance to talk about my work.) And then there are the countless articles, Web sites and blogs forwarded to me that play a crucial role in this analysis. Thank you to all who thought of me and continue to send me items of interest. In particular, I thank Professor Linda Morrison and that voracious reader Fred Will.

I also would like to thank James Cook, my editor at Oxford, for handing me one of the central premises of the book—the "everywhere and nowhere" of con-temporary feminism—and to the anonymous reviewers for their comments and questions. The manuscript is much stronger because of his insight and the proc-ess of review.

When I think back on what really helped me get this book finished, it is clear that without yoga and coffee shops (with lots of really dark, strong coffee) I would still be searching for ways to get focused and get the writing done. Thank you to yoga teachers Lynne and Patty for making me focus on my intentions on the mat and helping me take those intentions to computer. In addition to yoga, I found a support network through Facebook. Thank you to everyone who gave encouraging comments when I needed them (or made me laugh—ahem, brother Jim). I also thank my family for their love and support. And just as coffee, yoga and my family brought me joy and comfort, so do the two most important peo-ple in my life—Faith and Angel. With an Angel and Faith on my side, how could I possibly give up or fail? I thank you both just for being who you are and making time away from the computer feel rich and rejuvenating.

However, the most important acknowledgment I have to make is to the fem-inists who took me in, answered my questions and shared their lives. I find their enthusiasm, intelligence and feminist grace truly inspirational, particularly in a time when feminism is lauded as nowhere, yet embedded everywhere. You fig-ured it out, and I thank you for sharing your world and your insights with me. I hope I have done your lives justice.

Everywhere and Nowhere

Introduction

The Everywhere and Nowhere of U.S. Feminism in the Twenty-first Century

WHO ARE WE?

The Forum for Women is a matrimony of outspoken, ballsy girls. We're pissed. We're driven. We're going to get things done. Raise your hand if you dare. We may just enlighten you. We are the third wave of feminists who aren't afraid to stand up, step forward and get on top of that damn soapbox. We understand what it means to be ourselves. We have what it takes to raise our voices and tell it like it is. We know what we want, and by any means, we'll get it. We're tired of making sixty-four cents to their dollar. Our attitudes and opinions are anything but timid. Boys, don't worry, we're not man-eating barbarians. We like men. They're okay. However, some of us like women more. A lot more. Our message is haunting. Tongue-in-cheek. Risqué. Loud. Witty. Feminine. We're a kaleidoscope of cultures and backgrounds. Some of us fancy skirts while others opt for jeans and sweatshirts. But we all have one thing in common. We love being women. And quite frankly, we love our vaginas. Unabashedly outspoken, we are the luminous, uncompromising women of this generation. We will not allow for those women who came before us to be forgotten. We're inspired by our foremothers; for all of their contributions and achievements. Together, we will make a difference. We have what it takes. We are more than just the Forum for Women. We are a family.

That's who we are.

—Student group, Forum for Women
  Woodview University, 2005

At a university in the Midwest, Jaclyn, the twenty-year-old vice president of Forum for Women (FFW), pens these words as the mission statement for her group. To Jaclyn and the other group members, becoming a feminist is a powerful statement in their lives—one that explains the forces of injustice, prejudice and discrimination in the world around them. However, their enthusiasm for feminism can be puzzling when juxtaposed against the constant negative hype about contemporary feminism. Written in the first decade of the twenty-first century, the group's belief that feminism is relevant as a life-empowering ideology stands in strong contrast to the pervasive public discourse that feminism is dead, and no one, particularly young women, is interested anymore. This contradiction between the adoption of feminism and antifeminist declarations is not a new phenomenon. Social commentators have continually seen feminism as "nowhere," meaning no longer relevant or present in American society. Obituaries for feminism reoccur throughout the history of the movement. For example, the movement, after activists obtained the right to vote in 1920, was declared dead by the 1950s, due to media reports of happy homemakers who had no interest in feminism.[1] A contemporary obit is the 1998 *Time* magazine's cover story, "Is Feminism Dead?" complete with pictures of Susan B. Anthony, Betty Friedan, Gloria Steinem and TV character Ally McBeal in which the author claimed, "If feminism of the '60s and '70s was steeped in research and obsessed with social change, feminism today is wed to the culture of celebrity and self-obsession."[2] This quote illustrates that in addition to death notices, ridicule is also an aspect of the media's relationship with the women's movement. Take, for instance, the history of the Riot Grrrl uprising in the Northwest in the early 1990s. The emergence of a young, punk-infused feminism quickly became the focus of "dismissive, sexist and condescending" media coverage.[3] This coverage was so dismaying to women prominent in Riot Grrrl organizations that they declared a media blackout. While it effectively shut down the ridicule of feminism, it also ended any cultural discussion of the continued vitality of feminism.

Contemporary obits continue this combination of silencing and ridicule by stating that the nationally visible, organized and institutionally focused (alive) feminism of the 1960s and 1970s is gone and in its place is a (dead) apolitical feminism concerned with dress, appearance, and individualized empowerment.[4] Titles such as "Where to Pass the Torch?" (*New York Times*, 2009) and "The End of the Women's Movement" (*The American Prospect*, 2009) continue to surface in the media.[5] But why these repeated declarations of the end of feminism? Feminist scholars argue that these notices are not so much an appraisal of the movement but instead a strategy aimed at silencing it.[6] Myra Marx Ferree argues that movements that seek to change societal values, ideas and norms often face "soft repression," which she defines as the "means to silence or eradicate oppositional ideas."[7] Regardless of their intent, these obits serve to make young feminists who continue to identify and work in the movement invisible to the mainstream public.

While the declaration of the death of feminism is not new, there is a new twist. A number of older feminists are stepping forward to label contemporary feminism as apolitical and ineffectual. For example, longtime feminist Letty Cottin Pogrebin addressed young feminists at the 2002 Veteran Feminists of America conference by saying:

> We were action-oriented in a public, political context. We had to challenge laws, change patterns, alter behavior. Being able to bare your midriff . . . is fine as an expression, but it doesn't mean things are going to change.[8]

Phyllis Chesler, another longtime feminist, starts out her essay, "The Failure of Feminism," with the line "Is feminism really dead? Well, yes and no."[9] Pogrebin and Chesler are not antifeminists; instead they are two of many older activists who see young feminists as too concerned with the popular culture. They charge contemporary feminists with being too involved in sexual empowerment ("being able to bare your midriff") and feminist consumption (such as buying into Nike's slogan of "Just Do It"),[10] and not engaged enough in legislative or policy change efforts. Aligned with the notion that contemporary feminism is nowhere (i.e., dead) is the idea that feminism is also "everywhere."

"Everywhere" in this context is the idea that as social movements continue over long periods of time, their ideas and goals are pervasive, becoming a part of every-day cultural beliefs and norms.[11] Just as contemporary feminists exist in a time when they are told feminism is nowhere, they also live in a time where feminism is everywhere. For example, I examine a college town on the East Coast where a feminist student group exists on paper but languishes in terms of activity. Lots of self-identified feminists in the community know of the group but seldom engage directly with women's rights issues. Instead their attention turns to issues of racism, homophobia and transgender rights. Yet when you question them about these issues, they view feminism as the root of their activism. Here feminism maintains its relevance but is submerged into other movements, issues and groups. Feminism, in this context, is a set of ideas and identities diffused into the culture and structure of society, and informs, sometimes unconsciously, the actions of these college students. In this community, as feminist authors Jennifer Baumgardner and Amy Richards are often quoted, "Feminism is like fluoride, it is simply in the water."[12] Or as Ednie Kaeh Garrison describes it, feminism is in the airwaves around us.[13] Important in both of the metaphors and in this college town is the idea of feminism as present and active, yet undetected—everywhere and nowhere.

In this book, I examine the vitality and continuity of the U.S. women's movement and explore the idea of a "nowhere-everywhere" feminism through an investigation of community-level activism. I explore how feminism is created in three different feminist social movement communities as a way of understanding how the movement continues to challenge the status quo and mainstream society on issues related to women's rights. These three feminist communities, in the Midwest, East Coast and the Northwest, vary in some aspects but also have similarities. The communities differ in the relevance of established feminist organizations and the relationship to other feminist generations. In terms of similarities, activists in all three communities continue to embrace feminist identities, adopt mainly culturally focused tactics and strategies, and struggle with issues of racism, inclusion and gender fluidity. All contain multiple layers of the movement from the presence of national groups to the creation of local organizations and grassroots networks—although in different formulations.

These differences and similarities I argue are the result of a political generation shaped by the cultural and political environment in a community context. A political generation is a group of people who share a similar political awakening brought about by societal changes. Political opportunity theorists posit that movements emerge and respond to favorable (or unfavorable) openings in the social environment.[14] As such, community environments can be hostile to activists' goals or facilitate them. For example, open or accepting political fields may include sympathetic elected leaders, the existence of related groups and organizations, or a community tradition of progressive politics. Hostile, or closed, political fields may contain political leaders or organizations antagonistic to activists' agendas. These openings or opportunities can also be cultural in nature.[15] For example, Kimberly Dugan in her study of a local antigay ballot proposal illustrates how gay, lesbian, bisexual and transgender activists lost a cultural battle against conservative Christian forces when Christian groups drew on the cultural opportunities (e.g., images of gay and lesbians wanting "special rights") available to them to create a more "believable" public image that helped uphold the ballot proposal.[16] Holly McCammon and her colleagues also found that the cultural context of a movement, in their case women's right to serve on juries, shaped the discourse of their struggles. They call this "a discursive opportunity structure," which shapes how movement actors put forth arguments.[17] This example illustrates how community environments can be hostile toward, neutral about or accepting politically and culturally of movements, which in turn shapes the way in which a political generation of activists does activism.[18] Applying these concepts of generations and opportunity structures allows me to see the diversity of feminist communities as opposed to painting all contemporary feminism in broad strokes.

By focusing on the community level, I offer a corrective to perceptions of the U.S. women's movement solely based on observations of a nationally organized feminist presence. A community analysis captures how feminism has always existed on multiple levels, from the national chapters to the grassroots networks, within feminist communities. This complexity is captured by Steven Buechler's concept of "social movement community" and Raka Ray's concept of "fields of action." Buechler argues that movements have always contained a variety of organizational forms and networks, and in social movement communities, activists are loosely connected through formal and informal organizations and networks. They share in a set of beliefs, ideas and goals for social change, and interact with and respond to other actors such as the state, political parties and social movement organizations.[19] Ray conceptualizes communities in a similar way, seeing them as places where activists function within a political field, which is defined as "a socially constructed environment [in] which organizations and activists constantly respond."[20]

It is the community complexity of social movements that allow movements to continue even when declared in decline on a national level. In their article "Whatever Happened to the Women's Movement?" Verta Taylor and Suzanne Staggenborg argue that:

> The women's movement survives to the extent that it has developed feminist "fields" in a variety of arenas, devised tactical repertoires that have challenged numerous authorities and cultural and political codes, and permeated other social movements and public consciousness.[21]

Taylor and Staggenborg point to the everywhere nature of feminist communities as important in the movement's continuity over time. By "permeating other social movements and public consciousness" in a variety of arenas, feminist communities are shifting contexts of interaction and response that contain multiple movement forms and tactics. By moving the analysis of the women's movement from a national organizational perspective, an examination of feminist communities offers a structural and cultural "slice" of multiple layers of activism from the national groups, such as the National Organization of Women (NOW), to the local organizations (such as Forum for Women) to the informally organized network of feminists. To understand where this sense of nowhere originates from, I examine the wave metaphor and how it shapes our understanding of U.S. feminism.

Rejecting the Wave Metaphor

One challenge in studying the continuity of U.S. feminism is the terminology used. The metaphor of ocean waves is central in most investigations of a feminist movement, evidenced by the common usage of it in articles and books.[22]

U.S. feminism is often presented in a series of waves, with the first taking place in the 1800s, the second rising in the 1960s and 1970s and a third cresting in the mid 1990s. There have also been numerous efforts to identify a "fourth" wave, with one woman I interviewed asking me if I thought we were in the "fifth wave" yet.[23] The idea of a wave fits with how social movement scholars argue that social change efforts come in cycles.[24] However, the wave metaphor in the women's movement is troubling to many. In 2010, the journal *Feminist Formations* dedicated almost sixty pages of essays by feminist historians critiquing the wave metaphor.[25] While it makes for a neat historical package when telling the history of the movement, the wave metaphor has been charged with leaving out the efforts of women of color, lesbian, poor and working-class women, "washing away" much of feminist history.[26] Too often, scholars charge, the history of the movement's rise and fall becomes one of white, middle-class women who were visible nationally.[27] Other scholars point out that women who come to feminism between waves are left with no defining terminology for themselves.[28] To that end, as someone who came into feminism in the Reagan era 1980s, I have been known to call myself a feminist "tweener," between the waves with no neat label. In addition, identifying by waves does not resonate with all feminists. As noted by Suzanne Beechey in her study of young women who work in feminist organizations, many had not heard of or did not identify with the idea of third wave; instead they chose to identify as simply "feminists."[29] In addition, social movement scholars are increasingly critiquing the idea that movements only exist when they focus on state-centered political change.[30] Overall, when the metaphor focuses on waves of state-centered national mobilization and these waves are not evident, the movement is perceived as being in decline or nowhere.

As a scholar investigating feminism in the late 1990s and twenty-first century, avoiding the reification of the wave metaphor is not easy. It does not work to talk about "today's feminism" (too temporally oriented) or "young" or younger feminists (too age oriented).[31] To avoid reifying "waves," I adopt the terms "contemporary feminism" (which still has some temporal connotations), referring to a feminist generation that emerges in the late twentieth and early twenty-first centuries, and "second-wave generation" to describe feminists coming of age in the 1960s and 1970s.[32] These feminist generations are the result of experience, ideologies and identities forged by the time they are living in and not by rates of mobilization or a type of activism evident in the overall movement. While not all activist generations are defined by age, in the case of contemporary feminism, I find this to be largely true of the participants in the communities studied. While some argue "third wavers" are under the age of thirty, others argue that any age range leaves out activists and stereotypes feminists by age.[33] While I agree that age ranges are problematic in characterizing contemporary feminism, age turns out to be an important factor in the communities studied.[34] The average age of the community respondents was 22½ years old in the college communities of the East and Midwest, with the Northwest having a slightly older population, the average being 26½ years old.[35] I speculate that this is because in earlier generations of feminism, particularly in the 1960s, women of all ages discovered it in a similar time span, often spurred by specific events. For current generations, feminism has been integrated into the U.S. landscape since the 1800s, leaving mostly a younger generation to come to a feminist identity for the first time.

Using the term "generation" allows me to situate different groups of feminists active in the movement without conceptualizing U.S. feminist activism as ending with one wave and beginning with another. By using the term "contemporary feminist," I draw upon ways in which interviewees conceptualize different generations of feminism as coexisting, yet having distinct differences. With this terminology, the movement becomes one of overlapping generations instead of waves framed by temporal events. This follows the thinking of Lelia Rupp and Verta Taylor who argue "that waves do not rise and crash independently of each other" and neither do these generations of feminists.[36] To show this interconnection, I employ social movement concepts to illustrate how the second-wave feminist generation influences contemporary feminism. Although feminist historians argue that the movement's history is problematic because of its reliance on waves as a central framework, I draw on various aspects of this history to illustrate the continuity and dynamics of the movement.[37]

Theory, History and Contemporary Feminism

Overall, the movement has had periods of growth and accomplishment as well as times of backlash and low mobilization. Working within these times are generations of activists who come to see the movement in a particular way based upon their own contexts. Throughout its history, feminist issues and corresponding tactics and strategies have ranged from institutionally focused to those of personal empowerment and cultural change. Along with changing issues and tactics came variation in feminist identities and ideologies, creating a movement with a variety of structures from formalized local and national organizations to more amorphous groups and networks. Throughout it all feminists have continued to struggle with creating a diverse and inclusive movement. Overall, the history of U.S. feminism foreshadows the topics to come in this book, in particular ideas about continuity, movement structure, feminist generations and identities, tactics and issues, and inclusion. I begin by describing how the U.S. women's movement has theoretically expanded conceptions of social movement continuity.

Movement Continuity and Organizational Diversity

How and when movements emerge, peak and decline are questions concerning social movement scholars. Often theories of movement continuity are based on activity within formal social movement organizations.[38] However, feminist scholars such as Taylor and Staggenborg, interested in revising and expanding conceptions of continuity, draw on the women's movement to propose a different view.[39] They argue that continuity emerges from movements with multiple organizational forms, not solely limited to visible, national formal organizations, and is maintained in fields where movement actors respond to and interact with the social context. These movement communities contain a variety of tactics, strategies and goals that continue to resonate with new generations of activists.

The history of the first-wave generation is one of national and local organizations with a long agenda of movement goals that narrow over time, changing as activists responded to shifts in the social and political environment. While the early years of the movement were primarily structured around formal organizations, activists also worked on issues through networks of women's church groups, clubs, missionary societies, the College Women's Alumnae Association and a coalition of working women.[40] Within these organizational structures, feminists entered the movement in different generations, sparked by new tactics, ideologies and a changing political and social environment.

The movement emerged during a time of social upheaval in the nineteenth century: a time of geographic expansion, industrial development, social reform and a growing debate on individuals' rights.[41] As women became increasingly more visible politically, they attempted to work within the abolition movement and other social organizations of the 1830s. Outraged at their treatment of being shut out by their fellow abolitionists, Lucretia Mott and Elizabeth Cady Stanton held a convention for women's rights on July 14, 1848.[42] At the Seneca Falls Women's Rights Convention, both women and men drafted a Declaration of Sentiments and twelve resolutions demanding women's rights to determine their own lives, particularly in areas such as the law, marriage, employment and the church. What followed was a period of mobilization that led to the eventual development of multiple organizations and networks focused on women's rights with a goal of passing suffrage. In 1869, there was a split in the movement over tactical and ideological questions. Susan B. Anthony and Elizabeth Cady Stanton, longtime friends and well-known leaders, formed the National Woman Suffrage Association

(NWSA), an organization with a broad scope that addressed issues outside suffrage with more radical tactics. The NWSA focused on working through the courts as the fastest way to gain women suffrage. In 1875, the NWSA suffered a setback when the Supreme Court ruled that suffrage was not a privilege granted by the Fourteenth Amendment, which guaranteed the rights of free men. Suffragists also failed to get women added to the Fifteenth Amendment that prohibits the denial of suffrage because of race. Believing suffrage would be won working state by state, Lucy Stone founded the American Woman Suffrage Association, which had a narrower scope on the issues and more mainstream tactics.

In 1890, the two organizations merged to increase their efforts and now the movement focused almost solely on suffrage. The National American Woman Suffrage Association, as it was now called, was in the hands of a second generation of women leaders when Carrie Chapman Catt succeeded Anthony as president in 1900. However, the group was not to be the only voice of women's organizing. In 1919, Alice Paul formed a small radical group called the Congressional Union, which later became the National Woman's Party. The Congressional Union reinvigorated the movement through its use of militant techniques such as hunger strikes and mass demonstrations.

After the passage of the Nineteenth Amendment in 1920, feminists in the National Woman's Party turned their focus to the passage of an Equal Rights Amendment (ERA), a constitutional amendment guaranteeing equal rights for the sexes.[43] However, as the climate grew increasingly hostile to feminism, the amendment got little attention. By the late 1940s and early 1950s, images of the domestic role of women dominated American culture, putting once vibrant feminist organizations into a state of "doldrums."[44]

The resurgence of the movement in the 1960s and 1970s with the second-wave generation tells a similar story of changes in the social contexts and organizations, informal groups and networks. The second-wave generation of the movement was not a "new" movement but a continuation of the movement with similar stories of shifting social and political times, multiple organizational forms and exclusion from other movements. While this period is characterized as the second wave, it contained multiple strands of activists entering the movement for different reasons and with different goals ignited by changing social contexts.

As women increased their labor force participation and educational attainment in the 1940s and 1950s, they also began to experience more divorce while marrying younger and having more children. For white women in particular, increased employment and educational opportunities conflicted with constraining domestic roles. At the same time, young women in the New Left began to articulate the sexism they experienced working with men, particularly in the antiwar movement.[45] It was those strains that led to the revitalization of the women's movement in the late 1960s.

The second-wave generation of feminism is often divided into two different strands, with different organizational structures as the foundation of each. On one hand was the founding of women's rights organizations such as NOW, Women's Equity Action League and the National Women's Political Caucus, which are all formally organized organizations with national offices. These organizations, such as NOW, also often had regional, state and/or local chapters that created multiple levels of engagement in the movement. These women's rights activists were classified as the "older" or bureaucratic strand and were mostly professional women with extended communication networks developed from organizations such as the President's Commission on the Status of Women, state commissions and groups such as Business and Professional Women, and trade unions. Whereas the women's rights branch developed from a context of older, more established women, another branch emerged from a different social context. Just as earlier feminists were excluded from the abolition movement, these activists experienced exclusion and ridicule within the civil rights, student rights and antiwar movements of the time as well as in the emerging women's rights organizations.[46] As a result, women's liberation groups such as the Redstockings, The Feminists and the New York Radical Women appeared.[47] Characterized as the "younger" or "collectivist" strand, these groups consisted of college students who drew on networks and organizing skills acquired in other movements. The emphasis on social networks in recruiting and the ideology of radical feminism led to the development of collectivist organizations that discouraged the development of leaders and hierarchical structure, instead organizing to allow every woman equal say in the group.

These two strands experienced a peak of activity between the years of 1972 and 1982. The women's rights strand celebrated a number of successes, including the passage of Title IX, which banned sex discrimination in publicly funded education, the passage of Roe v. Wade, a U.S. Supreme Court decision legalizing abortion, and the 1977 National Conference on Women. At the same time, women's liberation groups were successful at drawing national media attention and were a source of art, music, literature and critical analyses of women's lives.[48] Just as the earlier movement created, merged and dissolved organizations and networks, so did the second-wave generation. Over time, the collectivist groups began to dissolve and activists from both sides came together. One issue that mobilized thousands of activists was the state-by-state struggle to ratify the ERA. The ERA state campaigns illustrate the importance of community-level analysis with national and local organizations working for the amendment, connected often through networks of activists involved in multiple levels within communities.[49] The ERA campaign soon encountered opposition from antifeminist organizations such as Phyllis Schlafly's national STOP ERA group as well as local and regional anti-ERA organizations. By 1982, the amendment had not met the ratification deadline for Congress and was defeated.

Because of anti-ERA and other opposition, the overall pace of feminist activism began to decline in 1983.[50] One contributing issue was the continued fragmentation of the movement because of dissension about race, ethnicity, class and sexual orientation and the movement's lack of inclusivity. In addition, the movement faced a conservative backlash against feminism, erosion of the movement's gains and the rise of what was labeled the "post-feminist era."[51] However, activists did continue to achieve some victories. For example, women's studies programs, largely initiated by radical feminists in the second-wave generation, flourished, increasing from 275 in 1978 to more than 900 by 2009.[52]

It is in this time of the constant chipping away of the policy and legislative gains of earlier feminists with few victories that contemporary feminists come to the movement. For example, while many second-wave-generation feminists fought to legalize abortion at the national level, contemporary feminists face a series of state-by-state attacks on abortion and birth control providers. The political context has also changed dramatically. Feminists active in the 1960s and 1970s describe the "rush" of accomplishments in a time open to political gains.[53] During this period, feminists experienced a number of important legislative and legal gains including Title IX guaranteeing equal co-education, *Roe v. Wade* and several Equal Employment Opportunity Commission (EEOC) rulings. In the 1980s, signaled by the defeat of the ERA, the political climate changed from one where feminists could advance their agendas to one of a backlash. For instance, Susan Faludi details how feminists went from being media darlings in the 1960s to being named as the reason for modern women's woes in the 1980s.[54]

In sum, although simplified, this history tells of a movement that grows and declines in response to the social context of the times, and experiences organizational growth, mergers and division. It also tells of generations of sustained challenges that included the ERA and working for women's employment, education and religious rights as well as cultural change. These generations were not monolithic, but instead were made up of activists with different identities and ideologies shaped by the social context around them. Contemporary feminism is clearly situated in this history. Contemporary feminists work in organizations founded by their older sisters such as NOW, National Abortion Rights Action League (NARAL) and Planned Parenthood. They also founded their own national organizations such as the Third Wave Foundation, started by Rebecca Walker and Shannon Liss, a group focusing on direct action, education and leadership training for young women.[55] They work in organizational settings such as

Ms. Magazine and a variety of social service organizations started by the second-wave feminist generation.[56] They also continue to create community organizations such as local Web sites that direct activists to activities and actions in the surrounding area.

As further evidence of their feminist legacy, contemporary activists continue to address many of the same challenges. In *Manifesta*, one of the first popular books to articulate a vision of contemporary feminism, the authors lay out an agenda that includes both institutional and cultural goals.[57] Their institutional goals are issues familiar to second-wave-generation feminists such as reproductive rights, the ERA and accessible and affordable health care. The top three issues for community interviewees confirm this, listing abortion and reproductive rights, violence against women and pay equity in that order. However, some of the goals in *Manifesta* are also cultural and deeply personal. Contemporary feminists advocate for the idea of nonjudgmental choice in their personal lives, an agenda repeatedly mentioned in the communities studied. In particular, community interviewees talked about choosing sexual and gender identities, their experiences of sexuality, along with concerns about body image and eating disorders. As I will discuss in chapter 1, how strongly these personal choice issues shape feminism depends largely on the community context.

By opening up the lens of how we understand continuity, it is clear that the movement exists today with a variety of organizational forms and works to promote both institutional and cultural/personal change. While the movement may surge and ebb, activists continue to work on multiple levels seeking to make change where it seems possible. How those goals are pursued depends upon the tactics and strategies activists draw upon.

The Shifting of Tactics and Strategies

Scholars have argued that in long-lived movements, activists constantly revisit and revise tactics and strategies of past generations, learning from a "tactical repertoire" created throughout the history of the movement.[58] Understanding what tactics and strategies a movement utilizes is important for two reasons. First is the debate over what tactics and strategies are the most effective: institutionally or culturally focused? Often, movement continuity has been measured by the movement's ability to engage the state with movements that have no or few challenges with the state perceived as in decline.[59] Some scholars have refuted this focus by arguing that more culturally focused tactics such as changing participant identities and altering cultural norms are legitimate movement outcomes and indicate movement continuity.[60] Indeed, social movement scholars have argued that culture is a missing piece in understanding movements.[61] Secondly, it is important to understand *why* movements shift or combine tactics. Nancy Whittier argues that as repression from the state shifts in form, so does activism from social movements.[62] Therefore, movements and movement communities may shift their tactical and strategic focus when they perceive one direction (e.g., institutional or cultural) as being the most effective in making change.

Throughout the movement's history, feminists have consistently sought equality through both institutionally focused actions and attempts to change cultural norms. In the early years of the movement, women and men fought to increase women's political and public rights and responsibilities. While the fight for suffrage was largely fought in the legislature and the federal courts, early activists also drew upon demonstrations, parades and hunger strikes as a way to accomplish their goals. In addition, as many feminist historians have noted, activists embraced cultural tactics. However, attempts to change culture often faced severe backlash. For example, in 1851 a dress reform movement called the Bloomer movement began when some women began to dress in loose and comfortable clothing called "Turkish trousers." After gaining popularity as a fashion fad, the bloomer began to draw ridicule and was dropped by movement leaders.[63] Another example occurred in 1898 when Elizabeth Cady Stanton wrote the *Women's Bible*, a critique of religion and women's positions within the church. However, she drew severe criticism from feminists who felt the work detracted from the movement's main purpose, which was seen as suffrage.

This focus on institutional and/or cultural tactics was also evident in the resurgence of the movement in the 1960s and 1970s. The difference between the women's rights organizations and women's liberation groups was immediately apparent in their tactics. Women's rights activists lobbied and networked with state officials to bring about major policy and legislative changes. One of NOW's first actions was to petition the Equal Employment Opportunity Commission to ban categorizing employment ads by sex. A few years later, focusing on individual empowerment as a collective way to change the culture, the New York Radical Women began the process of consciousness raising. Consciousness raising groups allowed women to explore their personal experiences and analyze issues such as housework, sexuality, sexual orientation, relationships, motherhood, day care and work with the goal of changing society through collective empowerment. One often cited cultural protest is the 1968 demonstration against the Miss America pageant in which a sheep was crowned the winner. This protest set off a cultural firestorm that continues today with the myth of the "bra-burning" feminists. However, each strand did not stay within the confines of institutional or cultural strategies and tactics. The ability to attract the media or influence the legislature often shaped tactics and strategies. NOW, headed by then-president Betty Friedan, spearheaded the 1970 Women's Strike for Equality, which capitalized on media attention for the movement. As the deadline for passing the ERA neared, women's liberation activists began to work with women's rights organizations for its passage, hoping to influence the legislature. In sum, feminists of all generations have drawn on a varied tactical repertoire that ranges from lobbying the state to challenging cultural norms through symbolic action.

Contemporary feminists continue to draw on this repertoire of institutional and cultural tactics and strategies; however, they do so in different times. Coming into feminism in a time when overt feminist bashing is popularized in the term "feminazi" coined by conservative talk show host Rush Limbaugh, contemporary feminists work within a time in which institutional change can seem difficult, if not impossible.[64] Although the identity "feminist" has always had negative connotations, the 1980s and following decades are ones in which it became an especially pejorative label many did not want to adopt. This sense of backlash and hostility is evident in statements from the feminists in the communities studied. When Lana, a twenty-four-year-old self-identified queer in the Northwest, compared herself to her mother (and her mother's feminist generation) she saw contemporary feminism in a really different point in time, a time where even major legislative backlash would not reinvigorate the movement. She said:

> If I just compare conversations with my mom of what it was like when she was my age versus what it's like now ... there's part of me that wishes that something horribly terrible would happen like a bunch of women are going to get pissed off and take off their bras and say "fuck you to the man" but I don't really see that happening. I mean unfortunately I think even if *Roe v. Wade* was overturned, I don't really foresee ... I mean it might take something like that to piss off enough women that they're going to be like "This is crap."

Anna, a twenty-four-year-old lesbian from the Midwest, agreed. In answer to the question "What does the movement need?" she said, "What do they need? [She sighs.] Young feminists and everyone need a sense ... of change—a sense of progress; that we are not taking steps backwards."

For many feminists interviewed, the antidote to the inertia was not a large national-scale protest or campaign, but instead focused changing the movement and individual empowerment. They echo the call from feminist theorists such as bell hooks and Patricia Hill Collins who call for a resistance from the margins and argue that social change does not have to focus on the state but can happen through new forms of resistance.[65] For Marley, a twenty-four-year-old, self-identified queer from the Northwest, the resistance needed is about personal empowerment.

She said, "This younger generation of feminists—[they] aren't only concerned about women's issues." For her, the movement was not about "trying to pass a bill." She said, "ERA, no ERA—where are we?" To her, contemporary feminism needed to be different from the second-wave-generation feminism she saw as characterized by NOW and other national organizations. She wanted issues to be reprioritized with corporate advancement at the bottom of the list and personal development at the top. She said:

> Economic justice is important but it's not our emphasis—it is not at the top. It's at the bottom.... It's about having a valid identity and a safe space and exploring your own individuality outside the boundaries of gender and refusing to let society prescribe "the book" upon you. I think it's a major emphasis of [the] third wave which is ... at least from my perspective, not really addressed in any meaningful way by established feminists or organizations.

As contemporary feminists struggle to define the movement in a time of backlash and hostility, they illustrate how tactics and strategies are often shaped by the generations that came before. As Leandra Zarnow puts it, "We can see how feminists work within inherited intellectual and organizational spaces."[66] These spaces give contemporary feminists a range of tactics shaped by the society around them. What tactics they embrace is influenced by the relationship between their political generation and their community environment. This creates unique feminist identities that have political generations as a part of their foundation.

Multiple Generations and Identities

A political generation occurs when "common and historical experiences during one's youth produce a common frame of reference from which individuals of similar ages would view their later political experiences."[67] Political generations are then the result of experiences that bring together a group of people and politically "awaken" them at the same time, influencing their future beliefs, values and political involvements.[68] Scholars argue that late adolescence is often a time for political generation formation.[69] As young adults interact, they reflect on the ideas that they have internalized through interaction with their families, peers and communities and develop a sense of their own place in society. Richard and Margaret Braungart argue that young adults are most likely to be critical of the political legacies of the generations before them in the formation of their worldviews.[70] This process is labeled "disidentification," a time when one generation intentionally distances itself from another within a movement.[71] In addition, one's sex and gender (in a society without gender equality) can prompt a political experience and promote the development of a political generation.[72] Feminist political generations are shaped by the experience of being an aged, gendered and sexed being in a particular social context. As such, feminist generations are not easily categorized into discrete time periods (e.g., "first-," "second-" and "third-" wave) but instead are the result of a series of political understandings generated by the social environment that challenge and build upon preexisting generations. As such, political generations can overlap, depending on the social context, with multiple generations coexisting.

The existence of multiple generations has had a powerful effect on the women's movement. Generational dynamics were salient in the 1940s and 1950s as members of the National Women's Party entered their eighties and nineties.[73] The perception of this aging cohort of activists set the stage for the disidentification of the next generation. Garrison writes:

> Historically locating and specifying the "first wave" allowed those who recognized themselves as "second wave" to draw specific boundaries around themselves and consequently argue for their viability as a legitimate social movement.[74]

Similarly, Astrid Henry argues that without this generational disidentification, second-wave-generation feminists would have had a harder time asserting their differences and consequentially unique identities and ideologies.[75] This is not to argue that second-wave feminist identities were all the result of generational disidentification. Different social contexts and experiences played a role in the construction of multiple feminist identities.

An essential part of social movement communities is how activists interact with each other creating a collective identity. Collective identities are shared ways of viewing the world within a group and are located within a specific time and place.[76] When communities of activists form meaningful and strong collective identities, they contribute to movement continuity.[77] Just as many activists may share the individual identities of race, sex, gender and/or sexuality (as illustrated in the interviewee demographics in Appendix A), they also participate in the construction of a shared collective identity that creates a sense of "we" as a group and a sense of "them" outside the group. That is, social movement actors interact within their own groups to identify both internal and external boundaries, a process referred to as "boundary framing."[78] To adequately frame identity boundaries, social movement actors must identify three groups: protagonists, (i.e., members or potential members of the activist community and outside supporters), antagonists (i.e., those targeted as the enemy or the "other") and an audience (i.e., observers such as the bystander public or the media).[79] Activists collectively create all three groups through their identity work by drawing on their intersubjective definitions of "reality," that is, the context of their communities and their understandings of the movement.[80] Boundaries then are created through the identification of a target or oppositional group and depend upon the interplay of internal activist dynamics and external social factors. Antagonists, or the "others," identified within a community may include other groups of activists, or as indicated by Garrison and Henry, other generations of feminists.

The women's movement has always contained a variety of feminist identities situated within feminist generations. The early years of the movement had different organizationally based identities that saw the struggles for rights differently. For example, Alice Paul's radical feminist group, the Congressional Union, was a homogeneous group that allowed no deviation from the tactics and strategies of the leaders. The National American Woman Suffrage Association was in contrast a more open, heterogeneous organization that welcomed diversity in support and tactics. Both of these dynamics shaped the feminist identities of the organizations.[81] In the second-wave generation, feminist identities are often characterized by theoretical outlooks that emerged as feminists articulated their view of gender inequality in groups and networks (e.g., liberal, radical, lesbian separatist, Marxist, socialist, multicultural, etc.). One of the founders of NOW, Betty Friedan, is credited with mobilizing many women to a liberal feminist identity that saw social change as happening though working within a patriarchal society to change it. Her book, *The Feminine Mystique*, addressed "the problem that has no name," a form of emotional oppression suffered by primarily white, middle-class, educated homemakers. Women's liberationists experienced a different set of forces bringing them into feminism. Many of the women who came to women's liberation were younger and did so after experiencing sexism within student rights, antiwar, civil rights and New Left organizations. Women such as Casey Hayden and Mary King, dissatisfied with sexism in the New Left, began to articulate their experiences, drawing a connection between sex and oppressive class systems. These experiences led to more radicalized identities such as radical, socialist, Marxist and lesbian separatist feminists.

Missing in most discussions of political generations and collective identities is the link between the two. Whittier provides the conceptual bridge when she argues that political generations are not solely the result of age or life stage, but are the culmination of experiences set in a particular community context. These experiences forge multiple groups, or "microcohorts," of people who enter a movement at different times in the same location but have unique political experiences.[82] Therefore, political generations are broad groups of people who forge a common life perspective due to the social times and context around them. Within a political generation, people are set in particular community and social contexts that may vary in experiences. These experiences form groups of activists who enter into and create movement communities and construct unique activist identities.

In the women's movement, the link between the broad (political generations) and the specific (activist identities) is especially clear when examining contemporary feminists. As I will discuss in chapter 2, the formation of contemporary feminist identities are responses of a political generation within a community context (elaborated in chapter 1) as well as the existence of a second-wave feminist generation (see chapter 3). The generational disidentification between second-wave and contemporary feminist identities has been the source of much attention to the movement played out in the media particularly around issues of abortion. *Newsweek* magazine published an editorial entitled "Remember Roe! How Can the Next Generation Defend Abortion Rights When They Don't Think Abortion Rights Need Defending?" which set off a myriad of responses in the blogosphere.[83] It was also evident in the 2009 election for the NOW president when the candidates were often portrayed in terms of generation. Running for president were thirty-three-year-old Latifa Lyles and fifty-six-year-old Terry O'Neill. Lyles directly addressed the generational divide by stating she could attract younger feminists to the organization. However, O'Neill won the election despite the fact that Lyles had the endorsement of past president Kim Gandy.[84] While generational disidentification can create a sense of "us" versus "them" in the movement, other social factors throughout the movement's history such as race, ethnicity, class and sexual identification shape the way contemporary feminism is done.

Continued Struggles with Diversity

Social movements have long struggled with the issue of inclusivity when building a sense of the collective with diverse groups of people. As Rachel Einwohner, Dan Myers and I have argued, "Disagreements about who 'we' are—or should be—can become quite costly, taking time and resources away from other activist tasks and even alienating participants or fragmenting the movement."[85] Issues of diversity have been a part of the U.S. women's movement since its inception and have two dynamics. One is a documented history of exclusion and prejudice. The other is a historical record that overstates the middle-class, heterosexual whiteness of the movement, omitting the activism of marginalized groups of women and men. For example, the popular historical record of suffrage is almost entirely of white women, such as Elizabeth Cady Stanton and Susan B. Anthony, two of the most visible leaders, even though a range of activists including black women and men initially worked together on black and female suffrage.

Both the first-wave and second-wave generations have been accused of leaving out women of color and poor and working-class women, with the second-wave generation also charged with homophobia and heterosexism. Part of these charges stem from an ideology embraced by many feminists—universal sisterhood—that makes sex the most salient social category. This universal sisterhood, articulated by the mainly white, heterosexual strand of activists, was seen as having the ability to unite women in a common struggle for women's rights.[86] For many non-white, non-middle-class activists this created a sense of being "either/or" in the movement, that is, either a woman *or* a person of color, working-class or non-heterosexual.[87] The ideology of universal womanhood led to multiple divisions in the movement throughout its history. Acting on this, white feminists often engaged in strategies and tactics that distanced other women from the movement and exacerbated the issues of racism. In the early movement, Stanton argued that white women should be given the vote to offset African, Chinese and immigrant men, a sentiment resulting from a sense of betrayal by feminists' white male allies.[88] Racism was also evident in first-wave-generation organizations. For example, although generally a popular speaker, Sojourner Truth, a former slave and women's rights reformer, often faced white audiences hostile to her message, and did not hold particularly powerful positions in the organizations she worked in.[89] The second-wave generation was also not free of prejudice and discrimination. Scholars have documented how often feminist organizations ignored issues of race and class in the formation of goals, ideologies and strategies.[90] Although the years from 1972 to 1982 were times of success for feminists, it was also a period of conflict, fragmentation and growing discord in the movement. Lesbians, working-class women and women of color critiqued second-wave-generation feminists and their control of the movement.

Working-class women, believing that their work and family lives were not being addressed, created separate organizations. For example, the Coalition of Labor Union Women was formed in 1974 when 3,000 women met to address sexism in the unions and also women's inequality in society.[91] Women of color also worked with and separated from both the first and second waves of the movement. Black women, along with Chicana and Asian-American women, created organizations—including the National Black Feminist Organization, the Mexican American Women's National Association and the Organization of Pan Asian American Women—specifically designed to address their issues.[92] These organizations are in addition to the ways in which women of color often worked as feminists in groups not labeled as such. As Premilla Nadasen notes, "Feminist activity can and often does take place in race- and class-based organizations, including labor unions, nationalist formations, and civil rights and socialist groups."[93] It is also within the second-wave generation that issues of sexuality came to a head. For example, NOW experienced dissension and division over the presence of lesbians in the organization when Friedan called them the "Lavender Menace." Her view was that visible lesbians would detract from the ability of the movement to reach the mainstream public. As a result, some lesbian feminists began to organize separately in the 1970s even though NOW did change its position and supported lesbian rights in 1971.[94]

Feminist theorists addressed the racism, classism and homophobia of the earlier feminists by dismantling the concept of universal womanhood. Feminist activists and scholars, such as the Combahee River Collective, Deborah King and later, Patricia Hill Collins, conceptualized an intersectional feminist paradigm that views race-ethnicity, class, gender and sexuality as interlocking systems of oppression, forming a "matrix of domination" in which one social identity cannot be understood completely without considering all aspects of a person.[95] Another response was the groundbreaking anthology *This Bridge Called My Back,* published in 1981, which gave voice to women marginalized and silenced in the movement.[96] It is this anthology along with the concept of intersectionality that provides the foundation for contemporary feminist views on inclusivity, diversity, racism and classism.

Overall, the ideology of universal womanhood as well as racism, classism and homophobia contributed to a movement that often focused on middle-class white women. The historical record with its focus on white women's achievements and organizations reified this story, erasing the collective action of women of color, working women and lesbians. Benita Roth and Becky Thompson argue that the history of U.S. feminism, told through the wave metaphor, leaves out vibrant strands of organizing by women of color "whitewashing" feminist history.[97] Roth argues that this simplified history creates an understanding of the movement that is focused on individual rights and equality with men with little regard to class and race analyses.[98] One way feminist historians and sociologists have worked to correct this one-sided view of the movement has been to revisit the historical record to see who has been left out. Historian Nancy A. Hewitt argues that when stories of early feminists focus on the 1848 Seneca Falls Convention, they miss the racial and class diversity of activists. She documents how African-American women were particularly important as orators and advocates of women's and slaves' rights through literary societies, reform associations and antislavery groups, a fact often left out of feminist history.[99]

Many contemporary feminists enter the movement only knowing this simplified history, which states that women of color, poor women and lesbians had been shut out of the movement. Drawing on this history and anthologies such as *This Bridge,* contemporary feminists have openly taken earlier generations to task and made inclusivity a major theme of their feminism.[100] While I address the community dynamics of inclusivity and race, class and sexuality in chapters 5 and 6, the interviewee demographics illustrate how the struggle for truly inclusive organizations is easier to achieve in terms of sexuality than it is for race and class (see appendix A).[101] The interviewees in two communities, the Midwest and Northwest, were largely white (90 percent or more). The East Coast community was the most diverse, with 65 percent identifying as white while the rest identified as biracial and/or Chicana/Latina. As I will discuss, this was also the community most likely to address issues of racism. By focusing on these communities, I am not arguing that there are no diverse communities of feminists in the United States. Indeed Kia Lilly Caldwell and Margaret Hunter document how women of color build feminist communities and the difficulties they face.[102] In addition to being largely white, the interviewees were predominantly middle class, with a range between lower and upper middle class. None of the feminists defined themselves as upper class and few defined themselves as poor or working poor. This middle-class status could be inflated by the number of college students in the sample; however, many of them, particularly on the East Coast, had a variety of scholarships and financial aid, and at the Midwest site, the student population had a wide range of class status, even if the feminists did not. The place where diversity was the most apparent was in the sexual identities claimed by the community members. Instead of aligning with the notion that the women's movement is made up of heterosexual women, the majority of interviewees identified as lesbian (46 percent in the Midwest) or queer (on the East and Northwest coasts, 41 percent and 50 percent respectively).

I argue the makeup of the community networks depends more on the community context and the opportunities to organize even with an ideology of inclusion. For example, in the communities based around colleges, I find a slightly younger group of feminists. In communities exposed to ideas of the fluidity of gender, sex and sexuality, feminists were more likely to adopt identities of queer and/or genderqueer. Communities with little overall diversity in race-ethnicity also have less diverse activist networks. In other words, activists often mirror the communities around them, sometimes creating networks that are in opposition to their ideologies. I address the issues of race-ethnicity, class, sex, gender and sexuality in chapters 5 and 6, exploring how community context shapes their discourse of diversity, privilege and oppression.

Reflecting on the movement's history and its continuity, tactics, identities and diversity, I conceptualize contemporary feminism as continuing in social movement communities made up of a variety of organizational and interpersonal networks ranging from the national to the personal. These communities face shifting cultural and political opportunities that influence strategic and tactical choices. Present in these communities is a process of generational disidentification, which along with the community context, influences the construction of feminist identities. Returning to Leandra Zarnow's insight, it is clear that feminists work within "inherited intellectual and organizational spaces," shaped by the past and situated in the present, each set in a social context that produces unique patterns of action and identity.[103]

Relevance for Social Movement Studies

Feminist scholars argue that women's movements, in the United States and abroad, offer social movement theorists an opportunity to expand and elaborate concepts such as continuity and outcomes.[104] I continue this line of theory building and argue that a community-level analysis of the contemporary U.S. women's movement offers valuable insights to social movement scholars. Social movement studies often veer from the micro of identity construction and grassroots networks to examining the macro of national, international and transnational contentious politics. By locating this study in the meso community level, I highlight the importance of examining a context where the individual, organizational and broader society all reside. Social movement communities are not defined by geographic boundaries, such as the marking of cities, counties or regions, but instead are demarcated through activist centers or focal points and the construction of activist identities. These activist centers, similar to collective identities, shift over time, changing as the groups adjust to a shifting social and political environment. Therefore, what is salient in one social movement community as an activist center may not be in another. For example, in the feminist communities studied, activist centers range from a single feminist organization, to a hate crime incident, to personal and organizational networks of feminists and queers. In sum, a social movement community surges and wanes in activism depending on the political and cultural opportunities and environment, creating a shifting context of interaction and response that is not always evident on the national level.[105] As I will argue, even when the national level of a movement looks nowhere, in the communities the movement can be everywhere—in classrooms, coffee shops, bookstores, restaurants, co-ops and bars.[106]

Studying Communities of Contemporary Feminism

I selected three communities through convenience sampling based on access and entrée with an eye for potential variation. Although I was not seeking regional variation to represent all U.S. feminism, the regions of the communities are interesting in terms of the history of feminist organizing. The East Coast and the Northwest have been sites of reinvigorated feminist activism with phenomena such as the Lesbian Avengers and Riot Grrrl in the 1990s and the growth of a vibrant feminist zine culture in the twenty-first century.[107] The Midwest has also been a site of considerable, but less visible, activism.[108] Because much of contemporary feminism is visible in university settings, two of the case sites are focused on college-oriented communities, also due to issues of access and entrée. My goal was to come into contact with feminist networks that could pull me into a feminist social movement community and once engaged, I could then identity the major organizations, events, institutions and actors (as identified by the feminists) that make up the community. The result is an examination of specific community dynamics in an extended case study. Methodologist Michael Burawoy argues that the extended case method is a way to construct theory even when presenting representative and generalizable statements for entire populations (or, in this case, movements) are not possible.[109] This approach has yielded three cases in which different institutions (i.e., college or universities), organizations (i.e., national to the local) and focal points (i.e., one organization or a community event) are the center of the communities. Examining these dynamics and drawing on Burawoy's case method, I am able to generate theoretical connections between issues of environment, identity and generational relations. With this perspective in mind, my goal here is to produce an understanding of patterns of contemporary feminism overall, as well as expand social movement theory by emphasizing the importance of community-level studies, more so than generating definitive statements on contemporary feminism as a whole.

To construct these case studies, I drew on my own lived experience as a feminist, interviewed activists, gathered a variety of documents and spent time in these communities. For as complete a picture as possible, I interviewed forty self-identified feminists on topics such as definitions of feminism: stories of becoming a feminist; views of contemporary and second-wave-generation feminism; and their goals for an organization, network or community.[110] In addition, in two of the communities I sought out informants to provide me with background and context. To provide anonymity, I created pseudonyms for the communities, colleges, interviewees and organizations. The purpose of these pseudonyms is not only to foster a sense of anonymity and confidentiality among activists; they also allow the broader patterns to emerge without being confined by perceptions of locality.[111]

At the Midwest site (e.g., Woodview with Woodview State University), the thirteen interviews drew participants from the only visible feminist organization on campus, Forum for Women (authors of the opening statement). This group served as the activist center of a feminist community and networked with the local and national organizations around it. At the East Coast site (e.g., Evers with Evers College), the seventeen interviewees were from a more diverse mix of progressive, antiracist, queer and feminist organizations, with many of the groups either being legacies from past organizations or arising in response to events. The activists were joined through a variety of personal and/or organizational connections and the community's activist center was formed around a specific incident. At the Northwest site (Green City), the ten interviewees belonged to a wide variety of community groups focused on such topics as fat acceptance and queer networking groups including national organizations such as NOW, National Abortion Rights Action League (NARAL), Planned Parenthood and Human Rights Campaign (HRC). Some belonged to no organizations but were in a network of activist friends and acquaintances. The community's activist center was a link between the feminist and queer networks and organizations. The Green City interviewees were also predominantly college graduates.

Across communities, the respondents were predominately female (97.5 percent) although many identified their gender as other than "woman" or "feminine," often adopting the identity of genderqueer. I purposively did not seek out a diverse racial sample (i.e., obtaining a number of interviewees from each race) but instead investigated the racial-ethnic makeup of the networks in light of the focus on inclusivity in contemporary feminism.

To understand the layers of activism in the communities, I immersed myself in as many events and locations as possible and took field notes as my second source of data. Some of the events included a drag king show in Green City, a meeting with first-year students at Evers College and performances of the *Vagina Monologues* on Woodview's campus.[112] I also spent time in community venues that were central to the feminist/progressive community, such as bookstores and coffee shops. It was at these venues, along with organizational meetings, e-mail lists and Web sites, that I gathered documents relevant to each community, such as meeting minutes, Web site content, e-mails, flyers, brochures, zines, newsletters and posters. To understand the broader perceptions of contemporary feminism, I collected and analyzed locally and nationally distributed feminist magazines and newsletters, and read various blogs and Web sites on a regular basis. I use this material to juxtapose the community activism and dialogue against the media discourse on feminism.

Organization of the Book

This book first examines the state of contemporary feminism and then explores the community and historical dynamics that give it its current form. Section 1 analyzes the continuity of contemporary feminism in the United States through a description of three community case studies, an analysis of the ongoing adoption of a feminist identity and a discussion of generational dissension within the communities. In chapter 1, I describe each of the communities' political, social and structural environments and give voice to interviewees' experiences of feminism in those communities. The result is three distinct portraits of feminism—each the result of a different context. These descriptions document how community factors come to influence the construction of feminist identities. Chapter 2 explores how feminist identity is adopted and defined in the contemporary era. Here I examine the patterns by which young people come to feminism at a time of movement diffusion and backlash. In particular, I look at how mothers, family and educational experiences (in particular women's studies) bring women, men and transgender people to continue to adopt a feminist identity, and how these identities are shaped by the level of hostility or acceptance faced by the community. Chapter 3 addresses the perception of discord between generations of feminists. I examine how contemporary feminists respond to a second-wave feminist generation depending on the community identity and the environment, and how these feminist identities are affected by these perceptions.

SECTION 2 EXAMINES the way in which contemporary feminism departs from and continues to resemble prior feminist activism. In particular, I examine how contemporary feminists construct tactics and strategies as they work toward the goal of inclusion, and how they talk about the focus on deconstructing gender and sexuality.

Chapter 4 investigates how feminists draw on a tactical repertoire by assessing the environment around them, with most of their tactics being largely cultural except when faced by a crisis that demands interaction with policymakers. In the communities, studied tactical focus moves from education to personal empowerment to challenging cultural norms. Chapter 5 explores how these mostly white feminist communities address race, ethnicity and social class in the movement and the differences between the communities. I conclude that without a concentrated commitment to move dialogue into practice, dilemmas around diversity and privilege in the U.S. women's movement will continue. As long as feminists continue to organize in communities that are segregated by race, the important dialogue about what race and ethnicity mean will not happen. In chapter 6, I find that compared to the discourse on race-ethnicity and class, it appears that contemporary feminists are not only talking more about the deconstruction of sexed and gendered identities, but they are creating communities where these discussions are ongoing and infused with feminist sensibilities. I end the book with a characterization of contemporary feminism from the patterns that emerged from the communities and lay out the framework of community-level analysis relevant for social movement scholars.

The Continuity of Contemporary Feminism

1

Life in Three Feminist Communities

TAKING A STAND. In a Midwestern town, a group of white female college undergraduates hang up the Clothesline Project on a cold winter day in front of the university's student center. The Clothesline Project consists of a series of T-shirts with poems, drawings and stories of women's testaments of their sexual abuse and assault experiences. As the group stands shivering in the cold, they garner little attention, but huddled together they are convinced of the importance of "airing the dirty laundry" of rape and sexual abuse in their community.

Talking Out Racism. In a dormitory parlor, twenty women gather to watch a documentary on the racist and homophobic incidents that happened at their East Coast college a year ago. Most of the students are in their first year and the room is evenly divided between white women and women of color. As the video plays, some of the first-year students begin to cry. Following the video there is an impassioned discussion about racism and homophobia on campus, with the women of color leading the discussion and the white women mostly silent.

Playing with Gender. It is a crowded night at a local nightclub. The room is filled with young women and transmen who have gathered for a drag king show to benefit a local queer organization. The theme is "Drag Stars in Uniform: We Want You." On the stage, drag kings lip-sync and act out songs. All the performers wear uniforms of some sort, with the armed services well represented. Occasionally a woman is portrayed onstage and these performances are sexually suggestive and largely heterosexual in nature. The standing-room-only crowd holds their drinks and cheers loudly for each performer.

Described here are three different social movement communities with three different types of activism—public protest, group consciousness-raising and cultural celebration—and three different activist centers—an organization, an incident and a network. Despite the fact that feminism is often painted in broad strokes as a single identity or set of ideas, taking a close look at feminist communities reveals how they vary from each other. For the three communities studied, being a feminist could range from: feeling isolated as an individual yet united as a group in a conservative environment; encapsulated in a feminist bubble and focused on race and transgender issues; or having the experience of creating over-lapping feminist and queer activism. The first community is in a midwestern county within a large regional university. The second is in a small town with a women-only college on the East Coast. The third is in a large metropolitan area in the Northwest. These three feminist communities each have unique feminist identities and experience surges and ebbs of activism, yet they reveal overall pat-terns in the contemporary women's movement. In this chapter, I show how these patterns are influenced by the political, cultural and social environment. I find the less open the community is to feminism, the more feminism is articulated as a significant and salient ideology, focused on a tight core of activists.[1] Hostile communities have the ability to generate strong activists who see themselves as vanguards struggling against a culture that perceives feminism as "nowhere." In communities more open to feminism, feminism is not as strongly articulated. Instead, feminism is seen as "everywhere," and activists are more likely to take feminism and feminist identities for granted. In these communities, feminism is submerged, serving as the foundation for action or linked to other forms of activism.

The use of the term "community" in the social sciences comes with specific understandings. Political scientists argue that communities have a "shared com-mon political culture" and have characterized regions in the United States as ranging from liberal to conservative.[2] Woodview is situated in a region identified as "moderately liberal," with Evers and Green City in the "most liberal" regions. Along with political cultures, community also incorporates the idea of "place." Katja Guenther notes that "place" has three sociological dimensions: as a site of the practices of daily life, as a geographic location (where social and political cul-tures are located), and as a place of collective identity and belonging.[3] In this chapter, I draw upon the idea of "place" as the context in which social movement communities are formed and describe the overall areas that these communities are situated in.

Shaped by these dimensions, I note three distinct forms of feminist identity that are constructed. Woodview's feminist community, in the most hostile envi-ronment of the three communities, creates a *focused feminist identity* centered on women's rights and concentrated on a single organization with some connection to other groups. Evers's feminist community—the other campus community—is located in a progressive environment that allows for the construction of a *sub-merged feminist identity* that puts feminism at the core of all issues but does not make it visible organizationally. Instead, Evers activists engage in a variety of organizations and activist networks. In the most progressive area with a multitude of activists and organizations, the Green City feminist community constructs a *linked feminist identity* that connects the feminist and queer communities. While feminism in Green City is not taken for granted as it is in Evers, activists focus on issues that align with the queer community such as gender and sexual fluidity, and the body as a site of the political. So what does it mean that the feminist communities create different feminist identities?

There is a temptation to assume that when movements experience diversity in identities, factionalism is the result.[4] I have argued that groups, such as NOW chapters, can often accommodate new ideologies and identities, thereby expanding the social movement organization instead of fragmenting it.[5] I find the same to be true in the overall women's movement. Variation in feminist identity does not indicate a fragmentation or decline of the movement, but instead points to the importance of factors, such as different levels of political and cultural opportunities and the overall nature and size of the political, social and structural environment. To illustrate the role of these factors, I examine each of the areas in turn and then discuss the overall community patterns that emerge from this analysis. To do so, I draw on geographically defined factors (such as registered voters for political parties and racial-ethnic and class demographics presented in Appendix B), presenting them as the context for the feminist social movement communities that are constructed in these environments.

Woodview: Focused Feminism Among Conservatives

Politically, the Woodview area is conservative, evidenced by a 52 percent approval of a 2005 antigay marriage amendment. Historically, the county has had a Republican majority, as high as 67 percent of all registered voters. The county is made up of multiple cities, villages and townships and had a population of 1.2 million as of 2008. Most residents are employed as professional managers at the large corporations headquartered in the area with an average income of $100,453 as of the 2000 U.S. Census. Average housing costs are an estimated $260,000, but many of the residents live in subdivisions of expensive homes dubbed "minimansions." Racially, the area is predominantly white (88 percent) with small percentages of Asians (7 percent), Blacks (2 percent) and Hispanics (2 percent).[6] Central to this community is a regional public university that draws students from the surrounding areas. What this creates is a community in which the residents are primarily white, conservative and middle class. (See Appendix B.)

University Culture. The university reflects the larger area in many aspects. Because it is a mainly a commuter campus, students come from the affluent areas as well as working-class towns and a large impoverished metropolitan area. Most students and faculty describe the university and, in particular, the board of trustees, as conservative in nature. Professor Bette Hanson, a longtime member of the community, said the school had become increasingly more conservative after twelve years of Republican appointees to the board of trustees. Although the university's women's studies program with a major and minor was not made official until 1999, a group of women faculty and staff worked to bring feminism and other more liberal viewpoints into the environment.[7] However, this push to expand the ideologies was not without resistance. Professor Hanson, who worked to start the program, said that the harder the faculty pushed for women's studies, the more "nervous" was the administration's response. She recalled that when faculty started offering classes with a gender focus in the 1980s, "We all felt like we were doing the right thing. We were trying to advance the consciousness of women who were very suburban, very Republican." The lack of enthusiasm for women's studies and feminism was also evident after the program started; for instance, when the first director of women's studies brought the author of the book *Cunt*, Inga Muscio, to the campus in 2000, she had a difficult time getting the university to advertise the event.[8]

The area's conservative culture led Professor Hanson to conclude that the main student ethos was an "unwillingness to critique the [dominant] culture" and many of the students were 'apolitical.'" Laura, a twenty-four-year-old women's studies student, agreed. Laura, who was a driving force in organizing the feminist student group, described the culture among women on campus:

> Anna and I were eating in [the student center] and these girls next to us [were]. . . . analyzing everything about that person [who walked by]. How terrible their hair looked; how their jeans weren't long enough; how they were *da da da da da*. And . . . you just don't want to be in an environment like that, you know? It is so sad to me. Anna and I were sitting there talking and I am like "It is so sad." I said, "Isn't that sad to you that these girls just—they don't even appreciate somebody's a human being or another woman." . . . And so that is really frustrating on this campus and I think there is a lot of that.

Despite the environment, the area is not without feminist organizations. A local NOW chapter, made up primarily of women in their thirties, forties and fifties, is active in a nearby community and the state NOW organization holds yearly conferences. Other groups, mostly social service agencies such as domestic violence shelters, are at times active in the area working with students. Also, the campus has been the site of more progressive activism, including a gay students' organization, which surges and ebbs in membership depending on the student leadership at the time. As a result, in spite of the multiple layers of feminist organizing in the community, Woodview feminists largely exist in a relatively small network.

Activist Center—Forum for Women. In this environment, a feminist core did develop and largely depends on the existence of the women's studies program and Forum for Women [FFW], a formalized group institutionalized through the university (e.g., all student groups must register with officers, attend trainings and are given a budget pending university approval).[9] While a formal organization, FFW also serves as an informal network of students who seek out like-minded others. The group, established in 2001, provides a central meeting place for feminists, holding weekly meetings with anywhere between ten to twenty-five people attending. Many of the members are women's studies majors and the group works closely with the women's studies program.

FFW has been one of the most active and visible student organizations on campus. The group has organized very successful productions of the *Vagina Monologues*, the antiviolence Clothesline Project, a women's fair involving other campus and local progressive groups, and several other initiatives.[10] The group was instrumental in advocating for a gender and sexuality center on campus to provide resources to women, gay, lesbian, bisexual, transgender and questioning (GLBTQ) students. Along with its actions, FFW's main purpose is to connect like-minded individuals on campus and the community. According to Leslie, a twenty-two-year-old sociology major, "[FFW] is community seeking each other and then figuring out the issues and directions. [The] importance is in finding each other." Emily, an English and women's studies double major, saw the group as having a similar purpose—that of connecting people. She said, "Lots of young people hold these [feminist] opinions but don't know where to go." FFW provides a place for like-minded individuals to find each other and often advertised itself as such. For example, in a 2003 newsletter, then vice-president Jaclyn issued a call for all those who were curious about feminism to get involved. She wrote, "Together we can offer a non-threatening, fun and supportive environment to welcome an open floor discussion."[11]

Despite its success in making itself a visible place for feminists to gather, campus response to FFW has been mixed. When Laura talked to other students about FFW, a common response was, "Oh, you are a male bashing club." To fight this stereotype, she discussed plans early in the group's history to hold an open panel about feminist stereotypes. She said:

> I would love to do that on this campus because my own experience just running into students or whatever, they're "Oh, you are a feminist. Oh. Are you lesbian? Oh, you're not? Oh, you don't hate men? Oh, you are not bitter at the world?" There are all these negative connotations that come along with [feminism] that really need to be addressed and I feel they really need to be addressed on this campus in order to get a progressive movement going.

During the group's first years, it faced a variety of antifeminist reactions. When FFW printed up flyers stating 85 percent of all girls and women had been sexually harassed, someone took down the flyers and printed "That's because 85 percent of them dress and flaunt like sluts" and hung them in the residential halls. When the group brought the Clothesline Project to campus, FFW hung tape that read "rape free zone" around the exhibit. One male student asked the organizers if that meant he could "rape someone for free." In addition, members report that the campus administration is not always as responsive as it could be and the school newspaper did not always cover or publicize their events. The group has also clashed with other more conservative student organizations, in particular the College Republicans. According to Jaclyn, the relations with other groups ran the gamut:

JACLYN: If we're talking about [Gay-Straight Alliance][12] and stuff, we're still in the same social movement nonetheless. When you start going on to the other end of the spectrum you have the College Republicans . . . They know we're very liberal and for being such a conservative campus and conservative county, they see us as a threat. They have flyers going around comparing us to Nazis . . . did you see those?

JO: No, I didn't.

JACLYN: Oh my god! [The flyer was] comparing us with fascists with these little scales with feminists on one side and fascism on one and they're equal. And Nazi symbol in the background with little 'Fs . . .

JO: Who did that?

JACLYN: No idea—we have no idea. But they were posted all through the residence halls, like everywhere—everywhere. Soo we know it is someone who probably lived on campus, that's about as much as we know.

Ben, one of the few active men in the group, agreed that the FFW stirred up the campus. He said, "People are very intimidated by us . . . very intimidated . . . because we are the most liberal group on campus. And [Woodview's] a fairly conservative campus and we definitely ruffle some feathers a lot." As a result of his visibility as a member, Ben began receiving hate e-mails that called him a "feminist fag." FFW members suspected that the messages came from a man who was a member of one of the campus's conservative organizations but had no evidence to prove it. The idea that feminism is antimale and no "real" men would want to participate was pervasive on campus. Even Ben, a political science and women's studies double major, struggled with how he should fit into the group. He said:

Part of me understands the reason for having all-women groups and things like that because I know it's definitely empowering to women and I see the purpose for that, so part of me has this conflict within myself. I don't ever want to get to the point where I feel like I'm stepping on toes or I—that I feel like it's just another man coming in and taking thing over and stepping on people's toes. So part of me—at first it was like that. I was very nervous. I was very—I was struggling to find out what I could do without trying to taint the group in a way. . . . But then I gradually grew because I definitely had people who respected me and showed me that they respected me because I didn't step on toes and I was very open to doing whatever. I mean there were no limits really to what I was going to do and I was very supportive of everything they were doing with the Clothesline Project and other things and the *Vagina Monologues*.

FFW leaders worked to make sure men knew they were welcomed, adding "pro-men" to many of their flyers. Even though the group openly advertised itself as pro-male, sympathetic men were hesitant to join the group. After seeing me at meetings, John, a student, e-mailed asking if I thought the group was open to men. He wrote, "I didn't get the impression that this was a meeting exclusively for women only, but then it may be; I've never taken part in any extracurricular activity @ Woodview before so I wouldn't know."[13] John did eventually join the group and worked with Ben to launch a white ribbon project to get men to commit to working to stop violence against women. But he and Ben remained two of the few men who worked with the group.

Despite the hostility the group faces on campus, there are also moments of support. In 2001, the first year the group put on the *Vagina Monologues*, it raised more than $6,000 for charity. Since then, FFW has won yearly leadership and activity awards on campus. Members report that some of the events, in particular the Clothesline Project, have touched many students and made them aware of sexual assault issues. Jaclyn remembered what it was like to staff the Clothesline Project exhibit. She said:

I've talked to women when I would do the Clothesline Project who had never heard of FFW, but they would come to the Clothesline Project and hug me because they thought what we're doing is so important. [They were] crying and sharing their stories with me. So for a lot of women, we're very positive.

Not only were women influenced, so were men. She recalled how one young man, after seeing the display of Clothesline T-shirts, wrote a poem for the group advocating against sexual assault. During a pay equity bake sale, in which men pay more for baked goods than women based on income inequality statistics, one of the FFW members reported having a male student so shocked by the numbers he vowed to write a paper on it. So, despite the hostility, the group does reach some students and provides a feminist presence in the Woodview environment. Judith described it this way:

> I think there's this good liberal bubble. We have a good liberal little core in our campus, and . . . I always tend to think there's—there are rings on a tree. There's an absolute core where everybody's feminist and then there's the next one who are like "feminism is cool, but we're not feminists" and then it keeps going out and out until you reach the right wing, scary Christian conservative weirdos.

As Judith points out, FFW was the small center "ring" in the Woodview "tree," shaped by the environment around it. However, this core group of feminists did change the atmosphere on campus. Professor Hanson said:

> The difference between then and now is really marked, because now with the Clothesline Project with all of these things, to my knowledge, there was nothing like that. I think today the level of consciousness and the self-starting quality of these women is remarkable. I mean remarkable.

As the group grew in size, so did the sense it provided a place of belonging. Almost all of the interviewees talked about how FFW became a "home place" for them. Leslie, who often dressed in "punk" style with pigtails and short plaid skirts, recalled searching for other women to be friends with on campus by noting what they wore and what classes they took. After joining FFW, she felt the sense of connection that she had been seeking. She said, "FFW has been so incredibly important in my life, as a student, as a young feminist. That's where it all came together." Jaclyn, who also dressed eclectically and has a larger-than-life personality, echoed her thoughts:

> FFW? Oh God, it means so much more to me now. I mean, for one, the community. The community, it's more than just a place to go . . . Because I was also struggling with "What is my identity?" at that point in time too. "Who am I?" I really didn't feel like I had anything that—that gave me drive, something that I was fighting for, and then just becoming involved with FFW and I started taking women's studies classes and identif[ied] as feminist. I feel like I have an identity now. So the people that [sic] are in FFW, that's my community. Those are people—we're all

socially conscious, we're all fighting for the same things. . . . It's a sense of community and those are my friends and especially with what we do on [Woodview's] campus with it being such a conservative campus.

But this sense of home did not come without tension. Movement activists do not easily slip into constructing a collective identity—it often involves dissension and debate. In particular, FFW struggled over how "feminist" they were. One issue was that the organization's name, Forum for Women, did not include the word "feminist," something Laura, a founding member, regretted later when the group's executive committee was working on a mission statement. The group also struggled with how to present feminism to the campus. In a 2003 flyer entitled "You Don't Look like a Feminist!," the group selected nonthreatening images of a man and a woman dressed in business suits to challenge feminist stereotypes even though this did not reflect the appearance of the membership.[14] In addition, some of the members had more radical ideas than others. Paulina, who had been involved in anarchist organizations before coming to FFW, saw herself as different ideologically and somewhat outside the group. She described the feminism in the group as "complex" and largely made up of "a lot of traditional women that [*sic*] are doing amazing things." But she concluded that the group overall did not want to look too radical in the issues they adopted. The group often embraced issues such as those geared at stopping sexual violence and breast cancer but struggled with issues such as sexual self-empowerment. When the group held a women's fair, bringing information on area services and organizations, a controversy arose around sex and sexuality. Ben remembers the debate. He said:

> Zoe had decided that she wanted to do a table involving sex toys. Well, her idea behind that was very intellectual. . . . She wanted women to realize that you have the ability to—you can please yourself sexually. You don't have to depend on a man in a sense. You don't have to depend on a woman, you can do it yourself. And there was just like *whoa* uproar! It was just crazy.

The controversy among the activists indicates how they themselves monitored the perception of the group in the larger culture. This was made evident when one of the women, performing in the *Vagina Monologues*, painted the word "slut" across her stomach. Two of the organizers found this potentially offensive and polled other performers on whether she should be allowed to do this. While she eventually performed with the word "slut," the leaders' concern for the reaction of the audience indicates their constant monitoring of the environment.

This hesitation in looking "too feminist" or "too radical" is the result of a community context that is hostile to feminism, mirroring the larger culture that finds issues such as breast cancer awareness acceptable but more radical issues such as sexual empowerment objectionable.

Complicating negotiations with the antifeminist environment was the sense that the group was cliquish. Because the conservative environment tends to keep the feminist core of FFW relatively small, with fewer like-minded students, FFW was vulnerable to internal dissension, cliquishness and periods of low activism. Personal networks became a source of connection and could leave some of the members feeling outside of the tightly connected core until they engaged in events that drew in large numbers of participants. Several interviewees recalled their first meeting as somewhat alienating. Jaclyn was particularly aware of this, writing about her first meeting: "I hung in the back, quietly observing until I had learned more on my own and got to know the people in the group."[15] She remained conscious of this when she became an officer and said that the group struggled with cliquishness, particularly after the FFW executive committee members decided to rent an apartment together one summer and realized that they needed to be especially aware of welcoming new people. It was only when the group did large projects such as Take Back the Night, a women-only antirape march, or the *Vagina Monologues* that members on the margins reported feeling included in the overall group.

Yet being tightly connected did not mean that FFW members never ventured outside the boundaries of their organization. Often, those personal networks connected them to other campus organizations such as the Gay-Straight Alliance (GSA) and the Woodview Greens. FFW leaders also often extended invitations to members to engage with other national and local organizations. In an e-mail from 2002, Laura wrote that NOW was doing a protest against Walmart in a nearby town and that if members were interested they could carpool to the demonstration.[16] In addition, while few FFW members also were members of NOW, they often joined the national organization in celebrating Love Your Body day.[17] Members also worked with other organizations in nearby communities. For example, they participated in a Wash Away the Hate demonstration with local churches after an antigay protest.[18]

Another organizational layer to the community was through the Internet where members connected with organizations such as Amnesty International and Women's News and their petition drives.[19] However, it was through personal networks that members engaged in these events, circulating e-mails on carpooling and meeting places. The importance of personal networks fostering activism is noted by Doug McAdam in his study of the 1964 Freedom Summer Campaign. Tracing personal networks, McAdam found that the more connections one has to other activists, the more likely a person was to engage in activism.[20] The importance of personal networks meant that Woodview feminists engaged in activism mostly within their organization, venturing into other community and national groups only with each other.

Overall, the political environment combined with the need for social connection contributed to the construction of a focused feminist identity. Despite the fact that multiple organizational levels of feminism exist in this location, Woodview feminists do feminism in a "nowhere" environment where they mostly depend on each other. Even with this environment, it is clear from Woodview that feminism continues even in difficult locations, and that the environment has a powerful influence on the type of identity and activism done. The feminist community patterns of Woodview differ significantly from the communities in less conservative environments.

Evers: In a Feminist Bubble

The population of Evers is centered on a town with about 29,000 people, with Evers College being a focal point of the area. The surrounding locale is largely rural, giving the town a sense of being an isolated liberal mecca. Unlike Woodview, Evers College students and faculty are generally liberal in their politics and the school's women's studies department is well established. In addition, the majority of students come from liberal East Coast areas, and the school is a residential campus that fosters a progressive, leftist student community. Moreover, the town surrounding Evers College is equally liberal, with a tradition of openness to gays and lesbians. In stark contrast to the conservative leanings of Woodview, only 7 percent of Evers's population are registered Republicans. However, like Woodview, the majority of the area is white (88 percent) with small populations of Blacks, Asians and Hispanics (2, 3 and 5 percent respectively). The median household income in the community is $42,000 and the median house value was $225,000 as of 2009. (See Appendix B.)

Evers College is home to a variety of student organizations that address gender and other forms of inequality. Among these are two specifically feminist organizations, as well as groups organized around lesbian, bisexual, transgendered students, students of color, and antiwar and labor causes. Feminists Together, the most overtly feminist group, has been in existence for several years and has held well-attended programs, especially on issues of reproductive rights and abortion. However, the group has an uneven history and often goes for periods of time with no visible mobilization, depending on the energies of student organizers. The community around the college also abounds with local progressive organizations including Quaker, environmental, Latino rights and domestic violence groups that students can participate in. In addition, Evers feminists also interact with a variety of national and international groups including Amnesty International, NOW, NARAL, Sierra Club and Pro-Choice America. As such, Evers feminists exist in an atmosphere with multiple organizational layers of feminism and related activism.

Evers Bubble. Yet despite the existence of these progressive organizations, there is no organized center of feminist activism. Most of the feminists interviewed know each other through a network of other organizations and movements. One reason for this is what several of the interviewees called the "Evers bubble"—a sense that feminism is so everywhere in the community that it does not need to be specifically articulated. In other words, Evers College is in such a progressive, liberal area that being a feminist sometimes feels unnecessary. Terri, a twenty-year-old sophomore, simply said, "Feminism is lazy at Evers [college]." She continued:

> I think it's really hard to be here and not have some understanding of feminism just because it's in the air you breathe, it comes under the doors and it's inescapable . . . Whereas out there in the real world, people just aren't exposed to it at all.

In a similar vein, Evers College Professor Nida Andrews described the environment as "universally feminist and yet apolitical at the same time." This perceived lack of feminist activism fits with Terri's first encounter with the group Feminists Together. Terri, who is active in a number of organizations, recalled:

> So I went to a meeting and there were three people there and I was like "*Whoa*, what is going on? Something is really wrong here. This is Evers [College] which has this HUGE feminist reputation known far and wide." I've heard so many things from my male friends about it—it's just a *scary* school [with all these feminists]. So I definitely expected that [the meeting] would be like a huge group of women and it really is a very small group . . . A lot of women also don't feel the need to be involved in it because there's such a "Women Can Do It" environment that they don't feel the need to actually be active so I think that's part of the problem.

Abby, who is a member of a campus transgender rights group, continued Terri's train of thought. She said:

> It's a sort of thing where we have the privilege of not having to think of feminism a whole lot here because this whole environment is for us. We forget what it was like to be drowned out by men in the classroom, which

I hear from a lot of people here their first year—like "It's so nice being able to talk."

Whereas at Woodview women struggled with the negative label of feminists as "man haters," putting them at odds with the dominant culture, at Evers ambivalence with the feminist label was different. For example, nineteen-year-old Sandra, who identifies as a feminist, also challenged her feminism. She said:

I think being in an all-female environment made me reevaluate [feminism] because I was put in a space [where] 90 percent of the school identifies as being a feminist . . . So it's definitely interesting to see how everyone [views] feminism. And I think it's also turned a lot of people away from being feminist [along with the] stigma of coming to Evers.

According to Sandra, many of the women distanced themselves from feminism with statements such as "I like men and I want to have kids, but I don't even know if I want to work—so am I really a feminist?" As her comment illustrates, some of the Evers women resisted what they saw as the dictates of feminist identity—having careers, not being interested in relationships with men or having families. As I will discuss in chapter 3, many of these dictates came from their perception of second-wave-generation feminism; aligning with the stereotypes of feminists was the stereotype of an Evers student. Because it is an all-women's college in a small, progressive town, stereotypes about Evers students abound and are often contradictory. Becca, a twenty-two-year-old English and women's studies double major, reported that people believe that everyone is either an activist, a lesbian or will "put out" for any man because they are desperate for male attention.

Unlike Woodview's student group, which worked closely with their women's studies program and often drew members from it, Evers students had a different outlook. Many of the self-identified feminists had not taken any women's studies classes. As Sandra noted earlier, she identified as a feminist but chafed at the women's studies courses that discussed specific feminist theories and ideologies. One reason for this ambivalence was that many of the interviewees came to Evers already identifying as feminists. Therefore, women's studies classes, instead of providing feminist revelations, could instead feel like ideological prescriptions. Compounding this relationship with women's studies was the everywhere nature of feminism at Evers. Skye, a senior and government and international relations major, looked back on her time at college and concluded that she really had not felt a need to take women's studies classes at Evers because so many of the courses were taught from a feminist perspective.

The role the environment with its "feminist bubble" plays in shaping feminism is evident in the comparison drawn by Mackenzie, a student at University of California-Berkeley attending Evers for a year in an exchange program. She noted that the two environments were very similar:

> I feel like [Berkeley is] really actually equal to Evers, there's a lot of complacency and there's definitely a crew of people who are really active. And we had that at Berkeley, we have that at Evers. Maybe Evers is a little—I don't know—I feel like Evers is a little more . . . maybe the people are less active. It's because they're consumed with their schoolwork. While at Berkeley maybe they're consumed with just being in Berkeley near San Francisco and the city and all the stuff that goes on with that. But I think it's pretty much the same deal.

Becca agreed with this perception of Evers activism and pointed to academic work as part of the reason. Drawing on her experience as an organizer with Feminists Together, she said:

> We can all get together and talk about all of these wonderful ideas and then they never happen because when it comes down to actually the work involved in making this the reality that is where people are like "Ha! No, I got to write this paper and I have all this reading to do and all this stuff" and I know that it's minimized my involvement in [Feminists Together] and everybody else's involvement too.

Activist Center—Through the Issues. The response to this "feminist bubble" is that activism is often prompted by immediate issues and less focused on planned actions like those at Woodview. The resulting feminist identity is then shaped by the issues that do influence the campus; many of those are not specifically women's issues. According to Julia, who belonged to no feminist organizations, "A lot of people just compound different ideas into feminism." Deborah, a member of student labor and antiwar coalitions, noted how feminism diffused into other activism on campus. She said:

> And it's really interesting lately, a lot of the activist groups on campus, at least the ones that I'm in, it's like a totally a new generation of people are in and it's a lot of women of color and now somehow we are not talking about the same things as we were. Now we are talking about a lot of different things. We are talking a lot about anti-racist work. We're talking a lot about anti-imperialist work; we're talking a lot about anti-capitalist

stuff... And now the feminism isn't there as much and ... it's not there in the same theoretical terms that it was and it's really interesting and there's also a lot of queer activism in those groups but the label of feminist activism isn't there anymore.

As a result, feminism becomes submerged in other issues. Mackenzie, who identified strongly as a feminist when she first came to Evers, is an example of someone with a submerged feminist identity. She got involved in a needle exchange program and with the campus transgender group instead of joining Feminists Together. She said she was clear about her feminist beliefs and that needle exchange and transgender rights were important and "related to the feminist struggle." In Evers's feminism, feminist ideology becomes a foundation or submerged base from which activists articulate issues. As feminist scholars have argued, feminist activism can take place in any kind of organization, not only feminist ones, addressing a range of issues from poverty to peace, welfare and race.[21] This submerged feminism is similar to what sociologist Mary Fainsod Katzenstein calls "unobtrusive mobilization" within institutions. Unobtrusive mobilization is an outcome of second-wave-generation feminism where activists draw on a gender consciousness and work for feminist goals through resistance within their social surroundings.[22] Whereas Katzenstein examines institutional settings, the Catholic church and the military, at Evers issues that spark the greatest submerged feminist responses are those around racism, homophobia and gender fluidity. For example, when a residential hall and another area of campus had the graffiti "die dykes die" and "die nigger die" scrawled on the walls in 2002, the campus activists galvanized and formed the group The Student Coalition. Stella, a woman of color and one of the group's organizers, recalls how a submerged feminism entered into the activists' demands. She said:

> A lot of it was about addressing... institutionalized racism, classism and homophobia at Evers but what really went into the demands was about support—supporting students—all different kinds of students—support for trans students, support for students of color, support for low income students. What [the administration] could do better to support us as students and make the community safer and I think that through all of that, just because of who was working on it—it was really feminist.

When feminism is submerged, it exists in community networks and is not tied to one organization or institution. For example, Sabrina, who was a member of a queer student of color group, came to the conclusion, "My goal as a feminist at Evers is that I will support whatever cause I feel. I support whoever is sponsoring it.

I don't care." Paulina, who transferred from Woodview State to Evers College, had a unique perspective comparing the two communities. Paulina had been an active feminist at Woodview and participated in a variety of events including the *Vagina Monologues*. After a time at Evers she concluded, "I feel like there is a lot more [overtly feminist] action at Woodview in a lot of ways." As a result, while Woodview feminists engaged in an agenda more consistently focused on planned actions around women's issues, Evers's activism was sparked by issues or incidents not necessarily related to women's issues.

So despite the existence of numerous organizations, a progressive environment and the idea that the college was a feminist institution, feminism at Evers was not as visible as at Woodview. While people talked about feminism and identified as feminists, the "bubble" environment submerged the need to specifically articulate and make visible feminism. This is the result of a social and political environment that is accepting of feminism, and consequentially reduces the oppositional stance of it. Evers activists are secure enough with feminism to challenge it ("maybe I want to stay home with my kids") or largely ignore it ("I will support whatever cause I feel"). As I will discuss in more detail in chapters 3 and 4, challenging feminism did not mean that Evers community members did not identify as feminists; but existing in an insular liberal mecca meant they created a different kind of feminism. I now turn to Green City, a progressive environment not centered on a college or university to examine how feminism is shaped in a metropolitan area.

Green City: Life in a Progressive Metropolis

Similar to Woodview County, Green City is an area with a population of 1.3 million that incorporates twenty-five smaller cities. Different from Woodview and Evers, it is a metropolitan area that has been called one of the most environmentally friendly places in the United States to live, with a mass transit system, bike paths and a comprehensive recycling plan. The area also has been featured on cable travel shows as a "green city" worth visiting. Like Evers, Green City has a progressive culture. The area's large and visible LGBTQ population is one of the largest populations of same-sex households, according to the 2000 U.S. census. As of July 2009, 76 percent of the registered voters were Democrats with Republicans, Libertarians, Pacific Green and Peace making up the remaining parties. (See Appendix B.) The city is also known for its feminist, LGBTQ, punk and anarchist communities, making it the most visibly activist of the three communities studied. Because of this culture, many of the interviewees described Green City as part of the "left coast." According to Steve, a twenty-six-year-old self-identified genderqueer who had grown up in the area:

There are so many [cities similar to Green City] like the whole Left Coast [she laughs and names several cities]. There's just so many people that move back and forth between those places and communities that overlap, and you'll be in one of these cities and run into people you know from another city and people just really know each other and network and they're connected.[23]

One distinguishing characteristic of Green City is the fact that since the 1980s, over one-half of its residents are not originally from the area, but are drawn to the city for a variety of reasons, including its progressive and eclectic environment.

Racially, the city is approximately 78 percent white, 7 percent Black, 6 percent Asian, 7 percent Hispanic or Latino with the remaining 2 percent from other racial-ethnic backgrounds including Native American and Pacific Islander; thus it is the most diverse of the three communities studied. The median household income for families of four was $63,800 in 2007, putting it in the middle of the communities studied. However, observers note that the economy has declined in recent years, with traditional regional industries losing ground and a slow replacement by high technology–based businesses. Average housing costs in Green City proper are about $201,000, with the metropolitan area costing slightly more with an average of about $225,000. The area has several colleges and universities including a large Catholic university with 26,000 students drawn from around the country. Yet because of the size of the metro area, colleges and universities contribute to the environment, but are not the center of activist networks making this area different from Woodview and Evers.

Because of its size, the area is divided into a series of neighborhoods; some are seen as more upper class and/or suburban than others and some more "gritty" and activist. Star, originally from Kentucky, described the area as divided into two main areas: a southeast neighborhood made up of activists concerned with the environment and more "hippie" in their outlook, and a northeast neighborhood now being gentrified by wealthy residents making it unaffordable to poorer residents. The city is also known for its multitude of bookstores, coffee shops, vintage clothing stores and activist organization headquarters clustered in different neighborhoods.

Activist Community. Activist organizations in Green City are abundant and encompass a range of groups focused on the environment, spirituality, human rights, poverty, sexuality, sex and gender and women's rights among others. According to Kelly, manager of the feminist bookstore, "There's great activist community and a cycling community and environmental community and people wear many hats." Much activism takes place at the intersection of feminist and queer institutions, organizations and networks. One example is

a monthly "dyke night" gathering that draws both queer and feminist participants and announces events through the Internet.[24] Other citywide organizations include groups to end fat oppression, Radical Cheerleaders, a rock 'n'
roll camp for girls and a grassroots socialist feminist group called Radical
Women that holds "revolutionary feminist" meetings. In addition, there are a
variety of other programs such as monthly coffees to bring the hearing and
deaf queer community together and an annual Dyke March for lesbian rights
and visibility. There is a chapter of NOW in the area, along with other
national and international organizations such as International Workers of
the World, NARAL and the HRC in addition to an active statewide gay
rights organization. Staying true to its punk roots, the city has also been the
site of much DIY activism, with a zine symposium and many feminist/queer
zines sold at the feminist bookstore. Also common in the neighborhoods are
shops featuring handmade crafts and arts, with a variety of crafting fairs held
throughout the year.

As a result, Green City has an activist culture with multiple opportunities for
activist involvement. Steve, who belongs to several organizations including fat
acceptance groups, noted, "It's just not unusual to be invited to seven things a
week. You know? There's something going on almost every night! And there are
just places to go and people to talk to and see." Natalie, originally from New
York, described Green City as full of "Web savvy dykes" with a vibrant online
community. Samantha, who moved from Kansas to Green City for the activism,
described it this way: "There are so many people that [*sic*] have similar interests
to you or me that you can choose. I can kind of choose to live in a bubble of people that I know get 'it'." While the "bubble" of Evers made feminism less salient
and visible in the community, the Green City bubble worked differently, with a
vibrant and evident feminism.

Feminist Community. Green City is home to several well-known second-
wave- generation and contemporary feminist authors and poets. In addition, the
region includes cultural phenomenon such as the Riot Grrrl punk rock scene and
several well-known alternative bands. One of the central institutions mentioned
by almost all the interviewees was the feminist bookstore, founded in 1993,
which remains a central but struggling institution within the community. In an
e-mail, Kelly, the thirty-three-year-old full-time manager of the bookstore,
described its mission this way: "Our core values are building, strengthening, and
supporting women's community, diversity of feminist perspective, education for
empowerment, and social change though grassroots activism."[25] For many of the
transplants to Green City, the feminist bookstore was one of the first places they
sought out. Kelly noted that it was a resource center for not just feminists, but
the whole activist community. She said:

There's the people that have just moved here and also the people that are traveling through. And [the bookstore] as a resource center is very well equipped in dealing with that and it's one of my favorite things—that it was their idea to come to the feminist bookstore first. And so, right away there's a load worth of politics and bullshit that got left when the door closed behind them and they entered the store. So you know you're on the same page and you can make those assumptions. But we've even started getting more people from the activist community . . . that come here and say, "Okay, where can I stay for cheap?" "What's a good restaurant to eat at?" "Where is the two dollar happy hour at night?"

Steve and Susan agreed with Kelly's description of the bookstore. According to Steve, "It's like this tiny little store, but it's like the little heartbeat of the feminist community in this city." Susan, who came to Green City after college, said, "I think that a lot of people transition through there at some time in their history in Green City, and I know that it's a place that a lot of people feel is kind of a cornerstone for feminists in the community."

While the bookstore does serve as a cornerstone for the feminist community, like many other feminist bookstores in the nation, it is struggling. Kelly noted that the current bookstore replaced a previous feminist bookstore that had been in existence until about 1989. While she did not want to pin its failure on a lack of community support, she noted, "It has to be a political decision that you buy your book at the feminist bookstore. Period. End of story." As a result, the bookstore was in "deep financial woes," according to Kelly. Because of this, Kelly noted that her main focus was on keeping the bookstore open. The store has four paid employees and thirty volunteers, and had received a variety of community grants. When asked if the feminist community valued the bookstore, Samantha, who worked there as one of the few paid employees, responded:

Not enough, I don't think. I don't think the community realizes the excellent intention the bookstore has or the resources that are available from the bookstore—that the bookstore is trying to get across as far as the community meeting space, as far as bringing in authors and hosting events, things like that. And trying to offer new books, current issues, small authors, independent press—things like that. And I don't feel like the community as a whole recognizes it as much as it should . . . I feel like the only people I know who are young who are into the bookstore are women's studies majors at [a local university].

Samantha's observations illustrate how Green City experiences the same sort of "everywhere" feminism as Evers. Both are communities with vibrant progressive and liberal activist environments infused with feminism but not firmly centered on feminist institutions such as the bookstore. Laurel's story is an example of how many feminists experienced Green City. After moving from New York, Laurel said she found Green City to be "rich in feminists" but had not connected with a feminist organization. When asked to participate in this study, she recalled thinking:

> When Natalie asked me, "Do you know any people who identify as feminists who could do this study?" I [thought of] all my friends. They're [all feminist] and that's who I've been attracted to and who has been attracted to me so that says something too. But even just walking around, someone you'll meet on the bus or something—you can get into a conversation with a lot of times . . . whether they identify as feminists or not, I'm not sure but they think the same way on a lot of the feminist issues that I think. So I think it's [feminism's] pretty abundant.

Activist Center—Linked Networks. This sense that there was a community of feminists but not a feminist community is the result of Green City's *linked feminist identity*. Being a feminist in Green City was accepted—the source of everyday conversations on the bus as Susan points out. However, Green City feminists were most evident in their connections with the queer community. I argue this, in part, is the result of the number of Green City feminists who identified as queer (50 percent) instead of gay, straight or bisexual. Because of the abundance of activist organizations, institutions and networks and the openness to progressive ideas, Green City feminists linked their activism to issues central to their lives, such as sexual and gender identity. Being queer and feminist was an accepted way of identifying. For example, Natalie identifies as a lesbian, but as a newcomer to Green City noted that she was "trying to transition to queer."

While trans, queer and lesbian activists are usually considered a part of one social movement and belonging to the same community, in Green City they were more distinct. According to Kelly, the lesbian community is focused on women-centered sexual orientation and contains some of the older residents. The queer community draws many younger residents and is more focused on gender, sex and sexual fluidity. For example, one queer community event was a DragUp-KnockDown party with a "genderfuck cabaret" featuring a burlesque show and dance party.[26] There is also an indication that the transgender community is starting to separate from the queer community. For example, in 2009, the Green City Trans March, which had traditionally marched alongside the annual Dyke

March, changed its name to Gender (Free) for All and organized separately. Despite the distinction between the queer and lesbian communities, there was some overlap in the networks between these communities and the feminist community. From her vantage point at the bookstore, Kelly saw the lesbian and feminist communities as intersecting at times. She said:

> There's a huge women's community. It's gigantic. [It's] not just feminists, but there's a lesbian community and those two groups overlap. They aren't subsumed by each other at all, but they definitely overlap. And there's definitely cooperation with other communities.

Even with the overlap, there were different philosophies between the lesbian and queer/trans communities. Kelly was especially proud of the way the bookstore interceded when issues between the two arose. She recalled one example:

> I think [the bookstore] is a great example of a feminist bookstore that has not completely reinvented itself but definitely taken clues from the community. The Lesbian Community Project [who uses the bookstore's meeting space] started its mission as being woman-born-only women space and inevitably more than a couple of years ago the trans community was like, "What?" And [The Lesbian Community Project] held to it for a number of years. And it definitely was divisive in that community and [the bookstore] saw that happen and said, "No way. We won't let that happen here," and immediately created a trans inclusive policy and has been trans friendly ever since. And we have both transwomen and transmen that [*sic*] work here and that have served on the board.

In the national media, some view the fight for acceptance of transwomen as the result of different generational responses. This is evidenced by the longstanding policy at the Michigan Womyn's Music Festival, founded in 1976, for only allowing women-born women into the festival. This policy has been the site of protests with a full-scale protest launched in 1999, and is often conceived of as the difference between second-wave and contemporary feminists' views.[27]

As noted, even though the lesbian and feminist communities overlapped, it was in the queer community that most of the contemporary Green City feminists could be found. Although the Green City feminists were slightly older than in Woodview or Evers, their relative youth helped forge a link with the predominantly younger queer community. For example, Steve, age twenty-six, moved between the feminist and queer communities as a member of a fat acceptance group, and as a drag king in local performances. When Steve performed in a drag king show and served as emcee for the event, several of the interviewees were present. Star, also age twenty-six, found the feminist community by first seeking out the queer community. She explained why she saw the queer and feminist communities as linked:

> Because the oppressions . . . are linked. . . . I think also that being aware of feminism is being aware of the world and being aware of yourself and so I think that people who identify as queer have to be aware of themselves to be able to sort of reject the mainstream culture that's imposed upon them and to be able to say, "This is who I am," and I think that that's similar with feminism.

The connection between social movement communities is documented by David Meyer and Nancy Whittier who argue that "the ideas, tactics, style, participants, and organizations of one movement often spill over boundaries to affect other social movements."[28] Spillover is achieved through movements being located in a similar culture and by the sharing of participants. Being a part of the larger Green City progressive, activist culture with shared networks of participants, Green City feminists connect the feminist and queer communities, creating a linked feminism that strives for an array of gender- and sexuality-related goals. While many feminists such as Natalie, who was "trying to transition to queer," did not find this a problem, others had trouble connecting because of this linkage. Caroline, a twenty-nine-year-old heterosexual public school teacher, said:

> [It's] difficult to kind of figure out—"Hey where do I fit in all of this? What do I believe?" . . . Do I have to meet a certain criteria to call myself a feminist? . . . If I'm just for women's rights or [the] advancement of women?

Caroline was the only interviewee who did not specifically interact with the queer community and was the only one to identify as heterosexual. Kelly and Susan are both in heterosexual relationships, but Kelly identifies as a "political lesbian" and Susan preferred not to identify by a sexuality category. Caroline's trouble in finding other feminists is potentially the result of how, as a heterosexual woman, her networks did not pull her into Green City's linked feminism.

In sum, Green City has a multitude of vibrant activist communities set within a progressive environment. While feminism is alive in Green City, as evidenced by the existence of a feminist bookstore, it is often linked to the queer community by the feminists who are situated in a common culture to form a network between the two. Consequently, the Green City's feminist community is not as focused as

Woodview's on women's rights and is, at times, indistinguishable from queer community. It also differs from Evers feminism, which does not overlap with a specific activist community but submerges feminism into the issues that arise in the community. It is tempting to view the difference between Green City and the other case studies as simply one of college- versus non-college-oriented communities. However, I argue that the difference is not that easily defined.

A Community-Level Analysis

To understand the variation of feminist identities in the U.S. women's movement, it is necessary to look at the community level of analysis. By focusing on feminist social movement communities and the way in which a sense of "place" is created in each, I explore the daily life, the intertwining of political, social and regional cultures, and the networks of belonging for three distinct cases. I find that the degree of openness to feminist or progressive thought significantly shapes the way feminism is conceived. Woodview's feminist community is located in a hostile environment (feminism as nowhere), which creates boundaries resulting in Woodview feminists' focus on FFW with some interaction in other campus, local and national organizations achieved through personal networks. This creates a focused feminist identity embracing more "traditional" issues of women's rights. Evers's feminist community is located in a more open progressive community, but because of its geographic location it remains small in scope. The "feminist bubble" of Evers (feminism as everywhere) means activists focus on a variety of issues not centered in feminist organizations. While Evers feminists interact with national feminist organizations, their submerged identity influences most of their activism, which is centered on issues within their community. Green City is also in an open and accepting environment, but by not centering on a single institution, such as a university, the geographic boundaries are much wider. Green City feminists draw on their social identities as feminist and queer, resulting in a linking of the communities, a connection cemented by a vibrant activism scene. This makes feminism everywhere when the networks are connected and appear nowhere when they are not. In addition, this multilayered examination illustrates the complexity of U.S. feminism, one more complicated than whether a community is based around a university.

When feminist communities vary like those of Woodview, Evers and Green City, what does this tell us about the continuity of U.S. feminism? In each of these communities, the feminist identities indicate the vitality of the movement. Feminism in Woodview is visible through FFW but can easily be missed in periods of low mobilization in the organization. Evers's feminism can also be missed because of its submerged nature, often only appearing in the strategic deliberations or as the ideological foundation of other issues. In Green City, the presence of feminist institutions, such as the bookstore, establish the existence of the movement, but again feminism can be missed if the focus is not on the networks between social movement communities. If we are only looking for a particular kind of feminism (i.e., that being done in large feminist organizations instead of in community networks), we lose our ability to see movement continuity. Community-level examinations reveal how feminism can be more diffused or, in the words of Baumgardner and Richards, "in the water." By moving to the community level, it is clear that feminism continues and the existence of different feminist identities is not an indication of movement fragmentation but instead establishes how the community environment creates patterns of identity that contribute to movement continuity. By establishing that contemporary feminism is a movement in the twenty-first century, the question becomes: Where do these feminists come from? If we believe popular media reports, young people are no longer coming to feminism. To address this, I turn next to how members of the three communities come to adopt a feminist identity and in doing so, focus on some of the broader factors that originate within their political generation.

2

Surfacing in Particular Waters

In Houston, Texas, a friend of mine stood and watched her husband step over a pile of
toys on the stairs, put there to be carried up. "Why can't you get this stuff put away?" he
mumbled. Click! "You have two hands" she said, turning away.

—JANE O'REILLY, *"The Housewife's Moment of Truth," Ms. Magazine, Spring 1972*

PUBLISHED IN THE first issue of *Ms. Magazine* in 1972, Jane O'Reilly's essay, "The Housewife's Moment of Truth," popularized the notion of the "click," the dramatic "finger snap" moment of becoming a feminist.[1] Clicks often were prompted by interaction in a group setting such as a consciousness-raising (C-R) group where a woman, in the course of sharing details about her life, such as housework, would come to see how her experiences reflected larger social injustices. This process reinforced the slogan "The personal is political" for the second-wave feminist generation.[2] One longtime facilitator of C-R sessions described it this way: "By sharing our experiences and perceptions, we come to feel the 'click'—the *dramatic realization* of how we have been affected by a society based on gender inequities."[3] In the 1960s and 1970s, having a click moment was a way in which many women came to adopt a feminist identity. Overall, having a click moment depends on the individual living with a certain circumstance (i.e., unequal division of labor, lower pay, domestic violence), and coming to realize that, more than a personal problem, it is a societal issue. In fact, the idea of the click was so widespread that *Ms.* regularly published letters of click moments.[4] While the click continues to be used in contemporary feminism,[5] others have argued that the process is more complex. Cheryl Hercus, in her study of Australian feminists coming to feminism in the late 1980s and early 1990s, argues that while the click experience is a familiar metaphor, the process of becoming a feminist is an ongoing negotiation with a series of stages moving from thinking about the world in a feminist way, to having feminist feelings, to identifying as a member and then doing feminism.[6]

Building on Hercus's notion of feminist identification as a journey, I argue that the click realization is inadequate in explaining how a twenty-first-century cohort comes to feminism. The dramatic realization of inequality like a click makes sense in the world where women have been socialized to restrictive roles in work, home and the public arena, and began to push against those societal limitations. Although the United States is not a society of gender equality by any means, growing up in a world that celebrates individualized empowerment for women through slogans like Girl Power and Just Do It! socializes young women and men to believe they have no limitations on what they can achieve and creates a culture where feminist ideas are present (like fluoride) in the culture but are not readily identified as such. For young women and men making up this "Generation Fluoride," the world around them encourages the belief that they are not limited in any opportunities, yet gender barriers are still in place. For many in this generation, these messages of empowerment make feminism as a political movement seem irrelevant. As Rose Glickman argues, all young women "whether they embrace or reject feminism are the daughters of feminism, heirs to its struggles, failures and successes."[7] However, some break through the slogans of empowerment to see the continued effects of social inequality in their lives in work, income, education and domestic relations, and adopt a feminist identity.[8] In other words, thinking about feminism for Generation Fluoride is somewhat like a fish thinking about water: It is so present that it becomes invisible—everywhere and nowhere at the same time.[9] Instead, I propose that becoming a feminist in the twenty-first century is more a process of *surfacing*. Surfacing is the gradual process of coming to recognize that one is feminist in thought and then adopting the identity of a feminist activist. To extend the fish and water analogy, surfacing is when the fish comes to realize they are surrounded by water and identify themselves as fish within it. This is different from the dramatically realized click or the step-by-step stages of moving from point A (not a feminist)—to click—point B (now a feminist). Instead, surfacing is coming to identify how feminist ideas have shaped an individual's life course, and then through a process of gradual, and sometimes unconscious, transformation, adopting a feminist identity. It is the unconscious nature of surfacing that allows individuals to claim that they have always been feminists; they just have not always identified as such.

The dynamic of surfacing is common in contemporary stages of long-lasting social movements such as the environmental, LGBT and women's movements. Oppositional movement ideologies often diffuse into a society over time, making them appear mainstream and stripped of political meaning. For example, consider how ideas of recycling and conservation are common notions in the twenty-first century, initially articulated by environmental activists as radical ideas in the 1970s. When recent entrants to movements come to understand how their life views align with a political ideology, they adopt social movement identities that encourage them to act. What I call surfacing, social movement scholars, in part, identify as frame alignment, which is the process of bringing people into a movement based on the way in which leaders present the goals and strategies.[10] The women's movement is a particularly good example of this process with its long history, diffusion of movement ideas and multiple generations. All of the feminist communities studied are a part of a political generation that experiences some amount of feminist ideology as mainstream and apolitical as the cultural norm. Therefore, coming to recognize their beliefs as feminists and adopting the identity of feminist is a form of frame alignment, or surfacing, bringing people into the movement.

Hercus argues that one trajectory in feminist involvement and identification is the belief that one has always been a feminist.[11] There were feminists in each community who reported that there were no gradual or dramatic changes in their beliefs or sense of self; instead, a feminist identity had always been a part of their self-concept. For example, Steve of Green City claimed she had always been a feminist. She said, "One thing I've realized is that even as I've changed over the years and all of these things that have been dynamic about my personality and my life change, I'm still a feminist. And I always have been." For Kyra of Woodview, there was no time when she could remember she was not a feminist. She said, "I honestly can't even tell you when I decided I was a feminist. I just know it was something I always believed and that I could put a name on it and that was it." Stella from Evers had a similar experience. She recalled, "I don't think that there has ever been a time in my life that I haven't identified as a feminist. . . . I really think that when I was seven years old, I had some sense of that identity." Abby of Evers, who counted both of her parents as feminists, noted that she just grew up knowing she was a feminist. She recalled, "How did I come to feminism? I was three years old and someone told me I couldn't do what I wanted to do with my life because I was a girl and I decided that wasn't okay."

To explain the sense that one has always been a feminist, I argue "always being a feminist" is the result of a cultural environment that provides enough feminist messages for a sense of self to develop that can later be labeled as feminist. For example, Julia, Terri and Bailey of Evers identified as always being feminist but all described this identification as a journey of self-discovery set in a context of feminist beliefs. Bailey hints at this journey when asked how she came to see herself as a feminist. She said, "Ever since I knew what the word was I knew that I wanted to identify as one even though I wasn't sure how exactly that was going to happen." For Terri, the process was going from knowing what feminism was to acting like a feminist. She said:

> So I think that I always took those ideas for granted as the way that everyone believed the world was, and then once I got to that place where they were being contested and I was under all of this pressure, I sort of found my way to it as an activist rather than just as someone who was raised with those beliefs. I began to think of what they actually meant.

While it may not feel like a process to the feminists who have "always been," I argue that adopting a feminist identity in the twenty-first century involves the process of surfacing, which is coming to see themselves as feminists in a time of ideological diffusion. All the feminists interviewed went through a process of surfacing as members of the same political generation. To explore this process, I identify the major factors that emerged from the three communities: mothers, educational experiences, experiences of sexuality and violence, and involvement in other movements. While there is a common set of surfacing factors for Generation Fluoride, the context of the social movement community (i.e., openness or hostility to feminism) could produce variation. Indeed, as I will discuss, what draws some into feminism in one community can be a source of disidentification in others, and in some communities, various factors do not appear to be present. Before describing the process of surfacing in the communities, I first describe each of the factors.

Mothers. One might speculate that it is feminist peers who draw their friends into feminism.[12] As noted earlier, McAdam found in his study of the 1964 civil rights Freedom Summer campaign, most of the participants were connected through a series of friendship and social networks that drew them into participation.[13] While friendship networks played a role in drawing participants into feminist organizations, such as in Woodview's Forum for Women (FFW), the most common influence on feminist identities mentioned in two of the communities, Woodview and Evers, were parents, mostly mothers. Through exposure to ideas in the home, whether they are labeled as feminist or not, the possibility of developing a feminist identity later in life is set in place. However, Woodview's and Evers's feminists revealed very different dynamics with mothers. According to their children, almost all Woodview mothers *were not* feminists, while almost all of the Evers mothers *were* feminists. In Green City, the role of mothers was mixed. I argue that how mothers play out as factors in the adoption of feminist identities is largely the result of differences in political culture between the communities. Woodview students primarily came from a more conservative environment in the Midwest; Evers students' families were mainly from the more liberal East and West coasts, whereas Green City feminists came from all over the country.

Experiences and Other Movements. Gloria Steinem is credited with saying that women come to feminism later in life as the result of their life experiences.[14] For 1960s and 1970s feminists, this was largely true as they drew upon feminism to explain difficult life experiences such as divorce or employment discrimination in a culture that did not label these as oppression.[15] For contemporary feminists, personal experiences, particularly around sexuality and violence, also contributed to adopting a feminist identity but in a different way. The availability of books,

Web sites, groups and other sites of feminist information, plus living in a social world that has been altered by feminism, or as Pamela Aronson calls it, "living feminism,"[16] young people have resources and information and draw on their knowledge of oppression to explain these experiences as oppressive. As a result, experiences such as violence or sexual assault are not a click moment but instead moments in which salient feminist ideologies are articulated as a feminist identity.

Identifying oppression also brought some of the interviewees to feminism through other movements. As Meyer and Whittier argue, movements spill over into each other, sharing personnel, ideologies and tactics.[17] Working in one movement could propel one to become involved in another through interaction with activists and ideologies. The women's movement serves as an example of this spilling over process. As women in the 1960s New Left movements began to discuss how they were being treated unfairly in the antiwar and student rights movements, they began to organize separately, leading to the rise of the women's liberation branch.[18] This separation from the antiwar and student rights movements was the result of women interacting with each other to identify how their experiences with discrimination were not individual but societal. For some interviewees, feminism was a focal point in the journey through other movements. However, the most common factor among the communities was contact with feminism through educational settings.

Education. Sociologists have long argued that the institution of education is one of the major socializing forces people encounter in their lives. Education teaches basic skills as well as social norms and beliefs, and serves as a site for peer interaction. Therefore, school, particularly high school and college, can influence the development of a feminist identity.[19] In all three communities, education was a major factor interviewees cited in adopting the identity of feminist. Education played a role in a variety of settings, namely through high school teachers, college courses such as women's studies and extracurricular groups. In each of these settings, feminism was articulated through a variety of interactions. While high school shaped many of the interviewees, the most influential educational experience overall was college. Since all the communities studied have colleges or universities that teach women's studies, one would also suppose that women's studies would play an important role in the process of becoming a feminist. However, the community context shaped how college is experienced. In Woodview, women's studies was a dominant surfacing factor. Only two of the Woodview feminists interviewed had not taken a women's studies class. In Green City, approximately half of the interviewees had taken a women's studies course, but most had their degrees from universities outside of Green City. However, in Evers, women's studies had a more ambivalent role. Only eight of the seventeen interviewees discussed taking women's studies classes at Evers and of them, four found it to be a negative experience. In the following sections, I discuss these dynamics in detail.

In addition to coursework, one of the opportunities colleges offer is a chance to participate in a variety of organizations. While Evers students participated in a variety of organizations on campus, these groups were seldom overtly feminist.[20] Green City feminists had little to say about college organizations influencing their feminism. This could be due to the fact that many had obtained their degrees before moving to Green City and were not currently in an educational setting. It was at Woodview that a feminist college organization played a significant role in the process of becoming a feminist.

In sum, while mothers, experiences and other movements laid a foundation, it was often in educational settings that feminist transformation happened. It is important to note that there is a generational dynamic to education and becoming a feminist. Women's studies as a discipline is the result of second-wave-generation feminists in the 1960s and 1970s critiquing academia and working to integrate women. One outcome of this is that contemporary feminists have a much different experience whether or not they take women's studies courses. The presence of the discipline creates a potential politicizing experience for the individual and changes the social context for the whole community. I now turn to each community to describe the ways in which the interviewees experienced surfacing to a feminist identity.

Woodview: Empowerment, Disjuncture and Education

In Woodview the process of surfacing started with a foundation of empowerment imparted in the home, mainly through mothers. While the mothers did not identify as feminists, they gave their children a set of ideologies that resonated with feminism—that is, being strong, independent and capable. However, the disconnect between these empowerment messages and their lived experiences created a sense of disjuncture that was transformed mainly through college classes such as women's studies and their involvement with a feminist organization such as FFW. In a conservative environment like Woodview, feminists were much less likely to have interactions with other social movements, and instead the process of surfacing came mostly from their home life and educational experiences.

Identity Foundation. In Woodview of the thirteen interviewees, only Emily's mother identified as a feminist. The rest of the mothers distanced themselves from feminism and did not work to foster any sort of conscious feminist identity in their children. As such, these midwestern mothers imparted a form of apoliticized feminism. Laura, whose mother is a Pentecostal Christian and whose father died when she was eleven, described how she came to understand her mother's messages. She said:

It is so awesome for me to look back at that because she never deemed herself as being independent. She never deemed herself as being a feminist. She was a very conservative woman but she was so independent. She still is very independent, very strong willed. She instilled a lot of that in me. I remember my senior year in high school I was given an amount of money and over that I had to [get] a job in the summer. And I had to pay for my own things and I had to learn how to balance my checkbook and I had to do all of my own laundry . . . And so from that point on I think it was something that registered in my mind but I didn't identify it as feminism.

Laura's experiences are an example of the process of surfacing. Growing up, she learned many of the lessons of the second-wave feminist generation without the politicized label of feminist attached to them. While the mothers encouraged their daughters to see no limits to their potential, they stopped short of endorsing feminism. Maura remembers being shocked when her mother, whom she initially saw as very supportive of women's rights, told her that she did not want her to take women's studies because she was not sure what Maura would learn. Maura recalls her mother was particularly upset when her daughter learned about the 1970s abortion collective, JANE, in a women's studies class, a subject she deemed too radical. Sally's mother is another example. Sally described how her mother approached feminism with a "I'm not a feminist, but . . . " perspective:

My mom understands it and more so than my dad. She's one of those types of people who will be like—and even though she was in college in the '70s and stuff—she's like "I'm not a feminist but" . . . type thing. And she'll just say all these things that are pretty close to feminist ideas.

One message imparted by almost all of the Woodview mothers was the idea that girls and boys were no different and their daughters could achieve whatever they wanted. Emily's experience with her mother exemplified this. She recalled:

I think that she always implanted the idea in me that I could do whatever I wanted and that there was no difference between my brother and I. I'm the only girl. I have a couple brothers. And it was never different between them and me and so I realized—like she just taught me—I could do whatever I wanted and that I was strong and that if anyone tried to say that I couldn't do something because I was a girl, that was ridiculous and that was laughed at. So that just became the way I kind of thought about things.

A major emphasis of feminism in the 1960s and 1970s was the need for women to be financially independent, a message passed on to many of the Woodview feminists. For example, for Sally, a woman's need to work was a constant lesson throughout her childhood. She said:

> Both my parents worked [and were] extremely busy . . . My mom saved in my baby book an article . . . of my mom and my dad [where] my mom [is] talking about [being] a dual-income family. And that's in the front page of my baby book so I guess that right off the bat that was really important to my mom.

However strong the message that they were capable and equal, part of the process for surfacing was experiencing a disconnect between these messages and their experiences.

Ideological Disjuncture. The empowerment messages of their childhood were often contradicted by their experiences, particularly in a society where sexual assault and violence are routinely experienced by women. Sally experienced a sexual assault her freshman year that eventually led her to women's studies and FFW at Woodview. She summed it up this way:

> So a lot of my introduction to feminism came through the sexual assault and it came through dating [her girlfriend's name] and it came through just going to her bookshelf and we just like started talking and I sort of formulated ideas.

While girls were often the recipients of empowerment messages and victims of violence and assault, boys were not unaffected. Ben's mother's abuse and sister's rape led him to feminism. While mothers advocated empowerment and independence for their daughters, Ben's experience was different. Although he heard his mother encourage his sister to be strong, it was seeing his mother's abuse that brought him to feminism. He said:

> Well there's also [he pauses] this is probably another very important element to my—how I came to feminism—when I started realizing things were wrong. My mom was abused [he pauses] all throughout her marriage. There are probably five times in her marriage that she was actually physically abused but those are things that definitely stick with children when they see that. And it's something that always stuck with me and I always—I always wondered why that was happening and I didn't get it. My sister and I were just [he pauses] I remember the terrifying nights of

being up and listening to screaming and yelling. I was extremely close to my mom. I've always been close to my mom. And it takes a toll, definitely. . . . One of my main focuses [*sic*] just now particularly is violence against women.

Often the factors of surfacing occurred simultaneously, making young adulthood a time of transformation. Zoe's story combines her coming to terms with her sexuality, her sexual assault and her introduction to women's studies. She recalled events from the year before:

Last year was crazy. All of a sudden I like a girl and all of a sudden I'm dating a girl and then all of a sudden I'm raped and it was because of my sexuality. He was like—like—banging my head against the ground [saying] "Fucking dyke," terrible things. And then my parents kicked me out and they don't know I was raped because I'm afraid they're going to think that's why I'm gay. There were so many things that went into last year. It was interesting because I had women's studies and that was where I went. I'd just read and learn about stuff and . . . It's my passion.

Zoe's story illustrates how adopting a feminist identity and coming to terms with her sexual orientation and her rape was facilitated by her immersion in an educational setting, one of the most important factors at Woodview.

Surfacing Through Education. It was in an educational setting that Woodview feminists began to resolve the contradiction of messages of empowerment and experiences of oppression. For a few, it was as early as high school that they began to rethink their understandings of the world and their identities. Sally, who grew up in the surrounding community, remembers taking a government class in high school and learning about women politicians. She said:

And our teacher brought up feminism and then I think tried to offer an explanation and I . . . initially I didn't really get it. . . . I was always raised with [a] "women can do anything" kind of attitude, so I felt it [equality] was just already sort of already there . . . She's explaining this whole thing and I was like, "*Whoa!*"

However, unlike Evers feminists who often attended private or alternative high schools with a broader curriculum, the Woodview interviewees were less likely to have come into contact with feminism in high school. Woodview feminists were more likely to have attended public suburban schools, with some coming from inner-city high schools. Instead, it was on college campuses that they began to adopt a feminist identity. One major setting for this transformation was women's studies classes. Some of them came to the classes because of a personal interest, but most Woodview students came to an Introduction to Women's Studies class to fulfill a general educational requirement. The common Woodview narrative is one of a student taking a women's studies class, having a feminist awakening and coming to see themselves as feminist. For example, Maura said, "I can see characteristics of being a feminist in me before that, but I never would've labeled it like that." Ben's experience illustrates this process. Ben, who had seen his mother's abuse over the years, remembers how feminism became clear for him:

> I'd been studying international relations for probably three years until I found women's studies. During the time I was studying international relations we read a book and it was about gender and international relations and that was the first time that I think I'd ever been exposed to feminism. . . . So I started to realize—that's where I drew the distinction and feminism stuck with me. And I took a women's studies course and it all came together and I was just like, "Wow." It all fell into place for me.

He continued describing his experience: "It was almost spiritual in a sense for me. Like I knew . . . I just . . . I just went there. Everything just led me there." Women's studies and the lens of feminism allowed Ben to rethink his mother's abuse in a new light. He labeled women's studies "a decoder of everything that happened in my past."

Both Sally, who had been raped on a different campus, and Emily transferred to Woodview University. It was at their previous colleges that both began to think about feminism. For Sally, the process began when the woman she was dating began to take women's studies classes and got involved in feminist issues. After attending a Take Back the Night march at her previous college, Sally went on to organize a showing of the Clothesline Project as a way to deal with a sexual assault that had happened to her on campus when she was a freshman. For Emily, a sociology class at her previous university left her questioning gender equality. When she saw an ad in the paper for a group called Sisters, she joined and spent time with other women discussing and reading about issues. For both Sally and Emily, these experiences at another university led them to search out a feminist group when they transferred to Woodview.

The experience of taking women's studies and getting involved in feminist organizations were linked for many at Woodview. Woodview University officially added a women's studies program in 1999, and in 2001, the group Forum for Women was founded largely through the efforts of a group of feminist students. Two of those women were Laura and Anna, who had become close friends and served as its first officers. It is through their recruitment efforts that many of the Woodview women initially joined FFW. For example, Leslie had a class with Laura and Anna and was delighted when they invited her to join the group. The relationship of Laura and Anna symbolizes the importance of friendship and social networks in the culture of Woodview, with many of the members coming to connect with other progressive women.

Joining FFW and being with other feminists did not spur an immediate adoption of feminism. Instead for many the process of interacting with the group was more gradual. In the meetings, I observed that several students came to FFW but sat quietly for several meetings before interacting with other members. As they grew more comfortable with the group, it had a transformational effect, as Jaclyn relates:

> I never knew what I was going to go to college for . . . I'm going through all these ideas. Do I want to make a lot of money? I don't know—that's not the thing that's going to make me happy. So before entering Woodview, I want[ed] to do something to help people, that's where my main idea was. So I was going to go on to English, so I'll be a teacher. I'll teach in inner-city schools. I remember what it was like to go to high school and not have an English teacher. I had a substitute the entire year, and it sucks. So I wanted to be a good teacher. And then I came into FFW and was interested in women's studies. And my whole idea changed now. I want to go into social work and maybe someday become a professor.

Jaclyn's experience of coming to articulate what she wanted to be was promoted by the camaraderie and feminist ethos of FFW. It was working with other feminists on issues of gender equality that allowed the Woodview interviewees to see themselves as not only having feminist ideas but to identify themselves as feminists.

Returning to Their Mothers. In Woodview, the process of surfacing was circular and reached back to influence mothers. As their daughters and sons came to identify as feminists drawing on the lessons imparted at home, the mothers also changed. Several of the interviewees found that their coming to feminism was liberating for their mothers as well. Laura, Anna, Kyra, Ben and Judith all discussed how their beliefs and ideas led their mothers either to identify as feminists or become open to feminist ideals. One way this happened was by involving their mothers in their education and activities. Several mothers attended the *Vagina Monologues* put on by FFW to see their daughters perform. Laura remembers preparing her mother for the vocabulary used in the monologues (i.e., words like "cunt" and "vagina") in order for her mother to understand how the play was sexually empowering. Kyra jokingly said that her mother didn't use the word "feminist" "until I went to college and brainwashed her." Ben noted the same dynamic, saying that since he became a women's studies major, he and his mom have great conversations about feminism. Judith summed up her experience by saying that "except for the ten seconds where she kind of had a freak-out moment" she and her mom enjoy talking about feminism. According to Judith, these conversations left her mother wondering why more people don't call themselves feminists. Anna drew on her women's studies class and feminist perspective to analyze her mother's remarriage and subsequent divorce. She said:

> And me observing [my mother's marriage] and in the meantime, studying women's studies, I was able to articulate my opinions to her and say, "This is what I am observing. This is what I am seeing," and I think, for the most part, she wasn't closed to it. I don't think she got defensive. . . . So when I talk about women's studies stuff, she is very accepting of it. She enjoys it.

Overall, as their children came to identify as feminists, many of the Woodview mothers became more open to the idea of claiming a feminist identity or, at least, feminist perspectives. Fitting with Woodview's focused feminist identity as a community, mothers became allies to their children's identities and not antagonists outside the community boundaries. In a place of hostility to feminism, Woodview feminists did not shut out any potential allies, particularly those that had been encouraging their empowerment throughout their childhood.

In sum, the dynamics of Woodview fit with the idea that feminism is everywhere (i.e., diffused like fluoride) and nowhere (i.e., not always visible). Despite the fact that their mothers did not identify as feminists, the interviewees grew up with ideas that came from the work of previous feminist generations. The lessons of their mothers laid a foundation for the feminist identities of their children. However, it often took transformational experiences that did not jibe with these ideologies and the gathering of feminists in the classroom or in organizations for Woodview interviewees to come to claim their identity as feminist activists. In Evers, the story of surfacing took a significantly different pathway.

Evers: Creating a New Feminist Generation

Unlike Woodview, many of the Evers feminists had other feminists in their families and some had activist role models while growing up. Just as the ideas of empowerment served as the underpinning for a Woodview identity, growing up with an articulated feminism at home served as the foundation for the feminist identities they would come to adopt. However, where Woodview feminists experienced women's studies and organizations as a place of identity transformation and their mothers as potential allies, Evers feminists shaped their feminist identities largely through disidentification with their mothers and a strong critique of women's studies. By drawing boundaries that shut out second-wave-generation activists and achievements (such as a women's studies curriculum), they came to adopt an identity that was critical of the past.

My Mother's a Feminist, But ... In Evers, more than half of the mothers (nine out of seventeen) identified themselves as feminists, and all were from either the East or West Coast. None of the Evers feminists had mothers who were antifeminist and several had family members other than mothers who they considered feminist in their beliefs. Of the mothers who identified as feminists, most were activists. For example, in the 1970s, Stella's mother went to the University of California-Berkeley in search of activism and became a Marxist economist who continues to address issues of gender, race and class in her work. Mackenzie's mother, also in Berkeley, is active in reproductive rights and often took her to protests as a child. Skye, who grew up in Boston, described her mother, who is a feminist minister:

> My mom is definitely a 1960s child. She identifies as a feminist and ... she is a minister. She is a fifth-generation minister in our family, but our religious leanings have always been very feminist. Like the use of "God" has always been changed, but then my family has been a champion of inclusive language in the church. I was the taught the Lord's Prayer to say, "our father and our mother" or "our God who art in heaven," so that was very rooted and my father was a feminist. He died when I was eleven, but he definitely also really believed in women's rights and in feminism in a similar way that my mom did, and I think she taught him lot. She was more politically involved, I think.

Lila's mother was also an activist in her youth. Lila recalled a conversation during one family vacation with her boyfriend and parents:

> My mom was quite the feminist back in the day ... all the marching and fighting for reproductive freedom. She says that everything that comes around goes around. . . . We were in Washington, D.C. . . . me and my mom and my dad and my boyfriend who's like a super leftist. And he was sitting there arguing against the war in Iraq with my dad, "Blah blah blah." And I was like arguing with them and then my mom was like, "This could have been the same conversation thirty years ago with me screaming at my dad about the war!" [She laughs.][21]

Mothers did not always have to be activists to influence their daughters. For example, Terri from Massachusetts said of her feminist mother:

I think that my feminism came largely from a feminist mother who exposed me to those ideas very early on, which was phenomenal and I think is one of the best things she could have done for me. She was a feminist. She wasn't extremely vocal. She wasn't an activist so much, but she was growing up during the women's movement.

Overall, at Evers having a feminist mother and/or growing up hearing feminism articulated was common and served as a foundation for their feminist beliefs. For Bailey, stories of her mother's life were important lessons on how to be independent. Her mother did not change her name when she married and requested the newspaper that published their wedding announcement print a correction stating she had not changed her name. For Bailey, the fact that her middle name was her mother's last name was evidence that "my identity as my name is really deeply invested in my mom and dad's feminism."

Yet Evers illustrates how the relationship between feminist mothers and daughters is not straightforward. Indeed, Glickman, in her study of the daughters of fifty feminist women, found that parental beliefs do not necessarily create a similar belief system in their children.[22] Terri noted that feminist mothers could face a backlash. She said:

But it's interesting because I know that having a feminist mother is not necessarily something that ensures that you turn out to be a feminist. I think that it helps tremendously, but my roommate has a feminist mother . . . and she's not antifeminist, but she is absolutely not a feminist and it kills her mother. She's like, "OH GOD!" [she laughs] . . . I don't really think there's anything that absolutely ensures feminist consciousness, but I think that it's really important to be exposed to it.

In sharp contrast to Woodview, Evers mothers often found themselves being judged by their daughters and found lacking in their feminism. Ava dismissed her mother's feminism despite the fact that her mother had fought to be successful in the corporate world. She said, "I think at one point she was a feminist, but I think right now she is just comfortable." Others thought their mothers had given in to traditional gender roles, forsaking egalitarian ideals. Terri recalled her arguments with her mother over household work:

It's interesting because I think that my mother sort of has two different feminisms that are living within her. One is from the past and one is how she is right now—her feminism as a wife and mother—which are kind of two very different places to be. . . . But I think at her age and at her position, she has sort of modified her views over the years, and I know that when I was in high school, a lot of time I would be reading about feminism and I would get really mad because here was my mom who had all of these feminist ideas and principles and had taught me so well, and here she was doing the dishes and getting stuck with the housework. And I was like, "Mom, how could you say this and look what you are doing?" We actually did have a few conversations about it and she admitted that when you get married things change, and that when she and my dad first got married, the first five years he would cook some nights and do the dishes and they had this whole system and it worked for a while, but ultimately, even though she was a feminist, it didn't prevent her from falling into the stereotypical female role, which was hard for me to accept, and I was really angry about that for a while.

Others found their mother's feminist views outdated and too "second wave." Queer and transgender issues along with ideas about multiple oppressions were used to distinguish between a mother's and daughter's feminism. Sandra, who grew up in Connecticut, noted:

I used think my mom was a feminist until we discussed queer issues, and I think that one of my big issues was understanding that she is still stuck in the 1960s, 1970s mentality of women [who] want equality from men under the system of heterosexual normativity.

For Skye, it was her mother's lack of interest in other forms of oppression that was a point of contention. In Evers, a place of submerged feminism that merged feminist ideals into all issues, particularly those of race, sex and gender, the more focused feminism of their mothers was problematic. Skye said of her mother:

She says occasionally that she's not interested in black people's issues or issues of other cultures or learning about other cultures, but she's very interested in feminism and that sentiment is absolutely abhorrent to me. That's where we clash.

Evers's Professor Andrews noted that the phenomenon of distancing oneself from one's mother was a common dynamic, a form of disidentification between generations that placed mothers as outsiders to the feminist communities and identities that their children created.[23] It is this process of disidentification that led daughters to define their feminism as different and separate from their mothers. This process of distancing from their mothers is largely facilitated in their educational settings.

Education at Evers. Feminists in all three communities discussed how high school teachers and courses fostered their beliefs. However, the type and form of education varies considerably by community. Lila's experience in a conservative private high school outside of Detroit illustrates some of the dynamics of an educational environment hostile to feminism. Lila went to an elite private high school where she was a middle-class student in the midst of the very rich and very conservative. In ninth grade, she recalled an all-school assembly was held for a speaker who described how she had kept her virginity for her husband and would only ever have sex with him in her lifetime. Another speaker was brought in to discuss how sexual harassment did not happen and conservative politician Alan Keyes was the speaker at her graduation. In addition to the conservative political and social culture, Lila also found the school sexist. While most schools have equal or slightly higher populations of girls attending (55 to 60 percent), Lila's school had a population she estimated at 35 to 40 percent. She saw this as an indication of parents not wanting to spend their money educating their daughters and instead sent their brothers. Sports were another area where girls and boys were not treated the same. She said:

> For instance, we got a brand-new beautiful—beautiful brand-new turf system—before the Lions had it and they only painted [she laughs] the lines for men's lacrosse, men's football and men's soccer so that when we wanted to play field hockey, we had to go out like a half hour before, everyone had to get tape and we had to go around and tape around the field where our lines would be.

However, just as feminist mothers do not always create feminist daughters, conservative environments can give rise to feminist identities. For Lila, the beginning of her feminist consciousness came when the school got a brand-new performing arts center and named it after a prominent donor who was facing charges of rape and had several class action sexual harassment suits filed against him. She said, "That really, I think, turned me into a feminist."

While Lila's high school was exceptionally conservative, her experiences were mirrored by others who had attended public high school. Many reported that identifying as a feminist in high school meant dealing with a variety of stereotypes, including "icky feminists," "man haters" and "angry women." According to Terri from Massachusetts, "I think the hard thing about high school was that girls were either scared of feminism, the word, or no one would say they were a feminist." Having a feminist mother and attending a school where feminism was negatively stereotyped could spur feminist awakenings. Sometimes it was the lack of information presented that served as a catalyst. For Julia, of Evers, it wasn't the teachers but a textbook that sparked her feminism. She recalled:

I didn't see women reflected in the classroom so much. It was always a secondary or even a third status as you know, Betsy Ross did this, or this woman was a nurse or . . . But it was always like men did this, men did this, maybe women did this. I have an awful, awful memory. I can't remember many things, but one thing that I've never forgotten is in my—one of my history books in high school. I still remember the exact layout of the page and the paragraph in which they mentioned Jane Addams. It was the only time that they mentioned a woman in that entire chapter on settlement houses. And I was like, "Wait, this is a paragraph. It's not even a full story."

Julia's ability to recognize the inequity in women's historical coverage is grounded in the sense of feminism that she brought to her educational surroundings. Without some concept of women's importance in history, the textbook would have likely gone unnoticed. Some Evers feminists had positive educational experiences. Evers feminists, primarily from the East and West coasts, were more likely to have attended private high schools or public high schools that had women's studies curriculum or materials. For example, Abby's parents both taught at a private boarding school and it was through the out lesbian librarian recommending feminist books that Abby learned about feminism.

Coming to the "feminist bubble" of Evers College with its women positive courses would seem likely to encourage students to transform their taken-for-granted ideas of feminism into an articulated feminist identity. As discussed in Woodview, women's studies and college organizations can be places of transformation for students. For Becca, from Philadelphia, having a feminist mother immersed her in feminist ideas, but it wasn't until college she began to really think about feminism. She said:

It just became a part of me, so I didn't really have to think about it actually until I came here [Evers College] and started doing women's studies, and I was, like, "*Whoa*, [she laughs] there's so much else in this world."

Terri had the same experience of not questioning or identifying her ideas and beliefs as feminist. Her experience exemplifies the process of surfacing where she came to identify as a feminist after leaving home for college. She said:

I think that I always sort of took those ideas for granted as the way that everyone believed the world was. And then once I got to that place where they were being contested and I was under all of this pressure, I sort of found my way to it as an activist, rather than just as someone who was raised with those beliefs.

However, women's studies as a curriculum played a different role in Evers. Where women's studies played a positive role in Woodview and Green City, Evers students were much more ambivalent about it. Some reported having positive experiences in women's studies classes. For example, Deborah, a women's studies major and chemistry minor, found that her classes complicated her understanding and had the potential "to disrupt societal institutions." Mackenzie, a women's and Afro-American studies double major, found the classes to be safe spaces to delve more deeply into issues. However, just as Evers feminists critiqued their mothers, they also leveled criticism at women's studies courses and the overall discipline. Many of them said they found most of the courses at this all-women's college were feminist in content. Despite this focus on women and feminist theory throughout the curriculum, women's studies was not a fashionable major. The biggest criticisms were that women's studies was too academic, too much like therapy, and not activist enough. Becca, a women's studies major, said:

> Well, honestly [she laughs], I can't figure out why I am a women's studies major at this point because I feel like we just sit in class and we make up new words and crazy terminology that no one is going to understand except for other women's studies people, and we're going to corner this off like a new business plan. It seems like the main objective is to get this respected by academia so much that we are forgetting the origin of this social movement. It is so academic now and it's like real women get left out of discourse and when you talk about postmodernism versus this, that and the other thing and all of these crazy theories that aren't even going to be applicable to their real lives.

For Abby, a religion and philosophy double major, it wasn't the content of the courses that bothered her as much as the other students. She recalled:

> The people in the class—I just wanted them to stop talking about patriarchy. Yes, we're oppressed. We get it. And a lot of them would just make these really sweeping statements that really bothered me a lot of the time, they got too universal and I hated them for doing that.

Bailey, a women's studies major with an international relations minor, found women's studies to be too "self-indulgent" and found herself wondering if a class she was considering taking would just be a "group therapy session." Her response to women's studies is also noted by feminist scholar and professor Marjorie Jolles in what she calls the "theory/practice dilemma" she identified with her students. She defines this dilemma as:

The belief that there is a gap between the ideal and the real, perceived as a gap between what we do with our heads and what we do with our bodies, a gap between thought and action, and a gap between the solutions we envision to social problems and the challenges inherent in putting those envisioned solutions into practice.[24]

This, she argues, leads to a critique of women's studies as not dealing with real women and being disengaged from "real life." Jolles notes that this is a common contemporary feminist critique meant to "redress the failure and weaknesses of feminist scholarship of earlier generations."[25] As I will discuss in chapter 3, Evers's reaction to women's studies is largely a response to second-wave-generation feminism. Women's studies emerged from the same generation as their mothers' feminism and distancing oneself from it was another way to claim a new feminist identity, one separate from the feminism they had seen at home.

When comparing Woodview and Evers, the process of surfacing is significantly different. Woodview feminists grow up empowered but apolitical; they experience some sort of disjuncture between empowerment and oppression that leads to a search for answers. These answers are provided through women's studies and the camaraderie of a feminist organization. Evers's feminists grow up with feminism clearly articulated around them. As a way of defining their own feminist identities, they engage in disidentification from their mothers and women's studies, both situated in the second-wave feminist generation. It is interesting to note that none of the interviewees identified experiences with violence or sexual assault as factors in their coming to adopt a feminist identity. Green City with its connection to other social movements, slightly older feminist cohort and transplanted residents provides yet another way in which the social context shaped the process of surfacing.

Green City: Life Experiences and Feminism

While Woodview feminists came into a feminist identity in their midwestern hometowns and Evers feminists drew on their hometowns on the East or West coasts, only one-third of the Green City feminists grew up in the area, with the rest moving from regions around the United States such as the East Coast (e.g., Connecticut, New York and New Jersey), East Central (e.g., Kentucky), South (e.g., Texas and Louisiana), Midwest (e.g., Kansas) and Southwest (e.g., New Mexico).[26] This contributed to a less identifiable pattern of surfacing into a feminist identity. Many of them came to Green City with a sense of being a feminist, and in some cases, it was their search for a progressive community that drew them to Green City. For example, Star recalled:

I went to Green City kind of on a whim and a feeling. I was living in New Mexico and I was applying for the Peace Corps and I had a few more months left to go and I decided that I wanted to move again and Green City—I heard really good things about it and so I just moved there and then I loved it and I wasn't ready to leave so I didn't go.

As a result, Green City feminists' stories as a whole are not of growing up in a particular environment as they are in Woodview. Instead, their stories are often a mixture of coming to adopt the label of feminism in a political generation that encourages girls' empowerment but also limits girls' potential, and then seeking a progressive community in which to live out their feminism. I explore some of the factors common in Woodview and Evers and then present some Green City surfacing stories that draw on several dynamics, including involvement in other social movements.

A Mixture of Mothering. The role of mothers is a mixed bag in Green City. Two of the feminists did not mention their mothers at all in the narratives of becoming a feminist (e.g., Kelly and Natalie), two had homes that were openly antifeminist (e.g., Steve and Samantha), and three (e.g., Caroline, Lana, Star) had homes similar to the Woodview feminists where feminism was modeled through a strong mother but not articulated as a political ideology in the home. Only two of the Green City feminists reported having feminist mothers (i.e., Susan and Marley) and one had a feminist sister-in-law (i.e., Laurel) who influenced their feminist identities.

Samantha, who eventually left Kansas City in search of a like-minded progressive community, remembers how her mother gave her mixed messages about feminism. On one hand her mother often referred to feminists as femi-nazis. But there was also another side to her mother and her family:

> But my mom was a strong role model in some ways where she always worked, and she's always kind of loud and outspoken and asserted her needs and didn't necessarily—sometimes she bowed to the role of men as far as wifely duties of making dinner and being home for her husband—but otherwise she taught us to be strong, independent, and outgoing and assertive. And I had two older sisters who are ten and twelve years older than me who maybe were my early feminist role models. One of them ended up being an artist and a lesbian and living in San Francisco and doing a lot of activism and work. And the other one is a strong woman but maybe not an open feminist.

The idea that an antifeminist household (and life experiences) could spur a feminist identity is also expressed in the story of Steve. She said:

I think a lot of being a feminist comes from being raised the way that I was. I was raised in a very fundamentalist Christian home. I was raised Quaker when I was young and then in a fundamentalist environment. And I lived a lot of the time just with my mom and a lot of the time just with my dad. And I had a lot of trouble in school; I was picked on a lot. And when I grew up—I left home when I was fifteen—when I grew up, I realized that I didn't want to let people push me around anymore and a lot of that is where my strength came from. And when I joined that together with looking at the causes that I believed in and being a feminist, I started to be really analytical about the word [feminist]. I resisted using that word for a long time because I think that my identity politics have changed over time and will continue to change. I mean—I'll always be who I am now— but one thing I have realized is that I probably always will be a feminist because I believe in understanding gender and gender studies and what the implications of the binary gender system are on how they affect us.

Green City feminists did share some commonalities with the other communities. As stated earlier, three of the Green City feminists had parents similar to the apolitical yet feminist Woodview mothers. That is, they imparted a message of empowerment while not always identifying it as feminist. For Caroline, it was the role model her father set forth as the nurturer in the family that created a "feminist undertone" in her childhood home. She said:

> My parents were married until I was fourteen, and in that household my mom was the main breadwinner. So I was raised by a dad who did the cooking, the cleaning, doing my hair, buying me my first bra, talking about sex, doing all of that. So I really was never brought up with any idea of that that was unusual. I didn't think it was strange that mom couldn't go grocery shopping and so . . . But my parents never made the decision, saying, "We're going to raise our kids this way." They are high school educated and pretty conservative at the same time.

Just as the Woodview feminists illustrated that a feminist identity could flourish in a conservative area, so too did the stories of Green City feminists. Lana grew up in the South where her mother contradicted the norms of southern femininity. She said:

> How I came to identify as a feminist? Well, I grew up in the Deep South in Louisiana where [it was] very traditional, very [she pauses] debutant kind of upper middle class, white America in the South. . . . Fortunately,

my mother was a teacher. She is very highly educated and I grew up expecting, "Okay, you're going to go to college and graduate school."

For Star, growing up in Kentucky, her relationship with her mother had a similar effect of counteracting some cultural expectations. When her mom divorced her father and got a job, Star noted that she served as a good role model, but this did not mean that feminism was articulated during her growing up, a trend that continues in her adulthood. She recalled:

My family definitely wasn't against feminism by any means, but I don't know that—I mean we definitely didn't talk about it. . . . My mom is supportive of everything that I do. I talk about not just feminism but all kinds of oppressions. With my dad's family, I tend to get a lot of resistance. . . . My dad thinks that I feel like a victim a lot and that's his response to me.

Only three of the Green City feminist grew up with feminism articulated in their home, similar to many of the Evers feminists. Susan, who is a native of Green City, remembers:

I grew up in a home where my parents weren't really politically active, but I always knew that my mom identified herself as a feminist and so, from the very beginning, I was familiar with feminism and the idea of it. There was never an "uh-huh" moment [where I thought,] "I'm a feminist." It was part of my identity, I think, and then the more that I've learned about feminism as I've grown older, the more it's become part of my identity and my own definition of what that means. But so it was very vague, just sort of men and women aren't equal, very simple definition of feminism growing up, and then I started working in domestic violence and sexual assault movements when I was nineteen.

Her story exemplifies the idea of surfacing; feminism as an ideology exists for her until through a politicizing experience, she gradually comes to define an identity. Marley's mother also identified as a feminist, but it was her activism for her daughter that, in part, led Marley into feminism:

I don't I think I've always identified as a feminist. I think my mother would identify as a feminist. I don't think she participated at all in the 1960s in the feminist movement, but I think that for her feminism was like a value structure that was always part of our family. . . . My mother is a little bit more accomplished than my dad, and I think that growing up with that as the dynamic of my family--I think it helped. There wasn't ever a moment that I thought, "Oh I'm a girl, I can't do anything." . . . I think a lot of it was just growing up with a known reality of equality and then seeing that that wasn't everyone's perception. So I think also bringing the activist side into it actually started when I was younger. I was diagnosed with a learning disability and my entire life my mother and I have fought to make sure that I had acceptance in teaching me to understand that I was intelligent but also had a disability that needed to be addressed.

Overall, these stories illustrate that, in a variety of ways, mothers (and fathers) established the foundation of their daughters' feminist identity. Green City feminists give credence to the idea that family can shape political identities, sometimes unknowingly, particularly those of this feminist generation. Also evident in the stories of Green City feminists are the patterns that emerge from Woodview and Evers. While mothers varied in their input, it was educational settings that provided a transformational experience for many Green City feminists.

Education Equals Empowerment. Just as in Woodview and Evers, high school could serve as a foundation for a feminist identity. All of the Green City feminists who found high school empowering went to public high schools. However, the path to feminist ideas was not always clear-cut. Kelly remembered a high school experience that led her to explore what feminism meant. She said:

> I sort of fell into [activism] with a wonderful high school English teacher [who talked about] animal rights activism. It felt very comfortable and very easy to me until he came up with the theory that you couldn't be both for animal rights and pro-choice. And I was—here I am in, what, eleventh grade?—I just said, "What?!" [I] knew that that wasn't right for me, and so that led me to explore why I wanted, why I needed to define myself as pro-choice and then that was my introduction into the women's community.

Star's experience in a Kentucky school system illustrates how teachers and courses did not have to be explicitly feminist to encourage a feminist sense of self. She said:

> I think it [feminism] was just around me and I took it in more. I had a couple of teachers in high school, a male and female, who were—I mean never explicitly feminist—but just in the way that they taught class and the kinds of literature they had us read and that kind of thing. I don't remember ever really talking about feminism, but I remember it just being around.

While Star picked up feminist thought from a variety of sources in high school, other Green City feminists had specific experiences that introduced them to feminism. Natalie, who grew up in New Jersey, had influential teachers in high school who suggested readings to students and served as feminist models. Other feminists, such as Lana, who did not hear about feminism in her high school in Louisiana, found it through books. She recalled:

> But I guess my evolution of coming from growing up that way to actually saying "Yes, I'm a feminist" . . . is a different story. I was probably twelve or thirteen when I started [reading]. . . . So, probably when I officially was saying, "Yeah, I'm a feminist," would probably have been seventh grade. I think that for me books helped connect me to the fact that there are feminists out there . . . I did eventually find a community of people.

While some of the Green City feminists learned about feminism in high school, it was college where many of them were able to identify that they were indeed feminists. Star, who felt surrounded by feminist ideas in high school, remembers sitting in a college seminar on Virginia Woolf and realizing that she had been a feminist all along. For Caroline, the realization came in graduate school when she often was called upon in graduate-level English classes to speak as the class feminist. For some, the experience at home made adopting a feminist identity a moment of surfacing. Marley, whose feminist mother fought for her in the educational system because of her learning disability, remembers "it didn't take much" to identify as a feminist after taking a class on women and history. For others coming to a feminist identity was more of a journey. For example, Kelly, who had been told she could not be pro-choice and pro-animal rights, college was a place to continue exploring how she would fit feminism into her life. She recalled:

> The university that I attended didn't have a women's studies major, they had a minor but even that was loose. No one had been awarded a minor in several years and basically two professors that had been teaching there since the 1970s were willing to work with me, and so during my four years we created a women's studies department, which was so cool.

Her desire to create a feminist foundation for her college education was fueled not only by her belief that this was important but also by the activism she saw around her. She said:

But it was—it was really important. I went to a state school and it was one of the . . . less expensive schools, especially in Connecticut, and it just seemed fundamental to make feminist thought be accessible to whoever wants it. And the ironic thing is that the university did not approve the department until after I had received my degree. So, I actually had a major in English with a minor in women's studies. It is funny. In the university—it was in a college town and there were five or six colleges there—activism happened and this was when Daddy Bush was president and we were fighting for abortion rights and against the war and activism.

While Kelly comes to claim a feminist identity through educational experiences, she does so through involvement in other social movements. She worked in a feminist bookstore in Austin, Texas, and taught high school there, where she was reprimanded for providing too much information on birth control and abortion to her students. After leaving that job, she moved to an island off the coast of Washington to write about her experiences as a teacher and ended up taking a job as manager of the feminist bookstore in Green City.

While classes in English and history could spur the adoption of a feminist identity, women's studies classes, and the spillover into campus organizing were places this often happened. For Natalie, the foundation set in place through an influential high school teacher blossomed into a feminist identity at her East Coast private college. She recalled:

[College] was a great opportunity to allow my feminist identity to grow because there were opportunities to participate in things and to be active and to meet other feminists and to get together and organize things ourselves. . . . We organized Take Back the Night rallies and candlelight vigils and . . . I met a lot of young women who had similar experiences and having that forum in a college environment—being able to talk and until all hours of the night and getting to know people, make friends. It just was a really good environment to develop that side of me.

Laurel attended the same college as Natalie and remembers that being a feminist was not a big deal there, similar to the Evers East Coast "feminist bubble" environment. For her, the experiences and conversations with her feminist sister-in-law set the foundation for her feminist awakening in college. She recalled:

I had many discussions with her [the sister-in-law] about [feminism] and then I got to college and started thinking about it on my own and read books. . . . I took Women's Studies 101, but that was way after actually I started identifying as a feminist. Right at the start of college I started talk-ing to other people and realizing that "Yeah, this something that I care a lot about and this is something I want to identify with and that I want to fight a lot of the issues and I want to be involved."

For Steve, who attended a public university in the Green City area, women's studies put a name to the beliefs she had long embraced. She took a course on pornography and began to identify as a feminist. As a result, she double majored in speech and women's studies. Susan also attended a Green City public univer-sity and found women's studies when she began attending college and was search-ing for a major. She said:

> In looking at what I wanted to actually do to finish my degree, women's studies was the only program I found that kept my interest, intrigued me, [and] was anywhere near studying what I felt was important to me in this world on a passionate level. I could have gotten through other programs but that was the only one that really grabbed me.

Overall, common to all the communities studied is the importance of educa-tional settings, teachers, classes and organizations in the fostering of a feminist identity. Taking women's studies for Green City feminists is a similar experience to Woodview feminists. It allowed them to label their thoughts and beliefs as feminist. What is missing from the Green City stories is the antagonism felt by Evers feminists toward women's studies, a dynamic that reflects the lack of dis-sension toward second-wave-generation feminists, particularly mothers.

Surfacing Through Activism. Along with their home life and educational experiences, it was involvement in other movements that brought many Green City feminists to adopt a feminist identity. Often the act of identifying as queer, lesbian, bisexual or transgender brought about their surfacing. Natalie, in addi-tion to positive teacher role models, also credits her search to coming out as a lesbian as well as pro-feminist music. Marley also credits coming out as a lesbian in her path to identifying as a feminist. However, it was not just sexuality that brought the interviewees to feminism. Samantha's story illustrates how other movements were an impetus in adopting a feminist identity. She initially became involved in the male-dominated punk movement in high school.[27] It was there she began to articulate some ideas of herself as a feminist. She said:

> I was political and I was assertive, but at the same time, I was in such a male-oriented scene that a lot of times I felt like—see, even though I iden-tified as a feminist—I think I secretly kind of felt like within my scene the

only way to get listened to and the only way to be valid was to kind of function as a male just because of the scene I was in. . . . We would go to festivals for punks and hard-core kids and there would be political workshops, but I felt like the only people . . . who got listened to and said important smart things were men because it was male dominated and the women weren't really made to feel important. So I shaved my head and hung out with a lot of boys. I kind of dressed like a boy, and I think ended up trying to function as a boy and kind of isolating myself from women and trying to function but still recognizing myself as a feminist? Or trying to but not really understanding maybe what that meant.

To explore what feminism meant, Samantha tried to start a women's group in high school. She recalled:

I first started a feminist group when I was a teenager called Girl Positive that was a young feminist discussion group that we had in my parents' house. And I think that the first time I thought about doing that was when I read—I was really into zines and I read a book about zines that talked about something called the Revolutionary Sewing Circle or Knitting Circle. And so I heard about all these women coming together and talking about politics and their personal issues, and I didn't really have a way to connect to women because I was in a mainly male-centered punk scene. So I decided to start this group in high school. So that was my introduction to feminism—kind of a self-made feminist.

She continued describing the group's activities:

We would watch homoerotic movies, have sleepovers and then I tried to have discussion groups about just different issues, like we would talk about our families, we would talk about school, our relationships with men [and] other women. It was hard because I was the oldest in the group and the other ones were all in high school. I think that I had just started doing an independent study and had dropped out of high school. . . . Most of the girls in the group were still in high school and had a hard time. They weren't very confident and they weren't very good at talking about things in a group. So I feel like I went about it in a few wrong ways where it wasn't like a group of people that were already comfortable with each other talking about extreme issues. My goal was that we would make a zine for younger girls in middle school or elementary school just about the things that we knew, things that we had learned in mistakes that we had made. So that they could read it and know that they had allies and not have to make the same mistakes.

After the failure of the group, Samantha threw herself into other forms of activism. She went on an animal rights tour, organized political forums for people too young to vote, participated in zine symposiums and worked on censorship issues. When she moved to Green City, she continued to search for a place that was more women oriented. Her search brought her to work part-time in the feminist bookstore. She recalled her experience:

> Then moving to Green City, I was heavily entrenched in the male punk scene for a little while and just realized that when I was around them I felt like I shouldn't talk. I would come home but I wouldn't connect it [to] patriarchy or constructs of our social scenes or anything, I would just come home and be like, "You know, I just say so much bullshit. I don't say anything important. Maybe I shouldn't talk for a while. Maybe I should go for like a week without talking just so that when I say things they can be important." But really it wasn't that I was saying things that were unimportant, it was that [I was] being made to feel unimportant because I was with a strongly male punk scene where [I wasn't listened to] or respected or taken seriously because I was a sex object kind of or—[she pauses]—my friendships with them [men] were secretly sexually driven because they were all these young guys and when they realized that you aren't going to sleep them, the things you had to say were less important.

It is clear that for Samantha the journey to feminism came through a variety of personal and activism experiences. Even though she identified as a feminist at age thirteen, it was not until ten years later that she begins to think as a feminist. Her transformation is a process of coming to know the world around her, a world shaped by feminism. Aspects of her story are echoed in Kelly's interest in animal rights and protesting the war, Laurel's sister-in-law's teaching her about menstrual activism, and Natalie and Marley's engagement with LGBTQ movements as they were coming out.

Overall, the factors of mothers, education and other movements are present in the stories in Green City, yet the factors leading to a feminist identity are not as clear-cut as in Woodview or Evers. I argue this complexity is due to the differences in their formative environment, with Green City feminists coming from all over the United States. Yet the pattern of surfacing remains the same. Girls and boys grow up in a political generation that encourages no limits, while at the same time treating men and women differently. It is only through exposure to experiences in high school, college or other movements that the adoption of a feminist identity comes about. Having a feminist mother or father has the potential to encourage children to adopt the same ideals and identity but this is not a straightforward causal relationship. Contemporary feminists grow up in a society where it is possible to have feminist mothers or at least mothers who pass on messages of empowerment. This, in part, is the everywhere feminism of Generation Fluoride where feminist ideas are present yet not always expressed as political and feminist. Needed are other experiences to bring about surfacing to a feminist identity, and those experiences are often uniquely shaped by the community culture and environment, as the case of mothers in Woodview and Evers illustrates.

Surfacing in Generation Fluoride

The processing of surfacing addresses one of the questions that has long concerned social movement scholars. That is, how and why do people join social movements and adopt activist identities? Movement scholars have proposed several answers. People are drawn into movements on the basis of grievances (i.e., lack of opportunities or resources).[28] While the Woodview feminists do experience a disjuncture between empowerment and oppression that can be seen as grievances, many of the feminists in all three communities adopt a feminist identity based on experiences that allow them to articulate it as an already existing ideology, more than just the result of the "click" of understanding their personal experiences as political. Friendship networks and biographical availability are two other potential factors in movement recruitment.[29] While connecting with other feminists may serve to draw people into the movement or movement organizations, as seen in some instances in Woodview and in Green City, there are equal numbers of feminists who adopt the identity on their own, without the support of friendship networks. The large number of college students in the case studies would also support the idea that it is biographical availability (i.e., experiencing a time in life open to joining a movement) that brings people to movements. For many of the feminists in this study, college and particularly organizations and curriculum bring them to a feminist identity. However, not all the feminists had these educational experiences. Another explanation advanced is that of frame alignment where potential activists come into contact with movement leaders and ideas. This is true of many of the Green City feminists and their participation in other social movements. Yet, none of these explanations alone provides a complete explanation. Instead, I argue that the process of surfacing points to a more complex account. In a political generation where social movement ideas are in the mainstream culture, coming to identify with a movement and a movement identity is more a process of networks, timing and interaction set within a specific community environment. The role of the environment is particularly clear in the cases of Woodview and Evers. Woodview and Evers feminists come from particular places that shape their process of surfacing differently. It is by looking at the environment that we are able to answer the question: Why is there such a difference between Evers feminists and their dismissal of their mothers' feminism and Woodview feminists who are largely uncritical of their mothers? An important component in both Woodview and Evers is the level of acceptance of feminism. While all the contemporary feminists are of a similar political generation, an articulated feminist identity is not accepted in Woodview and consequentially feminism is not imparted to children as a meaningful ideology. Evers, with its private college that draws mostly from the more liberal East and West coasts, there are fewer sanctions against articulating a feminist identity. Evers mothers more freely express to their children their empowerment messages as feminist and political. So, then, why are Woodview children more open to sharing their feminism with their mothers and seeing them as sympathetic to their children's feminist identities? In a community where a feminist identity is accepted, such as Evers, the need for allies is not as great, leading to critiques and generational disidentification. It is these generational relations I turn to in chapter 3.

Dissension in the House of Feminism

Jessica Valenti, a 29-year-old blogger from Astoria (by way of Williamsburg), and Marcia Pappas, a 57-year-old life coach who owned and ran a hair salon in Albany for most of her career, might be surprised to find out how much they had in common if they ran into each other at a party. (Admittedly, it's hard to imagine what that party would look like.)

IN A 2008 *New York Times* column entitled "Feminists Find Unity Is Elusive," Jessica Valenti and Marcia Pappas were situated as generational opposites because of their presidential endorsements. Valenti is the founder of the Feministing. com Web site and author of *Full Frontal Feminism*, and Pappas is the president of the New York State chapter of NOW. Pappas argued that the late Ted Kennedy's endorsement of Barack Obama was because he "can't or won't handle the prospect of a woman president." Valenti, described as wearing three-inch heels and "fashionably bare legs" on the Stephen Colbert show, responded by saying NOW does not represent her. She added that the future of feminism does not lie in "old-school organizations" such as NOW. The columnist then (somewhat condescendingly) concludes, "The two women should probably talk. Surely, there's a message board somewhere big enough for both of them. We already know they have a lot in common."[1]

What this opinion piece makes evident is that age (i.e., 29 versus 57) is a dividing line between feminist generations, along with dress, appearance (i.e., "bare legs") and the belief that organizations make change. Presented here in the national media is the idea that feminist generations are at odds, like mothers and their daughters, who have little or no contact with each other. This dissension in "the family house of feminism" feeds the perception of the movement's "disunity," a view so commonplace that feminist writer Katha Pollit took the media (and feminist pundits) to task for perpetuating it. She wrote:

Can we please stop talking about feminism as if it is mothers and daughters fighting about clothes? Second wave: you're going out in *that*? Third wave: just drink your herbal tea and leave me alone! Media commentators love to reduce everything about women to catfights about sex, so it's not surprising that this belittling and historically inaccurate way of looking at the movement—angry prudes versus drunken sluts—has recently taking on a new life, including among feminists.[2]

As Pollitt points out, feminists themselves contribute to this sense of generational division. For example, although originally conceptualized as a "warm, personal, political, irresistible guide for young feminists,"[3] Phyllis Chesler's 1997 book *Letters to a Young Feminist* came under fire by a number of contemporary feminists who found her tone condescending.[4] In her book, Chesler writes a letter to an imaginary young woman or man, "somewhere between the ages eighteen and thirty five" as her "heir," someone to take on the "legacy" she has left her/ him.[5] Chesler attempted to rectify this young feminist's lack of knowledge stating, "You are entitled to know our war stories. We cannot, in good conscience, send you into battle without giving you a very clear idea of what may happen there."[6] Chesler is not alone in chiding the younger generation. Scholars Nancy Naples and Stephanie Gilmore both document the intergenerational dialogue at the 2002 Veteran Feminists of America conference where contemporary feminists were berated for not making meaningful social change.[7] Gilmore reports longtime activist Susan Brownmiller lamenting, "I don't hear strong, clear feminist voices today. I don't see women coming up with new theories."[8] Predictably, the contemporary feminist response to these messages is often anger. Feminist blogger Stephanie Herold responded to one such message in her essay "Young Feminists to Old Feminists: If You Can't Find Us, It's Because We're Online." She writes, "It's really irritating to read yet another article insisting that you don't exist. For young feminists, that happens all too often." She then proceeds to detail the online activism of young feminists across the country, including protesting the murder of abortion provider Dr. George Tiller and grassroots campus organizing.[9] The idea that young feminists are around but doing a different sort of activism is what scholar Astrid Henry argues is the central foundation of contemporary feminism, (i.e., the creation of disidentification between generations of feminists). Analyzing feminist contemporary texts, she concludes, "Younger feminists today seem to find their collectivity mainly through a *shared generational stance* against second-wave feminism and second-wave feminists."[10]

This shared generational stance often takes the form of sharp critiques by contemporary feminists based on their perceptions of feminist history—a foundation that the second-wave generation finds shaky at best. A reoccurring complaint about contemporary feminism is its historical understanding, or lack of it. Some scholars agree with Chesler that contemporary feminists are lacking a sense of feminist history and the context of their "inheritance." Scholar Catherine Orr argues that "the image of the monolithic, ideal, 'mainstream' feminism against which these young women battle is rarely examined as a *representation*; rather, it almost always is accepted as 'real.'"[11] That is, young people in the twenty-first century often come to feminism with perceptions of the second-wave generation and not a realistic understanding of its myriad of accomplishments, goals and issues, in addition to its problems.[12] This results in contemporary feminists judging the second-wave generation based on their understanding of several particular aspects of the overall movement. Those issues key in generational distancing include ideas such as all second-wave-generation feminists believed in essentialism (i.e., the belief women and men are distinct psychologically, spiritually, and socially from each other based on biological differences) and all advocated separatism (i.e., a stance proposed by lesbian feminists who believed withdrawing from patriarchy was the first step in dismantling it). Important in both of these ideas is the term "all." These were ideas embraced by some but were also hotly debated within the second-wave generation. Adding to these misconceptions is the contemporary belief that all second-wave-generation feminists ignored racism, classism and homophobia in the movement. Another predominant critique is that the second-wave generation was antisex as evidenced by books such as *Jane Sexes It Up* that seek to reclaim sexuality as a part of feminism.[13] Many contemporary feminists also claim that all second-wave-generation feminists advocated gender neutrality and androgyny (i.e., acting in a way that is either not gendered or is both masculine and feminine), arguing that these concepts stand in the way of understanding gender fluidity. Gender fluidity is a common contemporary feminist belief that there are no true gender or sex categories and instead people experience a form of gender and sexual fluidity that allows them to move on a continuum of action, thought and identity. This fluidity makes claiming identity categories like lesbian and gay (or heterosexual) outdated and instead the idea of queer and genderqueer is often adopted, indicating that no particular sexual, sex or gender category is chosen. Related to this idea is the common contemporary sentiment that second-wave-generation feminists discarded femininity as weak and subordinate and emulated masculinity as the key to gaining societal power. As a result, contemporary feminists often seek to reclaim femininity and its characteristics as powerful. On the whole, the generational critique of the second-wave feminist generation is that it made no strides to change cultural ideas and instead focused on institutional change, leaving contemporary feminists to correct their omissions, particularly those around class, race, sexuality and gender.

This focus on changing culture leads to a perception by some in the second-wave feminist generation that there are no young feminists or the ones that identify as feminist are not doing "real" activism. This is met with a contemporary feminist view that the second-wave generation created a historical legacy of exclusion and a denigration of femininity that needs to be fixed. With these generational perceptions in mind, I explore how contemporary feminists view the second-wave generation and I do so by moving the analysis away from the national and cyberspace dialogue to the local. Looking at the three communities studied, I ask: How do contemporary feminists view the second-wave feminist generation? Is this perception of dissension and discord, often repeated in news articles, blogs and Web sites, an accurate picture? To examine this dynamic, I continue to draw upon the argument that community environment can shape the ideology and identities of the activists within it.

Generational Relations in Contemporary Feminist Communities

By examining the community level, I move from investigating only how a political generation is characterized in blogs, articles and Web sites, and instead focus on the ways in which microcohorts of this political generation within particular settings construct beliefs about second-wave-generation feminism. I find that a continuum of generational relations emerges, ranging from the acceptance and admiration of Woodview, to the more neutral identification of difference in Green City, to the antagonism of Evers. This continuum is due in part to what social movement scholars see as a part of the process of constructing a collective identity, with activists defining who they are and who is not "them."[14] These decisions are based in ideas about the identities and attributes of groups seen as outside of "we."[15] In contemporary feminism, this can become a generational dynamic, and I find that these boundaries of "we" vs. "them" are influenced by the community context. For example, Woodview's focused feminist identity had the least critical and "gentlest" critiques with the most open boundaries to the second-wave feminist generation. I argue that this is in part due to the hostility of the Woodview community to feminism and the need for all allies to work together. Green City feminists with their interaction in established feminist organizations were critical of both generations but had permeable boundaries that allowed interaction to occur, effectively neutralizing criticism on both sides. Evers feminists were the most critical, drawing distinct, tight boundaries between themselves and the second-wave feminist generation. I now examine each community in more detail.

Woodview—Generational Allies. When asked to consider the difference between themselves and second-wave-generation feminists, Woodview feminists' answers ranged from there really was no difference to seeing the second-wave generation as the foundation of the work they were trying to accomplish today. Most of the Woodview feminists saw the second-wave generation as admirable and active. This view emerges from Woodview's focused feminism that continues to define the second-wave generation as a part of "us." Woodview feminists downplayed the idea of dissension as they worked to make change in a hostile environment. For example, Anna was skeptical of reports of movement dissension. She said, "My impressions are really based on the media and so I don't know how much validity there is to that." She added that she also believed that second-wave-generation feminists have shifted their goals "because times are different." This idea that dissension was not an issue and that feminism was changing to suit the times was a reoccurring theme in Woodview. For example, Jane said:

> I think that they've [second-wave-generation feminists] gotten us a long way and now it's to the point where it is. They've gotten us a lot of laws . . . and now where do we go from there? We've gotten to grow from that. I feel they had all of these issues . . . and now how do we use these and how do we educate people about these?

The theme of building on the past was also picked up by Emily. She said:

> I don't think that I or anyone else is doing anything else profoundly different. I think that we wouldn't know what to do if there hadn't been a feminism before us and we wouldn't even have any idea of where to go. But I think that we are just kind of building on that and taking—well, yeah— I guess taking the same issues and just continuing the fight for them.

The challenge then for Woodview feminists was figuring out how to build on the past. For example, Leslie said:

> We've just—we've made huge steps. It's a lot better than it was but there's still structuralized discrimination—and I think maybe people in the feminist movement are the ones who are most keenly aware of that—that we're not done and that we're far from done—even though we're totally appreciative and grateful for everything that's come before us. And that fight may have been much harder than ours because I have grown up being more or less more equal than maybe my mom was, and feeling that I have more there for me, more opportunities and that more is open for me than women in the past.

Leslie's statements are openly admiring of the second-wave feminist generation. She said:

> The one thing I've heard about the second wave is that it was big on consciousness-raising and that's something that I'm really passionate about. There's an element of that within in me, definitely. That's a huge thing. The word "awareness" comes out of my mouth 500 times on any given day, and people that are close friends of mine get so sick of it.

Kyra, who initially came to feminism through her local NOW chapter made up primarily of older women, saw the second-wave generation as still engaged and important to the contemporary movement. She said, "With the older feminists, they're getting involved. I mean there's [sic] people who just have regular bus seats for when they go to . . . their marches and stuff. . . . They're just so used to it. That's what I think is cool." Interacting with NOW members was an experience for Kyra that made her long for some of the relationships they had. Speaking of a NOW chapter president she knew, she said:

> But she's got these great friendships with these other women in the group, and they're all so different and they know each other so well. I wish it would be like that [today], but it doesn't seem like that. . . . I don't know them well enough to know if they live it out on a day-to-day basis or if they fight with their friends about it or they just have friends that believe the same things as them so they don't need to fight about it.

While acknowledging the continued efforts and achievements of the second-wave generation, some Woodview feminists did see some differences between themselves and this generation. While not labeling it as a source of strife in the movement, Sally wanted more intergenerational dialogue. She said, "I hold [to] the idea that there needs to be a lot of differences. People really need to disagree and that's . . . what keeps things going. And so there needs to be a lot of dialogue I think between—I don't know—older women and younger women." Ben was concerned that contemporary feminism would discard ideas such as women-only space *because* they were from the second-wave generation. He said:

> I personally am afraid of women-only spaces getting trampled on like the *Vagina Monologues* and that's something that I would never want to see. So that is definitely something that bears some watching to see how that with all these groups snowballing together—how do these women-only spaces—how does that play out?

For Zoe and Laura, differences between generations were hard to identify. Zoe noted that there were differences but could not specify them. She said, "I think there's . . . it's not distinct but there's a difference between second wave from [she trails off]. I think there is probably a difference." Laura also struggled to specify those differences. She said:

> I think that there's [*sic*] a lot of differences between second and third wave or young feminists and older ones from other generations in that sense because from my understanding of a lot of second-wave feminists or older feminists don't understand that [she hesitates] don't feel the [she pauses] I mean, they are still about the equality, they're still pegging those boards away, which is awesome because we still need that. . . . I think that's why [the movement] hasn't been maybe as successful as it could have been because of different opinions and the emotions attached to them.

Some Woodview feminists simply stated that there were differences (and similarities) in the generations. For example, Jaclyn noted that contemporary feminism had a new energy and focused on newer issues; Sally concluded that the movement was more inclusive now. Both Zoe and Jane concluded that they knew little of the second-wave generation and had little interaction with older feminists. Jane stated that contemporary feminists need to build on the work of the second-wave generation and not critique them. Paulina, who later attended Evers College, had the strongest critique. She said that the second-wave generation with its focus on separatism was a concern for her. However, she couched her critique in a context of not really knowing enough about feminist theories and history. She said:

> In my opinion, a lot of second-wave feminism comes from a lot of ideas about more—I'm making assumptions here—maybe some feminist theory with a lesbian sort of twist on it. [It is] by no means man hating or anything like that but sort of the separatist idea in a way and I think I'm so far from that.

Often, when a difference between generations was noted by interviewees, it was age that came up. Leslie recalled one protest she attended:

> When Laura and I went to protest at Walmart, we were the only two people there that didn't have grandchildren. They were all like these NOW old ladies that were still raging, going to meetings all the time, and Laura and I were like, "We can't wait to be retired so that all we have to do is volunteer." That'll be so much fun I bet because your whole life is just fighting a good fight.

Here age and dedication to the movement becomes an admirable trait and not a barrier between the generations.

Overall, Woodview feminists had little to say negatively about feminists who came of age in the 1960s and 1970s, and I should also note that when reviewing Woodview transcripts, I found that the critique of the second-wave generation was often initiated by me and seldom by the interviewees. There are two reasons for their lack of negativity. First is the lack of knowledge or interaction with the second-wave generation. Woodview feminists, as discussed in chapter 2, did not have many feminist role models in their families compared to the other communities. Also, as evident in the statements of Leslie and Paulina, their lack of historical knowledge made it difficult to critique the second-wave generation. This fits with the views of Phyllis Chesler and other second-wave-generation feminists who argue that one important aspect missing from contemporary feminism is an understanding of history and in particular the strategies, tactics and theories of the movement. However, this lack of knowledge was not completely negative. In Woodview, it contributed to an overall acceptance of second-wave-generation feminism. In fact, Woodview feminists have little to gain by critiquing other feminists and enacting identity boundaries. Woodview's environment is such that contemporary feminists need all potential allies and alienating the second-wave feminist generation would only increase their isolation. Therefore, the acceptance of the efforts of the second-wave generation contributed to the focused feminist identity of Woodview. Woodview creates a feminist community with open boundaries to the second-wave generation, and mostly through the local NOW chapter some Woodview feminists did interact with older feminists, even if infrequently. The generational differences are seen as largely the results of age and changing times, and dissension is downplayed and viewed as "different opinions." By and large, Woodview feminists continue to focus on wanting all generations of feminists to work together, seeing the work of the past as the foundation for the future.

Green City—Permeable Boundaries. In Green City, the issue of generational dissension is more pronounced than Woodview but overall was "neutralized" by critiques of both generations. Green City differs from Woodview in that it has a large, active second-wave generation of feminists and organizations, making multigenerational interaction more possible. A dominant theme in the interviews was that the second-wave and contemporary feminist generations often do not "get" each other and this dialogue is similar to that on the national scene (described at the beginning of the chapter). The generational relationship in Green City is expressed in two ways. First, the second-wave generation was seen as out of touch with contemporary feminism in general. This view was predominantly expressed by Green City feminists who had little interaction in established feminist organizations. Secondly, both generations were viewed as misinterpreting each other. This was most clearly expressed by two Green City feminists who had the most interaction with established second-wave-generation organizations.

Contributing to these types of relationships was the view that the second-wave feminist generation was simply different from contemporary feminism, a view not always based in an accurate history of the movement. For example, Steve stated, "I think [contemporary feminism] is a different type of feminism because the issues are different." Samantha continued in the same vein, outlining what she saw the differences as:

> I feel like for me the second wave seems like it was [about] predominantly major issues like abortion. [She pauses.] I feel like third-wave feminism is about being critical all the time about your surroundings and still being able to be a sex worker or be sex positive or watch mainstream TV but being critical the whole time and having dialogue within your community and discussing it. And [it is] being able to call each other or people in your community on oppressive language or different things that they do. . . . Everyday personal is political rather than these things are specifically political.

It is not clear that Samantha knows that the "personal is political" is a second-wave slogan as she views it through the lens of contemporary feminism, and much of what she is describing are the dynamics born from radical feminism and consciousness-raising. The lack of knowledge about the second-wave feminist generation was also evident in Star's critique. She said:

> I think that maybe older feminists don't—that I've met—some value that [spirituality] a lot and some don't value that a lot. Some [second-wave-generation feminists] value much more getting into the workplace and making the same amount of money alongside men.

Feminists active in the 1960s and 1970s would be quick to point out to Star that she is unaware of the long-standing focus on feminist spirituality and a large body of literature on women's spirituality.

While Samantha and Star draw their distinctions based on views not enmeshed in history, Natalie based her perceptions on her feelings about *Ms. Magazine*, a landmark feminist journal launched in 1971, and the coverage of feminism in newer feminist magazines. She said, "In magazines there's [*sic*] a lot of articles published by younger feminists, but right now I get *Ms.* and that's not part of that. [*Ms.*] doesn't feel part of that generation. It doesn't feel part of my feminist reality." For some Green City feminists, this sense of "not being a part" of their reality resulted in a sense of enmity toward the second-wave generation.

For example, Lana saw second-wave-generation feminists as potentially disrespecting her choices. While men at her work had more restrictions on dress, as one of the few women, Lana had more freedom. She said:

> Talking to the guys at work they're just like, "Oh my God, you get away with murder. You get to wear earrings to work and you get to do this and you can say things that we can't." [It is one of] the few times that it's actually somewhat [of a benefit] to be a woman at [work]. I'm going to fucking take it and run with it. And if old-school feminists want to cross me off the list and say, "Oh you're . . ." [she trails off.]

Here, Lana is not responding to actual comments from older feminists but her perception of how they would view her for taking advantage of being a female in a nearly all-male work environment.

Because Green City feminists interacted with the second-wave generation, their comments were more specific about the relationship. Susan's work as a sexual assault advocate and volunteer coordinator in a local organization brought her into contact with second-wave-generation feminists. Susan said that when the generations interacted, it could generate strife. An example for her was the 2004 March for Women's Lives in Washington, D.C. Susan, who was one of the older Green City feminists at thirty-two, said:

> It's like the concert thing when you're old and tired you want to sit down. [At the rally for the march] when all the young people stood up and you heard this: "Down in front! Down in front!" And then we didn't want to sit down, we wanted to stand up. "Just sit down—then we can all see!" I mean, this was back and forth tension. . . . I was at the women's march on D.C. in April, right? A million people, *a million people*! And we were actually really up close to the evening stage, just seven or eight rows back, and when all the different presenters and everyone started talking, the younger people in the crowd would stand up and the older people would sit down. I mean, I thought there were going to be some brawls going on! [She laughs.] And it did turn into—there were actually comments around about "this younger generation this and that" and "this older generation thinks this and that"—and I was witnessing this because of whether to stand up or sit down when people came onstage.

According to Susan, this generational tension symbolized by standing versus sitting was the result of each side's not understanding each other and this feeling emerged, in part, due to contemporary feminists' critical views. She said:

[There is] the criticism of feminism being such an essentialist movement and older generations feeling criticized for that and not being acknowledged for what they have done. I think that stems from a lot of the younger generation not looking at the history and where we've come from and being more critical than really understanding this as a movement. There is movement that happens—progression. There is a point A and a point B and on and on and on and it is going to look different. Yes, you need to look at that critically and explore what needs to change in order for it to move forward, but it doesn't necessarily mean that there has to be judgment and criticism when you look back.

While Marley agreed that contemporary feminists did not take the time to get to know the achievements and philosophies of the second-wave generation, she was also critical of the ways in which contemporary feminists were expected to interact within organizations founded by the second-wave generation. Marley, in her work as a political campaign manager, had extensive experience with organizations commonly thought of as second-wave generation, in her case NOW, NARAL and Planned Parenthood. An outcome of her experience was her view that the attempts by second-wave-generation organizations to appeal to younger feminists were a series of missteps. She said:

I think on a lot of levels [feminist generations] don't understand each other and it's weird to be—I feel like an interloper in some degrees because I'm—I love NOW and I love NARAL and I love Planned Parenthood and I totally see their participation and politics as really important, and then—I more culturally identify with third wave, and I think they don't understand each other in a lot of ways. I think that the more established organizations only see the obvious. They see, "Ooh, it's just about rock bands, girl rock bands." "Oh they're doing a festival with booths and stuff." And then they'll—[She laughs.] This is always my joke about HRC [Human Rights Campaign] and other groups is they think they "get" things and so they try to copy them and then they just totally bastardize them. [NOW will] see an organic booth and [think], "That's kind of third wave." And NOW will . . . invite Evian and MAC cosmetics and think that that's the same and it's not getting the point of it. . . . It's not [just] music . . . it's about a very particular message in music and it's about understanding that a group like Sleater-Kinney is different from The Donnas even though I'm sure to somebody who isn't intimately involved, they're both girl bands. They're both kind of rock.[16] One is a corporate sellout and one refuses to [sell out] and it's very important [to know that]. And that's what I think one of the hugest [*sic*] disconnects is that the establishment [groups like NARAL and NOW] don't get what it is about.

Implicit in Marley's analysis is that established organizations equal second-wave-generation feminism. The Human Rights Campaign is not usually considered a second-wave feminist organization but instead is a gay rights organization founded in 1980 to raise funds for congressional elections. In her equation, then, "organic," less structured action equals contemporary feminism, and profession-alized established organizations equal second-wave-generation feminism.

There are formally structured "third-wave" organizations such as the Third Wave Foundation that do organizing and fund-raising and give out grants. How-ever, in support of her observation, I also observed a disconnect between genera-tions in the one-way flow of communication at the 2007 Young Feminist Leadership Institute held during NOW's national meetings. Young women were encouraged to "grow" and "dialogue" with national NOW leadership, but nowhere did the publicity promote the idea that older feminists could listen and learn from the younger ones. According to Marley, the outcome of these organi-zations not "getting" contemporary feminism was that the second-wave feminist generation used contemporary feminists without integrating them or meeting their needs. She said:

> The second-wave organizations try to commodify you. They want you to be their poster girl. They want you to show up in a month when they want you. They want you to be in their fund-raising letters. They want to use you. HRC is notorious for that. They used Ellen DeGeneres. They used Candace Gingrich. They used Chastity Bono. That's what they do. They find the big gay and glom on. On a sick level they used Matthew Shepard. Do I disagree with what they were trying to do? No. Do a lot of people find that offensive? A little bit. And a lot of people see that [and say], "Oh, you're sold. You're now their bitch."

In Marley's view, part of the generational disconnect was the importance of fund-raising and the role that age and money play in these organizations. She said:

> I could go and show up and work with NARAL or NOW or whoever and my input wouldn't really be that important because one, I think age a little bit, but two . . . you're not on the board. Well, I'm not going to get on the board because I'm not going to write a $10,000 check. . . . If I was an

ex-congresswoman, sure, I could get on the board but I'm not, and so the ability to influence and mold the movement is a lot less unless you're like part of that power.

However, Green City feminists did not see this disconnect as solely the fault of established feminist groups. According to Kelly, manager of the feminist bookstore, it was not just the fault of older feminists. She said, "Definitely third-wave feminists have a disrespect for second-wave feminists. And that's a real general statement. I'm sure that somebody is going to yell at me for saying it, as they should." Echoing Susan and Kelly, Marley also took contemporary feminists to task. She continued:

> I don't think [contemporary feminists] appreciate the history and whys . . .
> Why did [a feminist organization] develop in these ways and why did they
> do what they do? Why do they have fund-raisers that cost $10,000 a table?
> I mean, they don't have them for $10,000, but you know . . . That is a huge
> turnoff, but there's a reason for that. [Established feminist organizations]
> could be really effective with a huge volunteer base, but that takes so much
> more energy than being able to have a war chest. Period. [Contemporary
> feminists] see it as, "Oh, this is an elitist group of women who once they get
> what they want . . . they'll not give a shit about working-class people, sexual
> minorities particular[ly] gender identity, and women of color." [Contem-
> porary feminists do] not understand who it is that these groups have to
> appeal to. How it is that they have to maneuver. [Established organizations]
> can't show up with a disabled transgendered punk person and lobby. [She
> laughs.] That's going to be incredibly ineffective. So they do have this poster
> look on purpose. Does it hurt them? Sometimes. Yes. Does it have a pur-
> pose within trying to reach the establishment? Yes. So it's a catch-22.

She acknowledged that these established feminist organizations could be more successful when the issues were urgent, such as fighting antigay rights ballot measures in her state. While she found contemporary feminists largely silent on the issue, organizations such as NOW were able to pull together countercampaigns to defeat the measures. She said, "They're not understanding how you fight a ballot measure. How do you do these things? That's very much the realm of the second wave that's been on the front lines for so long. Eventually there needs to be some crossover." She continued:

> In third wave, there isn't a good understanding of how decisions are made,
> how money is disseminated, and who makes those decisions. There isn't.
> And that's my hope that it will come. I don't think it will, but . . . And

there's like, "Are you with us? Or you're an idiot." Third-wave mentality, which does not get you much. . . . The flip side is you have NOW or other groups, established groups, that are very good at understanding who it is that they need to approach, where they need to put the resources, but they just don't get how to get the masses onboard. And I look at those organizations and I think the number one thing I want from them is a check because I can't count on them. They don't have a huge base. They're not going to be able to turn them [young people] out.

She noted that this lack of understanding between generations could have dire consequences as second-wave-generation feminists retire or leave these organizations. She concluded, "It is going to be younger people who adopt the second-wave mentality who will take over those organizations, and I think that they are either going to have to modernize or do something or they're going drop in ranks."

For some older feminists, Green City's equation that all second-wave-generation feminists participated in the building of formal organizations is sure to be troubling. Missing in this discussion are the informally structured groups common in the women's liberation branch of the movement, groups that have largely disappeared from the national landscape and local groups that have emerged in communities. However, it is this equation (i.e., informal equals contemporary feminism vs. structured organizations equal second-wave-generation feminism) that generates the notion that feminist generations do not "get" each other. Green City varies from Woodview where feminists have little interaction with the second-wave generation. Instead, Green City feminists take one of two paths. While one path is to see the generations as different based on perception, the second is to engage with both generations and find both lacking. It is this second view that creates a relatively neutral environment in terms of generational discord. Green City is a locale in which contemporary feminists can easily access the second-wave generation and established feminist organizations. Because of this accessibility, Green City feminists construct a permeable boundary between themselves and the older generation that they can easily pass through when desired. And in passing through these generational boundaries, Green City feminists such as Marley can see the problems with each. This differs from the generational dynamics of Evers, the community that expressed the most critical views of the second-wave feminist generation.

Evers—Dissension Through Evolution. Evers feminists saw the second-wave generation largely through the personalized lens of their mothers and their mothers' generation. Unlike Woodview, Evers feminists grew up with second-wave-generation feminists around them. Evers feminists also differed from Green

City in that there were no large feminist organizations actively involved in the community where feminist generations could interact. This resulted in the most closed boundary between the generations of the three communities studied.

In constructing their activist identity by directly opposing second-wave-generation feminists, Evers feminists created a feminism that was always evolving and responding to the perceived inadequacies of the second-wave generation. Evident in many of the Evers interviews is the conception of a "past" feminism that evolved into a "present" feminism. For Abby, who had feminist parents, the progression from one set of feminist ideas to another was a predictable evolution. She said, "The second wave definitely [goes] naturally into the third wave." Lila continued this train of thought. She saw the two generations as connected but shaped by different times. She said:

> I think a lot of it is a continuation, but I think today that we're living in a more—[she pauses] . . . I think in a grander picture it is a more conservative climate right now than it was in the 1960s and 1970s. . . . I think today it is a lot more [she pauses again]—I don't want to say more difficult, but there isn't that passion that's running through American youth today that had that massive separation with their parents. I think that it is a very big divide, and even though we have the Internet and e-mail and every other connection tool on the Internet available to us, I still think that [there is] the lack of that massive passion that was sweeping across in the early 1970s and really gave fire to the feminist movement.

This lack of passion and the differences between the two generations made younger feminists appear to be unappreciative. For example, Skye, whose mother is a feminist minister, said, "I get from my mom, 'I've done this for you. How can you be ungrateful?'" The creation of a generation gap made feminist activism seem more difficult. Tadeo, who had been an organizer on the West Coast since she was thirteen, explained:

> I'm tired of the generation gap, personally. I'm tired of not having—[she pauses]—I'm tired having to always make my own way in society. Always having to carve my own path, which is fine, it gives me character. It puts "hair on my knees," or whatever. . . . But I wish that I could have an older activist sit by my side and say, "It's going to be okay." And [to] talk with them about stuff or have them listen so I can share ideas. Or at least have—have that. And there's such a division between older feminists and younger feminists because—not just age, it's the politics primarily.

Fitting with Tadeo's statement, scholar Astrid Henry notes that there is a longing for intergenerational connection among some contemporary feminist writers, indicating that a generational divide is not always welcomed.[17]

However, the perception that there is a different view of politics works to separate generations at Evers. Although I discuss in detail issues of gender, sex and sexuality in chapter 6, it was often these issues along with perceptions of past feminist activism that Evers feminists drew upon in this conception of feminist evolution. For Abby, the change was from advocating gender neutrality and androgyny to one focusing on femininity as powerful and in need of reclaiming. She said that contemporary feminists tend to have more "popular appeal" than the second-wave generation's "more androgynous movement." Abby also noted how sexual identity (e.g., gay, straight or bi) was seen as very second-wave generation. She said, describing one of her professors:

> I mean she's—she's a little—[she] wears a sweater vest and has the fifty-year-old lesbian haircut kind of thing and went to Radcliffe in the 1960s and was married to a med student until she got divorced or realized she was gay kind of thing. [She laughs.] She's *so* second wave.

Moving past these "old" gender and sexuality identity labels is an important issue for Evers feminists. According to Sandra, who identifies as genderqueer:

> And I think that old feminism was very much a political response that didn't do anything socially or culturally. And I think now a lot of feminism has to [do with] queer advocacy because that's challenging the heterosexual normative, which I think [the second-wave generation] feminism wanted to do a lot of it but was scared to take that step and say, "Why are we ashamed to just to be how we are? Why do we have to have these labels?" [Contemporary feminists] want equal rights, but do we want [an] equal rights bill to say, "We're women," instead of just saying we don't have to fit into a label? We don't have to fit into this normal society, which is still based on men.

Viewing the second-wave generation as one who "didn't do anything" is harsh criticism; however, Sandra did acknowledge some of the gains of the second-wave feminist generation. She said:

> The second wave accomplished it being okay to be a woman and to feel like you could be equal to a man, but it didn't do anything to try and eliminate the differences. There's still a woman category. There's a man category. And I think the third wave is pushing that. It's not like there is a pink and

a blue. There's [*sic*] a lot of people in between and [the movement today] is definitely pushing for the stopping of labeling. . . . I would ask, "Well, why is it still when my mom [went] shopping for clothes for me [when I was] growing up was it the dresses for the girls and the pants for the boys? Why when I go to a job interview am I still expect[ed] to wear the nice dress suit or the skirt and dress up and wear earrings?" Did it really succeed or did it just reinforce a normative and we're just fooled into thinking it succeeded because society as a whole changed their perceptions? Maybe women didn't change all that much, just a little bit superficially.

Stella agreed with Sandra that what was needed was a critique of the notion of stable gender identities, something she saw Evers feminists as doing. She said:

> I don't necessarily agree with everything that feminists before me have done. [I am] taking lessons from that and also being able to critique the whole concept of women's liberation and within all these structures of race and class and especially dealing with issues like gender identity. "What does it mean to be a woman? Who is a woman?"

The idea that reinforcing sex categories as different keeps women (and men) oppressed is a tenet of queer theory—a theoretical framework familiar to many of the Evers feminists because of their college courses.

In addition to not making significant differences in terms of sex, gender and sexuality subordination, another common Evers sentiment was that second-wave-generation feminists failed on issues of class and race. Accordingly, this left contemporary feminists with a lot work to do. Becca elaborated:

JO: So it sounds like you are making this argument that in the past in the feminist movement, we'll say, like, the 1960s, 1970s, 1980s movement really left working-class women out of it. So do you feel like you are a part of this new movement that's bringing working-class women in?

BECCA: I still feel like I am fighting—that we are all fighting. I know that a lot of the other people that I talk to and organize with around here, they seem to understand it's along the same lines that the feminism of the past lacked a class analysis and that was always a problem, and that's why we have lopsided rights.

The idea that class was ignored was also linked to the conviction that the second-wave generation did not address race. Stella, a biracial woman with an activist mother, saw this as the result of focusing too much on empowering white, middle-class women. She said:

> I essentially agree in a lot of ways [the second-wave generation] was really white [and] middle class. And really, [they] were not trying to address those other sides of the power structure of American society. I think they were really focused on the man-woman thing, which is an important thing to focus on, but I think because they couldn't bridge those gaps, women of color never really could work toward that feminist goal, and so I think they could [have] gotten a lot further.

According to Evers feminists, the result of the second-wave generation's lack of inclusivity was that some groups of women advanced and others were left behind. Skye argued, "I see Hillary Clinton as a feminist political figure who I would say is a feminist and not a womanist.... I say [it is] primarily white, upper-middle-class women who have made strides but are not there yet."[18] By calling Hillary Clinton a feminist and not a womanist, Skye is making the argument that "feminist" as defined by the second-wave generation is a white, middle-class women's identity.

For many who would identify as belonging to the second-wave generation, the comments of the Evers feminists must seem like harsh criticisms. Each area of critique—sex, gender and sexual fluidity, class and race—has been the subject of activism at different times in the women's history and are not just contemporary feminist topics. What the comments of the Evers feminists reveal is a simplified understanding of feminist history, mixed with grains of truth. There are times in the history of the movement that activists, organizations and leaders acted on racist, classist, homophobic and transphobic (i.e., hatred and fear of transgender individuals) assumptions.[19] However, as feminist historians argue, there are also many moments of inclusive collective action that have yet to make it into the feminist historical record. As discussed in chapter 2, many of these distinctions and critiques at Evers come directly from experiences with second-wave-generation mothers. As Professor Anderson observed, the dynamic of mothers and daughters had much to do with the way the Evers feminists responded to second-wave-generation feminism. She said:

> I think a lot of them do have feminist mothers, activist feminist mothers, so they are sort of—they sort of admire their mothers and they don't feel like they measure up—but they also hate their mothers and they want to distance themselves from them. I think that's part of—they have this whole critique of second-wave feminism—that's partly about they see it as their mother's thing and they are different from it.

By drawing firm identity boundaries between themselves and the second-wave generation, the Evers feminists articulated what they saw as new and improved feminism. For example, Dana argued that the movement was more focused, radical and fierce. She drew these distinctions when comparing her feminism to her mother's. Her feminism, as she perceived it, was more inclusive and more global than the feminism embraced by her mom. Deborah also spoke at length about how her mother's feminism had influenced her own ideas. She realized that her mom viewed men and women as different, embracing the ideas of men and women's different value systems. She said:

> I had always kind of felt in my heart [the movement] had really been marginalizing to a lot of other people—that not everyone was also able to participate in [the] mainstream feminist movement that I saw when I was little, growing up.

This led her to clarify how her feminism was different from her mother's. She said:

> I think that a lot of contemporary feminism does see the work of maybe second wave—my mom's generation of feminism—as [founded] on an assumption now in society that women and men are equal or that women have rights equal to men, that women shouldn't be discriminated on the basis of their sex and that we can go from there and start . . . to get women into all of the institutions versus a lot of contemporary feminism that's still trying to say that we don't want these institutions. I think a lot of strains of contemporary feminism [are] still unwilling to assimilate into male-dominated structures and that seeing women entering those structures doesn't—isn't going to change what the structures are. Having the woman at the top of the banking firm isn't going to be enough because we don't want the bank to operate the way that it does anyway. Just having a woman there doesn't necessarily mean that the institution is now different.

As a result, Deborah labeled feminism, as seen through her mother and her mother's generation, as "vanilla" and not radical enough. She did acknowledge that maybe "vanilla" feminism was needed to pass "bigger pieces of legislation" and maybe "we don't see the controversy that went into having those milestones or getting those laws passed." But still it, in her eyes, did not go far enough.

Using their mothers and their mothers' generation to articulate their feminism resulted in the strongest boundaries between the generations and the strongest critique in the three communities studied. This is an idea played out in the national popular and independent media. For example, feminist writer Naomi Wolf, after noting that "third wave feminism came along, critiquing its staid mothers," states, "Third wave feminism is pluralistic, strives to be multi-ethnic, is pro-sex and tolerant of other women's choices."[20] This view of contemporary feminism builds on a critique of the feminism that "came before," and, in Evers, is the result of a political generation situated in a "feminist bubble" that interacts mostly with feminism through older women, mothers and professors and not local and national feminist organizations.

The variation in generational relations between the communities is apparent with all three communities reacting to the second-wave generation but in different ways. Woodview feminists had few critiques of previous generations and in fact, often said they had little knowledge of the "wave" lingo and didn't know the history of the movement enough to comment. Green City focused on miscommunications and created relatively permeable generational boundaries that critiqued both sides. Evers feminists had the most extensive critique, creating a "new" feminism to make amends for the "old." These community responses form a continuum that ranges from accepting to benign critique to disidentification. Each community is of the same political generation of feminism but is situated in different contexts. These contexts shape the boundaries between generations by infusing the interactions with a culture that is either open or closed to feminism. Part of the construction of a feminist identity is through the construction of boundaries between the "us" and "them" of the communities. In a hostile environment, feminists do not construct barriers between themselves as potential allies, needing all the support they can get. In environments open to feminism, different dynamics are in play. Green City is an example of community where generations of feminists interact and boundaries are permeable, even though relations are not always accepting of each other. Evers, with its feminist bubble, does not need to articulate a strong feminist identity since the assumption of feminism is embedded in all aspects of the community. Without a need for allies (or organizations) to support their actions, the Evers feminists draw the strongest boundaries between themselves and the second-wave feminist generation. Their feminism flourishes without a need to depend upon the support of older feminists. Yet, despite these different relationships with the second-wave feminist generation, feminism continues at Woodview, Green City and Evers.

Generations and Continuity

These communities illustrate how generational dissension is not necessarily the sign of a dying movement. All long-lasting movements experience generational change, which is the result of identity and ideological shifts of the movement that define new stages of the movement. Indeed, sociologists J. Craig Jenkins and Michael Wallace highlight generational change as one of the impetuses for involvement in contemporary protest movements.[21] This generational change is aided by the process of framing (i.e., the way that beliefs and ideologies are presented as meaningful), which allows generations of activists to distinguish themselves from each other.[22] In this study, it is clear that each community frames their generational relations differently, drawing on the context of their social movement community.

However, this study departs from social movement scholars and their assumption that as generations shift, they are sequenced with social and political factors creating a "new" generation that replaces the "old." Movement literature is full of these assumptions of "old" and "new."[23] As one example, Ruth Cherrington distinguishes between the 1980 "Thatcher" generation of young Chinese activists versus the "Mao" generation of the 1960s and 1970s.[24] This idea of sequencing is portrayed in the women's movement through the wave metaphor, in which one generation emerges, peaks and crests, making way for the next generation to emerge. As I noted in the introduction, this notion has come under increasing criticism by feminist historians, who advocate a less sequenced and more "messy" approach to understanding the movement. By moving away from the wave model and investigating the role of community context, this study offers new dimensions to understanding generational change in movements. It is clear that in the communities studied (and the dynamics reported in the media) feminist generations overlap, creating both cooperation and dissension in the movement. Also evident is the fact that dissension between generations is the product of a viable movement.[25] As contemporary and second-wave-generation feminists interact with each other, their negotiations bring forth a lively dialogue on feminism that ranges from admiration to antagonism. This replaces the common image of the psychological drama of mother and daughter or the view of feminism as just a "catfight" with no apparent momentum. In sum, I argue that generational dissension is not the last gasp of a dying movement; instead, it is evidence of the continuity of a movement where priorities and goals are defined within specific political environments.[26]

Yet, while generational dynamics illustrate movement continuity, it is troubling that so many contemporary feminists know so little of the movement's history. While some issues were not addressed in the same manner by the second-wave generation, it is a gross overstatement to argue that issues of sex, gender, sexuality, race and class were ignored. Feminists in the 1960s, 1970s and 1980s struggled with these issues. It was in these decades that feminist scholarship began to articulate ideas of gender, replacing the concept of sex roles. Lesbians worked alongside straight women in a variety of organizations and for a variety of goals, as did non-middle-class women and women of color. It is more accurate to argue that these issues have shifted, along with the political and social environment. Many of the issues addressed by contemporary feminists have long roots into the past, some going as far back as the first-wave generation. To return to the words of Tadeo from Evers, the solution to this lack of knowledge is for generations of feminists to interact, not through retorts on blogs and Web sites but through meaningful conversation. She longs for an older feminist to sit down next to her and talk as well as listen.

In chapters 1 through 3, I have examined the state of contemporary feminism and the role of communities, and despite the death notices constantly tolled, it is clear from the communities studied that U.S. feminism is not dead and instead continues to fashion feminism in accordance with the times and the "place." In the next section, I investigate how contemporary feminists are "doing" feminism as well as their discourse of inclusivity, diversity and identity fluidity, with an eye to how all this is influenced by the present and shaped by the past.

Doing and Talking Contemporary Feminism

4

Doing Contemporary Feminism

IN AUGUST OF 1968, women's liberation groups took a stand against "Miss America, motherhood and marriage" by protesting the Miss America beauty pageant. According to historian and feminist Sara Evans:

> With a sharp eye for guerilla theater, young women crowned a live sheep to symbolize the beauty pageant's objectification of female bodies, and filled a "freedom trashcan" with objects of female torture—girdles, bras, curlers, issues of *Ladies' Home Journal*. Peggy Dobbins, dressed as a stockbroker, auctioned off an effigy of Miss America: "Gentlemen, I offer you the 1969 model. She's better every year. She walks. She talks. She smiles on cue. And she does housework."[1]

Fast-forward to fall 2008—in a college course, The Contemporary U.S. Women's Movement, my students and I spent several weeks going over how contemporary feminists are doing feminism. As we discussed zines, blogs, crafting and the role of performance and presentation in everyday life, my students came to refer to these actions as "taking things out of the freedom trashcan." Instead of seeing those actions such as crafting as symbols of patriarchal control, they saw them as representing tools for women's empowerment. In their view, the ability to choose (one's appearance or activities) is what matters. This metaphor of the recycled trashcan was so powerful that after the semester was over, a former student posted as her Facebook status that she was learning to knit and was "taking it out of the freedom trashcan." The idea of recycling political actions is what social movement scholars call drawing on a tactical repertoire, meaning that movements often turn to a range of previous actions to bring about their strategies for change.[2] A strategy is the overall plan of a movement to accomplish broader goals. Tactics, then, are the actions meant to achieve these plans. As movement actors survey the resources, goals and opportunities available to them in the political and social climate, they decide upon the ways of accomplishing their goals.[3] For example, in the U.S. civil rights movement, a major strategy was to change the legislative and political policies governing the rights of black Americans. One way of accomplishing the goal of racial equality was through the tactic of nonviolent civil disobedience, which allowed movement actors to advance their cause in an extremely hostile (both socially and politically) environment. This also illustrates how movement tactics are decided upon in the environment of a political generation. As the larger social and political climate changes, so do the ways in which generations view their ability to make societal change. Just as the modern civil rights movement addresses a different environment, so does feminism in the twenty-first century. The contemporary feminist movement is often characterized (and criticized) as having a strategic focus on changing culture instead of addressing larger societal institutions such as the government, medicine, the economy and education. This contemporary feminist cultural focus is reinforced by magazines such as *Bitch* and *Bust*. *Bitch,* a monthly magazine with the tagline "Feminist Response to Pop Culture," was founded by Lisa Jervis and Andi Zeisler, both well-known contemporary feminist writers. *Bitch* started as a self-produced zine and eventually became a full-fledged magazine dedicated to critically examining aspects of popular culture from a feminist perspective. The magazine covers a variety of specific pop culture topics (e.g., music, television shows and celebrities). *Bust* magazine runs with the tagline "For Women with Something to Get Off Their Chests" and regularly runs a series of features on domestic activities such as crafting ("Buy or DIY") and appearance ("Fashion and Booty"). One of *Bust*'s founders and the editor-in-chief, Debbie Stoller, is often presented as a spokesperson for contemporary feminism. The focus on crafting, emphasized in *Bust,* carries over into the Internet and beyond. Feminist or progressive crafting fairs are common around the country, and Stoller is also the author of several books on knitting with feminist-oriented titles such as *Stitch 'n Bitch: The Knitter's Handbook* and *Happy Hookers: Stitch and Bitch Crochet*. A perusal of the Web illustrates how crafting is embraced by many feminists as a form of reclaiming a traditional feminine activity. For example, a pattern for making vegan fox fur is located on a Web site called Not Martha, referring to craft maven Martha Stewart.[4] A search of YouTube turns up a video from the cable show *The Colbert Report* of a woman doing "radical knitting," complete with a shot of *Bitch* magazine at the end of the segment.[5] In addition, both *Bust* and *Bitch* routinely cover culturally focused activism by different feminist groups, such as the Camel Toe Lady Steppers, a group that "owns their sexuality" and participates in a variety of public parades and functions in New Orleans.[6] While *Ms. Magazine* routinely covers legislation and policymaking, *Bust* and *Bitch* stay firmly within the realm of cultural criticism and personalized activism.[7]

Scholars confirm the characterization of contemporary feminism as cultural and see it as focused on the reclamation of femininity and the use of embodied politics.[8] Scholar Judith Taylor defines gender reclamation as recasting and taking ownership of group stereotypes rather than simply conforming to them.[9] Gender reclamation, then, is the act of "taking back" aspects of femininity seen as discarded by previous feminist generations. For example, in their essay "Feminism and Femininity: Or How We Learned to Stop Worrying and Love the Thong," authors Jennifer Baumgardner and Amy Richards argue one aspect of twenty-first-century feminism is reclaiming what past periods have discarded, such as embracing femininity.[10] Aligned with the idea of reclaiming femininity is the notion of embodied politics, which are creative acts of cultural resistance centered on the body as a way to disrupt power.[11] The body becomes a place "where cultural expectations about gender are rehearsed but also, at least, potentially, manipulated and resisted."[12] Embodied politics can take a variety of forms from using the body as a site to elaborate the need for social change (i.e., not wearing clothes made in sweatshops) to resisting cultural norms through dress and appearance (i.e., dressing in a sexual manner as a way to protest stereotypes of women's sexuality).[13]

In this chapter, I examine the tactical repertoire of contemporary feminists and ask: What are the tactics employed in the communities studied? Does community-level activism mirror the generational characterizations of the movement as solely cultural? Feminists in all three communities were aware of this cultural emphasis in the media, in part through reading magazines such as *Bust* or *Bitch*. For example, Sally from Woodview used *Bitch* and *Bust* as a way to educate women on her dorm floor about contemporary feminism. Stella, from Evers, talked about a Revolutionary Knitting Society in her hometown, and it was a Woodview feminist who made me aware of *The Colbert Report* clip on knitting and feminism. So does this national-level discourse on tactics then shape the activism in the communities? Are contemporary feminists only focusing on culture or does the interplay of environment and generation create differences between communities? The answer to these questions is not a simple yes or no. I find that while there is a focus on cultural change, symptomatic of a generation that has seen decades of backlash and policy backsliding, community environment and generational tension create a diverse range of cultural tactics. I find that in Woodview with its hostile environment, activists target the campus and local status quo with educational tactics. Green City is an environment where feminists have a large variety of organizations available to them, yet still focus on cultural change drawing on links between the feminist and queer communities. In Evers, an environment more open to feminism, feminists focus mainly on cultural change until a situation arises that brings them in contact with policymakers. To explore these dynamics, I discuss each of the communities and then elaborate on what this means to our understandings of feminism and social movement tactics.

Woodview—Education and Structure. Woodview feminists focused their efforts on educating the community outside of FFW. The group worked to inform the public around them of the importance of such issues as breast cancer, sexual assault and body image. These awareness campaigns became yearly events routinely organized by the group. An essential part of these events was building the group's infrastructure so new leaders knew exactly what to do each year. While breast cancer, sexual assault and body image do not seem radical issues, at Woodview, FFW was one of the only voices on these topics. For Ben, the fact that the group brought these issues to the community was radical. He said:

> The group is playing such an integral part on campus because I think there are very few groups willing to stand up for what they believe in and actually—and actually say it. That's important and that's something that the Forum for Women is definitely not afraid to do. And I think that— that definitely you have to start with the local first, and I think that plays such an important part on a societal level to have this one group in a small, conservative city . . . making the impact that we're making.

To make change, FFW focuses on altering the culture of Woodview. For example, Laura, president of the group, listed the events she wanted to see accomplished in FFW's first year:

> It will be interesting. It will be very interesting. Our biggest project for this year, being our first year, is the *Vagina Monologues*. So we are going to be doing those in April—along with doing those in April we are doing the Take Back the Night march on campus, which is going to be really awesome, and we are also going to do the Clothesline Project on campus as well.

Woodview feminists often drew on their personal histories in selecting the group's actions. For Jane, it was her grandmother's breast cancer that made her focus on breast cancer awareness. For Zoe and Sally, it was their personal experience of being raped that brought about their involvement in Take Back the Night and the Clothesline Project. Ben headed up a campaign to make men aware of their role in perpetuating violence based on his mother's abuse through the White Ribbon Campaign. Just as members used their personal lives to shape the group's goals, they also took the group's tactic of education into their daily lives. Sally described her efforts within the dorm, particularly on her floor. She said:

> I've introduced, I think, a lot of ideas about feminism to the floor, like my bulletin board this semester, or this month. I put some quote like if February is black history month and March is women's history month . . . just to get people thinking. . . . So I think I've had influence on people on my floor.

Sally went on to describe how she had made a bulletin board for the *Vagina Monologues* and cut words out of magazines to illustrate what feminism was all about. She said, "I think people see those words and they're attending these events. And they're seeing these words up there and they're not afraid to look at these words and what they mean." Her efforts at education carried over into her dorm room. She said, "My whole door is just covered with all kinds of stuff and people comment all the time like, 'Where'd you find this article?' And so I got to introduce people to a lot of things."

Equally important in Woodview's hostile environment was the need to educate the community on feminism overall. A common tactic of the group is "tabling" in the student center on a weekly basis. Jaclyn described what it was like to sit at a table and talk about feminism. She said, "Even having our tables out, something as minute as that . . . Just having a little table out there is making our presence known—answering questions. People come out to us, talking to us." The outcome of their educational efforts was a small but noticeable change. Maura noted that although "a lot of people don't know about our group. A lot of people don't know about feminism. We're starting to make I think a little bit of a wave."

Early in the group's history, organizers realized that in order to hold these events on a yearly basis, the group needed a structure—a goal articulated from the group's beginning. Anna, vice president during the group's first year, said:

> It's kind of difficult because it is the first year of the group. So there is absolutely no organization—that is what we are establishing. That is our goal—to implement some kind of a structure, some kind of an organizational structure so that this group is going to stick around and eventually . . . do things that are characteristic of feminism.

To meet this need, the group instituted a leadership system, including an executive board, applied for university funding and attended organizational trainings.

Emily, who joined the group a year after it started, was pleased at how FFW had been able to build an organizational structure. She said:

> Yeah, I'm really happy with [FFW] especially in comparison with my experience at [her previous college] because our group struggled for all the years I was there, and we never did anything and we had so many ideas but it just never happened. I feel like we actually accomplished a lot here, and we did raise the money for breast cancer awareness, and we did the *Vagina Monologues,* and we did the Karmanos [for breast cancer] walk. And we did all those things. And stuff actually happened. And people took notice of us, and I feel like that was really good and that was really different from my other experience.

When Jane took over for Laura as the group's president, it was the structure that Laura had put in place that allowed the group to continue its efforts at education. She said:

> The executive board [decided] here are the major things that we want to get accomplished. We wanted to do Clothesline [Project] again. We wanted to do Take Back the Night again. We wanted to do the [*Vagina] Monologues* again. And the new big thing was we wanted the benefit concert. . . . I went a lot by Laura's—she recorded all of the minutes and printed them out and all of the agendas in a book with all of the brochures and everything we did. So it's like flipping through . . . and just kind of comparing what we're doing to what they [did] because we wanted to keep a lot of the things the same and just build from that. I think that was our major thing was we had a template and we just built off that, and I think that was the major way we worked. It was like, "Here's what we did last year"—here are the things that we want to add onto that—and kind of just take it from there and let things happen.

While their tactics are aimed externally at community change, scholars argue that cultural tactics also have the potential to increase participant solidarity and identity.[14] This was true at Woodview where as FFW grew in size and structure in order to support its tactics, it also increased the connection between group members. Jaclyn noted how the group engaged in consciousness-raising as it developed:

> I think from a lot of things I've read and what I've seen [is that] consciousness-raising isn't appreciated as much as it should be . . . And I

think the members of FFW because we're all friends, we do a lot of consciousness-raising. And that's so important to me because I trust these people.

The events themselves could bring about a sense of empowerment and connection also. For instance, Jane said:

> I just remember me and Morgan [*sic*] would talk about it nonstop when we were first [she trails off]. And I think the most powerful thing was Take Back the Night. I mean, after Take Back the Night when we had been working with this group of girls that you really know them at the meeting but aren't really that close to them. . . . I think after Take Back the Night, after hearing everyone's stories that is—I just had this feeling like you are so emotionally drained—but the same time you are very uplifted with it. I was just like, "Wow, this is something I am so glad I am a part of."

An example of the external (i.e., education) and internal (i.e., solidarity building) aspects of FFW's tactics is the *Vagina Monologues*. Mentioned as a major event by all the interviewees, the V-Day organization established the college initiative in 1999, which gave permission for universities and colleges to perform the production and use the proceeds to stop violence against women and children in their communities as long as they followed organizational guidelines.[15] Woodview was the only community that made the *Vagina Monologues* a part of their tactical repertoire, in part because of the ability to educate the community around them and in part because of the empowerment experienced by the participants. The production helped build solidarity in the months the group spent preparing for it. In the play, the word "vagina" is said approximately 130 times in each performance. In 2002, while planning the Woodview production, cast members often discussed the production with visible discomfort. However, over the span of eight months of planning, I noticed that the women became more comfortable with using the words "vagina," "cunt" and "orgasm" even when the script was not being discussed. In addition, during these meetings it became common for the women to share amusing or disturbing stories about gynecological visits, and some women also began to talk openly about sexual experiences. By reclaiming the language and learning to express it publicly, group members began to collectively resist the words' negative connotations, reclaiming their voices and a vision of themselves and their sexuality.[16] Jane, who participated in two productions, said:

> The *Vagina Monologues* allows women to be empowered by their own bodies and existence. They make you question why you feel the way you

do about a particular word or phrase. You begin to question why you believe what they—society—have constructed you to believe, that many times language is pulling women down and we so often allow this to happen. The *Vagina Monologues* tells women to grab on to what they deserve, [not to] let language make you feel ashamed, but instead let it empower you.

This sense of empowerment was also aided by a "vagina workshop" attended by many of the women in the production. During the workshop, they performed "vagina exercises" in which they used their bodies and voices to express the emotions of their vaginas through movement, sound, voice or even silence. After each individual articulated an emotion, the group echoed it.

An important aspect of the *Vagina Monologues* as a tactic is the public nature of performances. At Woodview, the audience consisted primarily of other students, faculty, family members and some community members. The relations between the audience and cast removed any sense of anonymity from the performers and intensified their sense of "speaking out." Some of the women suggested that the play creates a type of sisterhood and community for women in the group as well as the audience. Paulina said, "It allowed women in the audience to identify with other women and realize that there is a community out there of people who go through the same things, and to be able to talk about it gives a sense of freedom." As evidence of the empowerment aspect of the production, some women from the audience joined the group the following school year. The group has continued doing the play each year, drawing audiences from the campus and local communities. Scholars have noted that oppositional performances, such as the *Vagina Monologues*, can influence audiences and the formation of collective identities. For example, in their study of drag queen shows, Verta Taylor, Lelia Rupp and Joshua Gamson note that these performances create a space for audiences to rethink ideas of gender and sexuality, just as the *Vagina Monologues* provide Woodview audiences a place to rethink gender, empowerment and feminism.[17]

Although Woodview feminists mostly drew upon education as a tactic, there were some in the group who employed everyday personal tactics such as fashion and dress as a feminist statement. For Jaclyn, dress has always been an important component of her feminist identity. Jaclyn, who often dresses in eclectic style (i.e., pink striped stockings, black skirt and heavy metal belt with dramatic hair and makeup), said of her style, "It's definitely a big part of my identity and being a feminist. Just not feeling like I have to conform to anything. . . . I don't think I'm playing your normal femininity. I'm not really participating in that all the way and for me that's important." Jaclyn here echoes some of the national-level dialogue on reclaiming femininity through dress. However, for the majority of the group, appearance and embodied politics were made political mostly through the *Vagina Monologues*. As noted earlier, during a performance in 2002, I observed that several of the performers had painted the words "slut" and "cunt" on their bodies. However, Woodview feminists' determination not to alienate any potential allies came into play the next year when one of the organizers questioned whether or not writing "cunt" and "slut" on the performers' bodies and clothes might be misinterpreted by audience members. Performing with the word "slut" painted on one's abdomen was viewed as potentially dividing feminist generations and creating a boundary not desired in Woodview. Sally elaborated on this idea, saying, "I think a lot of people, maybe older women feel alienated or they feel like, 'Why are you doing this or why are you presenting [yourself] in this way? You're oversexualizing yourself.'" So while the *Vagina Monologues* were seen as an important tactic, playing with appearance as a feminist statement was not embraced collectively and instead was seen as something that could weaken the community's efforts. Their lack of play with dress echoes sentiments in the second-wave generation. When some radical feminists adopted a style that included jeans, loose shirts, no bras or makeup; other feminists, such as liberal feminist Betty Friedan, described it as "scruffy," wondering why women would go to lengths to make themselves ugly. Friedan's logic was that presenting oneself fashionably and attractively was a tactic focused on accessing, not alienating, mainstream society.[18]

In sum, the tactics used by Woodview feminists were primarily those of education set in place by the building of FFW's organizational infrastructure. Most of their efforts were focused outward on the community around them, finding ways to explain feminism to a hostile environment with nonconfrontational topics. Breast cancer, rape, domestic violence—all are issues that can resonate with the larger public. Even the *Vagina Monologues*, with its themes of sexual and gender freedom, are a pop culture phenomena and are embraced by the larger community. These externally focused tactics of education also influenced the internal dynamics of the community by building a sense of solidarity. Overall, Woodview feminists do not resemble the characterizations of contemporary feminists in the media. While they focus on changing culture, their tactical repertoire largely consists of educational campaigns and solidarity building. Whereas the efforts of Woodview feminists focused on a single organization, the feminists in Green City, with its overlapping feminist and queer organizations, created a different repertoire of tactics.

Green City—Everyday and the Organizational. Green City draws on a number of more radical, personalized tactics than Woodview but situates these tactics within organizations aimed at changing the culture and making institutional change. Feminists entering the community find an array of organizations to join such as Radical Cheerleading and fat acceptance groups, a rock 'n' roll camp for girls and crafting circles. These groups exist within a social movement community that also contains more structured feminist organizations such as NOW, NARAL and Planned Parenthood. Together the groups illustrate the mixture of formal political organizations with more radical, informal groups. For example, Kelly, manager of the feminist bookstore, was a member of the Feminist Bookstore Network as well as the Green Party and the American Association of University Women, all formal organizations with national ties. Marley, as a campaign manager, often worked with groups such as NOW, NARAL and Planned Parenthood. In contrast, Steve was more locally focused as a member of the Fat Chick Cheerleaders, Fat Chick Speaks, Camp Love Your Body and WANDA, a direct action group—all being more informal community groups. This array of organizations differs from both Woodview and Evers by giving feminists a multitude of activist outlets.

In addition, many of the feminists in Green City came to the community from other places with social movement experience in place, changing the nature of their involvement. Samantha is an example of how activists entered this community full of progressive organizations. She recalled her move from Kansas City to Green City and the way she came to feminist activism.

JO: What kind of social issues were you doing there and here?

SAMANTHA: In Kansas, I was on the board of an organization called the Coalition Against Censorship and we had a yearly event where we had things for banned books and censored artists who we'd have come in. People who we had as keynote speakers came in and did events . . . And we had a Midwest underground media symposium, which was like a big zine conference that I helped organize. And I was on the board of that since I was sixteen or seventeen. I was the youngest person that they admitted to the board. . . . I organized an event for Rock the Votes, Rock the Nation, which is for the younger set of people who can't vote yet. [I] helped organize a youth forum for them— to have young people get their voices out and learn about activism and things they can do since they can't vote yet. . . . So [in Kansas] I felt like I wanted to do something more grassroots . . . something that was hands-on like animal rights activism or Earth First, somewhere where I was actually in the forest or I was in with the animals or something. But then I moved [to Green City] and I just, I felt like *it was already taken care of.*[19] I went to some primate and different animal rights things and it seemed that there were so many people that were already in it, already it got so much attention that when I just stopped going I didn't feel that much guilt because I felt like it was already getting taken care of.

Whereas in Woodview, feminists felt like they were starting from scratch and inventing a tactical repertoire and building structure, in Green City, the abundance of activism made it feel like much of the work was already being done. Samantha continued:

> So I tried to get involved with some vegan things here. Some people were going to start a vegan cafe that I was part of, but it didn't seem like it was going to pan out so I dropped out and then I got involved in an independent publishing resource center here. Which is [she pauses] a resource center for people [she laughs] who publish things like zines, chapbooks, book making and things like that. So, I work there now. I work here [the feminist bookstore]. I help organize the Green City Zine Symposium, which is a yearly event that's like this big zine conference that that [sic] draws about 900 people from throughout the country and also, I did some other things I don't remember. [She laughs.]

While Samantha struggled to find her place in the array of activism in Green City, she did so by investigating a variety of organizations engaged in a range of activism. As she moved from one organization to the next, she sought a place where she could make a contribution, settling into the feminist bookstore and continuing to build on her experience in organizing zine symposiums.

In chapter 3, I discussed how established feminist organizations in Green City were often perceived as not "getting" contemporary feminism, according to the feminists who worked within them. As a result, many of the Green City feminists were involved in local organizations or engaged in personal, everyday actions outside of groups. As a testament to the types of local activism available, I picked up flyers for an array of groups and events at a local coffee shop where I interviewed many of the feminists. Included in those are: Queen City Revolution ("An organization which seeks to empower the community concerning issues of fatphobia"), the Green City Zine Symposium, a TechnoDyke Hook Up—Dykey Dating Game!, a workshop on unlearning homophobia, Tart (a DJ performance playing old-school hip-hop) and Books to Prisoners work parties.[20] Many of these events and organizations link the feminist and queer communities. One reason for this linking (as discussed in chapter 1) is that half of the Green City feminists identified as queer. Natalie confirmed this linkage, stating, "There's a lot of overlap with the GLBT stuff in Green City." This overlap was also fostered by a local leader who started Fat Chick Speaks and TechnoDyke. Lana described her as an "amazing woman" and noted that for good or bad "a lot of feminists get pegged as queer automatically" in Green City. This link between queer and feminist politics forged a type of cultural politics in Green City that resulted in the popularity of drag king shows, queer dance nights at a local bar and TechnoDyke events. In fact, TechnoDyke was mentioned by most of the interviewees as a source of their connection to the community. TechnoDyke describes itself as a "mailing list which attempts to bring lesbian, bi, and trans-women together at a different venue bi-weekly."[21] One sampling of TechnoDyke events includes a variety show, a discussion of gay marriage, a group on reclaiming sexuality for women, a gender studies symposium at a local university, a monthly queer dance night and an open mic night for poetry. While Green City's feminist bookstore also holds a variety of events and meetings, it was not the central location for queer-linked-with-feminism happenings.

The connection between feminist and queer emerged in the form of embodied politics that celebrates the body and the blurring of gender distinctions. An example of this intersection is in the zine produced by Steve entitled "Fatty Fatty 2X4: A Social Commentary by a Queer Fat Chick," in which she writes that the zine is based on "my experiences as a fat, white, Queer, self-aware woman."[22] While Steve chooses to go by a masculine-sounding name and performs as a drag king, she states in her zine, "I have a Vagina (Vagina deserves a capitol [sic] 'V' don't you think?)!" Yet she sees a connection between fat (feminist) and queer empowerment. She often writes about how she is working to change size discrimination through reclaiming the word "fatty" with the people around her, including in her job as a nanny. In an article entitled "Say It! Fat! Fat! Fat!," she writes:

> One thing I have noticed recently is that I have had to train people to say the word "fat." I have assured them it's an acceptable term to me. It's the only one that really fits. Of course, I mean to say it in a positive way. It is very similar to how I helped coach my friends and family to say the word "Queer" when talking about queer folks. "Fat" is not a bad word.

This focus on the body is apparent in that two of the most commonly mentioned groups were Fat Chick Speaks and Fat Chick Cheerleaders, both focused on size discrimination and fat empowerment. Even when feminists were not involved with the groups, they knew of them. For example, Susan described the Fat Chick Cheerleaders, even though she was not involved in the group:

JO: So the Radical Cheerleaders—is it the same as the Fat Chick Cheerleaders?
SUSAN: No—There are two groups . . . They both use sort of cheerleading chanting as their form of political expression. But the fat action troupe [Fat Chick Cheerleaders] . . . they're just speaking politically about size oppression and so that's what their cheers and everything are about. And so those are all women of size on that troupe.

The Fat Chick Cheerleaders has drawn national media attention and were featured in *Bust* magazine as a group making cultural change. The group also performs at events around the community, often at Fat Chick Speaks events. Steve, who is one of the cheerleaders, said, "It's cool too because we've been invited to do things that really aren't even related to [fat empowerment]." Steve continued describing the group and how they try to change cultural norms about the body through their performances:

> We do cheers about body image and size acceptance and the dangers of gastric bypass surgery and how to not pay a lot of attention to the inundation of messages in the media about low carb diets . . ., and dieting and yo-yo dieting.

The group combines both messages geared at changing individual attitudes as well as critiques of the fashion industry and doctors who encourage surgery. For example, one of their cheers goes:

> 1-2-3-4 This is a body war
> 1-2-3-4 Tell me, girls, what's the score?
> One third wear over size sixteen
> Yet all fashions assume you're lean
> Fifty billion on products spent
> The industry loves every cent
> 1-2-3-4 This is a body war
> 1-2-3-4 Tell me, girls, what's the score?
> One in a hundred die on the table
> They'll kill us all if they are able
> 98 percent of all diets fail
> So throw away your ugly scale!
> 1-2-3-4 This is a body war
> 1-2-3-4 Come on, girls, let's even the score

Fat Chick Speaks and Fat Chick Cheerleaders are examples of two groups that draw on culturally focused tactics that are locally created, critique societal institutions and encourage personal empowerment. Lana recalled one Fat Chick Speaks event where plus-size women modeled lingerie. She said:

> There was one part of the show that the women went out and modeled intimate apparel like bras and panties and stuff. And they're all out there in muumuus because that's what fat women have always been told they

had to wear and they took off their muumuus. My girlfriend was behind the stage and she [said] that was the single best part of the evening just hearing the roar from the crowd. I remember that and I was just like, "That's awesome." . . . I was just like, "That's a fucking riot." I mean just 800 screaming people for these people onstage.

The concept of the body as a source of empowerment was also evident in Steve's zine:

> I'm a fatty and self-love is important to me. We learn in this country that size equals happiness, thin is in, stout is out. We learn that white and thin as a combination can lead to success and happiness. I learned by the time I was six what sexy was and that it was a high honor to be sexy in this country. Money and fame would surely follow whoever fit within the western beauty model.

This focus on making change through personal empowerment and cultural critique was echoed by others in the community. The average age of Green City feminists was the oldest of the three communities and, as a result, many of the feminists held full-time jobs, which could limit their ability to get involved in organizations, so instead they focused on everyday cultural actions. For example, Lana, who worked in UPS management, judged her current involvement based on her past activism in high school and college. She said:

> I support not really local [groups] but like the National Organization for Women, and I know that I support women-owned businesses like I'll go there and granted it might be 5 percent more—10 percent more—the bill ends up being, but to me that doesn't bother me. That's, I mean, that's part of being active in the community—just where you pick to go out to dinner or where you pick to buy your sex toys from or whose lip balm you picked to put on your lips. But as far as organizations that I'm actively involved with right now—I'm not.

As a result of the diversity of events and focus on personal activism, Green City feminists did not engage in solidarity building similar to Woodview. While many of the same people showed up to a range of meetings and events, they did not form a collective like FFW in Woodview. This, I argue, is the result of multiple organizations, groups and networks available to Green City feminists, as illustrated by Samantha's story. Whereas Woodview feminists had few allies and feminist-friendly organizations in their community, Green City has an abundance of groups in an open environment. This reduces their need to build a focused solidarity like Woodview and instead allows them to move comfortably through a series of linked networks and organizations. Despite the lack of a single organizational center, Green City feminists are situated within a social movement community that focuses on everyday activism and embodied politics in the intersection between queer and feminist communities. Green City feminists support national organizations and work within local groups. In this regard, Green City more resembles the national dialogue on contemporary feminist tactics. The coverage of groups like the Fat Chick Cheerleaders in *Bust* magazine promotes this resemblance. In addition, Green City differed in the amount of experience feminists had with activism before they entered the linked communities of Green City. As Samantha's story illustrates, the environment led some activists to search for a site of activism in a wide array of groups, networks and organizations. I now turn to Evers to examine an environment where feminist groups exist but activism often takes place outside those groups. Evers serves as a model of how contemporary feminism can be individually focused until a situation brings feminists directly into contact with marginalization and victimization.

Evers—"Ain't Your Mother's Feminism." By focusing on the second-wave feminist generation, Evers feminists distanced themselves from the institutionally focused tactics they perceived as originating in the past. Instead, Evers feminists turn to mostly everyday cultural tactics as a way of making change. This move away from the second-wave generation was obvious when Feminists Together "chalked" around campus the slogan "Ain't Your Mother's Feminism."[23] For Julia, the distinction between past and present tactics was clear. She said, "It doesn't help for me to go march or go talk to a senator." Instead she elaborated on what tactics would work:

> It's not so much a matter of protesting—marching on D.C. sadly doesn't have the same meaning it did thirty years ago; maybe starting a magazine in your suburb, which is what these girls do. Maybe that's more powerful now. So that's one of the things about the third wave that I really like is we're trying to find another direction. I've never been to a protest. That's mostly because I wasn't exposed to any protests in [her hometown.] I do plan on going to the March for Choice protests in April [2004]. So that will be my first one. I'm excited, but I don't see that as any longer being [at] the forefront of feminism and the most necessary action to take. And I would see writing and educating as the new thing, as the most important. I think that's really where the second and the third waves deviate in terms of the politics and the actions that are taken.

The notion that the second-wave generation was only interested in organizational tactics and large national actions further distanced young feminists from participating. According to Ava:

> I feel [contemporary feminists] deal with it in their own personal ways, through their own individual action other than a huge mobilization of people. We have NOW. We have [the] Feminist Majority and groups like that, but you don't necessarily have some sort of huge action around it and there's not really—both with Feminist Majority and with NOW—they're so all over the board you don't even know where to jump in and try to make a difference and I think that's—that's sort of reflective of the way—the problems that we have now. It's so across the board and you don't even know where to begin. [She pauses.] I say it's through personal actions—people picking their battles. I don't think we pick our battles as much as the second wave of feminism probably did because the feminists of that time made huge advances for us, but the obstacles still exist or are harder to pinpoint.

Tadeo concurred that the times had changed and so had the tactics. She said, "The direct action [of today] is very different than second-wave feminism. Nonviolence is a tactic; it's not a way of life and that's a huge division; huge, huge difference between second-wave feminism [of the] sixties, seventies." This division was ideological, but also, according to Tadeo, the result of generational dynamics. She said:

> I think a lot of [the] problem is that young people doing organizing don't have any guidance like I was saying before and don't—aren't—either don't have guidance or too much guidance [by older activists who] say they have to do it a certain way, like you have to be nonviolent. But what does that mean? What is nonviolence? I always thought it was a tactic. Like, what about self-defense? I like that better.

The perception that the second-wave generation of feminists did not make any comprehensive or complete changes to society, leaving contemporary feminists to "pinpoint" harder targets, led to the endorsement of more cultural everyday tactics. Terri described the idea of an everyday tactic:

> I think that whole—just the zines and women making movies—women claiming different [forms] of public expression—I think that's a big part of [contemporary feminism] whether it's performance art or painting or just getting your voice out there and making it heard. Whether or not

you are specifically addressing feminism, just by talking about your own experiences, that's feminist if it can help other women to realize they're not alone.[24]

However, communicating to women that they are not alone in their struggles did not mean an adoption of consciousness-raising as a tactic. Julia said that while she found the idea of consciousness-raising valuable, there were many who did not. She said, "The idea of consciousness-raising, it's kind of—it's silly now. People don't take it that seriously. They're like, 'You mean a bunch of women got together in the seventies and talked about housework and then decided they should get paid?'" Instead, personal expression as a feminist tactic took a different route.

For Ava, feminist activism was solely located in individual actions. When asked what issues she saw as important in her life, she answered by listing her everyday actions meant to make change:

My issues today? My right to play pool; dealing with everyday harassment. If you walk down the street and you're wearing a short skirt. Explaining to people that not all feminists are man-haters and educating people about how women are treated differently than men. For me, it's more through personal interactions with people because I'm still friends with the same guys that I was in high school and still really close with all of them and we'll have two-hour-long arguments over the phone because they don't understand. And making them understand would be my little—my activism. . . . I think for me it is very situational. Depending on the situation I'm in is how I'm going to act.

Fitting with Ava's characterization of contemporary tactics as everyday and the personal, Evers feminists embraced the idea that appearance and fashion could make change. Fashion as a form of politics in Evers can be seen as a direct rebuttal to the "freedom trashcan" of the second-wave generation and the related perception that a feminist appearance was a "nonsexual" one. According to Ava:

I think that a lot of women want to fight for their rights, but at the same time, they are not going to give up their sexual power that they have and instead use that to their advantage maybe. . . . It's just a completely different culture now than it was back then—completely different culture— in the way people dress, in the way people talk, and the way we interact with each other and what we do with our free time. I think it is a completely, completely different culture. I don't think that you necessarily need to be wearing baggy jeans and a baggy T-shirt to be able to call your-self a feminist. My favorite thing to wear is short skirts.

Drawing on the idea that contemporary feminists act as subjects rather than objects of sexuality, desire and sex, Evers feminists found fashion to be a potent way to state one's sexual empowerment. In this aspect, Evers feminists' focus on sexual empowerment echoed the sexual ethos that was articulated as a pro-sex answer to the second-wave generation, particularly in magazines such as *Bust*.[25] Deborah described her community's views on sex. She said:

> We've gone toward a very pro-sex, pro talking about sex, making sex okay [and] acknowledging and validating other kinds of sexuality, other kinds of sexual expression and promoting women's sexual identity [by] allowing them to talk about pornography and pleasure and all these things.

While incorporating sexuality into dress was embraced in Evers, there were other reasons for seeing dress as political. For some of the interviewees, the impact of globalization and sweatshop labor on women's work was a concern, prompting their dress. Bailey said that community members avoided wearing or buying clothing known to be made in sweatshops. Deborah noted how labor activism and feminism merged for her. She said, "So much of the anti-sweatshop activism has started to look at women in the global industries and women in capitalism, and I would really like to see the labor activism that I am involved in go more in those directions." Playing with appearance could be a way to express politics, but it could also be problematic. Bailey described these complex dynamics at Evers:

> And I think there are people who are . . . very, very, very much aware, especially on this campus, that clothing is political because it connotes a gender identity. You know? And so it's interesting. It can be extremely empowering to say I'm going to go all over the place and look at how much I can switch and look—I can identify as everything. But it can also be really, really suffocating . . . Because people do make assumptions.

While everyday tactics took prominence, Evers feminists also got involved in different groups. Despite the lack of involvement in feminist organizations on campus such as Feminists Together, there were organizations on campus that drew Evers feminists. For example, one group was the Radical Cheerleaders. Stella, who was a member, described the squad:

STELLA: I think it's very feminist. A lot of our cheers [are] appropriating traditional women's "Oh, let's be cheerleaders."

JO: Can you tell me a little about what you do as a Radical Cheerleader?

STELLA: We, as a squad, we make up cheers and we put little movements to them, but it's not terribly professional looking and organized [she laughs], but it's really cool and we cheer at rallies or protests or "just because" around campus when we want to draw attention to an issue or whatever.

While Radical Cheerleaders do reclaim the act of cheerleading as feminist, the cheers are often not overtly feminist, fitting with Evers submerged feminist identity. For example, one cheer goes:

> No Justice
> Here's a piece of my mind
> No Justice
> A piece of my behind
> No Justice
> Piece it together you'll find
> RADICAL CHEERLEADERS ON THE FRONT LINES!
> Revolution—not if but when!
> Revolution—I'll say it again!
> Rev Rev Rev REVOLUTION![26]

It is possible to deconstruct this chant and the phrase "a piece of my behind" as a form of embodied politics; however, I would argue the cheer is more abstractly focused on the notion of social justice and not on combating gender-based discrimination and prejudice. While Woodview planned out educationally oriented projects and Green City feminists gathered at queer and feminist events and meetings, Evers feminists were less institutionally focused in their personalized everyday tactics. Consider the difference between tabling informational literature on breast cancer citing statistics and how to do a home breast exam with the more abstract message in a Radical Cheerleaders chant.

Based on how Woodview feminists responded to the *Vagina Monologues* with its focus on personal empowerment and reclamation of language and voice, it would seem that Evers feminists would see the performance as opening up new ways of personal expression. Instead, the *Vagina Monologues* went the same way as consciousness-raising. Although the play had been produced on the

Evers campus by theater students, for many of the feminists, there was little in it that was relevant to their feminist identity. For example, Abby described her reaction to the play:

ABBY: For a lot of people it's [the *Vagina Monologues*] this "rah rah" feminist third-wave empowerment thing for a lot of people. It's cute and it's funny and it's touching. I mean, there are monologues that I think are absolutely amazing and there are some that absolutely everyone I've ever met hates.

JO: So when you talk about for some people it's sort of this third-wave "rah rah" thing—do you have any sense of how it's seen as a third-wave thing?

ABBY: Well some the monologues in it, especially "My Short Skirt," are very much [about] reclaiming femininity and feminism, which some people think doesn't always work together. It's sort of [a] fun "fuck you" kind of attitude and this is about a woman who, gasp, had a good experience with a man. . . . It's theater and fun and touches people . . . as opposed to sort of throwing feminist dogma in their face.

Another common Evers critique was that the monologues were too essentialist, equating women with their biology. This led one Evers transgender student to write an alternative set of monologues entitled "The Naked I: Monologues from Beyond the Binary," cast with "gender freaks" who argue that there are genitals that do not fit the male/female dichotomy. The revision of the monologues to focus on transgender issues illustrates how Evers feminists viewed the message in the original performance as "too staid" and not revolutionary enough.[27] Overall, Evers activists viewed the monologues as too second-wave generation, and instead focused on tactics that addressed a variety of issues, often submerging the feminist content.

This is not to argue that the Evers tactics resembled the national dialogue on contemporary feminist tactics in every way. For example, crafting as a tactic promoted as "third wave" by a variety of media was not all that common in Evers. Stella was the only one to discuss crafting as a topic and that was in relation to a group she knew from her hometown in California. She said:

I have these friends who started this Revolutionary Knitting Circle and it's really cool in a lot of ways because it encompasses so many different things than like just a knitting circle. They get together, they knit, they talk about social change and social justice work, so they are reclaiming women's work in a lot of ways and it's open to anyone of any gender, but they reclaim this concept of women's work and they say actually this is really important stuff to do and it's self-production. They are making their own things. It's not [about] consuming. So I think that's one of the biggest things about feminism now is making those connections between different issues and like gaps between all of these identities.

Despite her endorsement, crafting as a tactic reclaiming the domestic was not popular or common at Evers.

As introduced in chapter 2 (and to be discussed in detail in chapter 5), Evers feminists did form organizations and directly work to change the status quo when racist and homophobic graffiti appeared around campus. The Student Coalition brought together a number of new and preexisting groups that addressed the campus administration, asking for specific changes in housing and in the college's constitution. Along with these institutionally focused tactics, Evers feminists also kept up their emphasis on personalized, cultural tactics with such events as brown-outs (i.e., having people of color gather in a location), kiss-ins (i.e., having same-sex couples meet at a certain location and kiss) and dress as a form of protest. However, The Student Coalition lasted as long as the crisis and most of the organizations dissolved over the next year. In sum, while the Evers feminists did not advocate moving away from collective action, as evidenced by the reaction to the hate graffiti incident, they did move into more personal, culturally focused tactics. This was largely due to the distancing based on a perception of second-wave-generation tactics as too institutional and ineffective.

Feminism and Tactics

The reaction of Evers feminists to second-wave-generation tactics begs the question—what are the tactics of the past? While historical accounts of the movement tend to focus on legislative outcomes, a mixture of the institutional and the cultural has always been a part of the women's movement. Women seeking suffrage lobbied politicians and the general public as a way of gaining support for a constitutional amendment granting women the right to vote. At the same time, when these institutional tactics did not work feminists in the 1800s turned to more direct-action, confrontational tactics such as hunger strikes and an extremely unpopular picketing of the White House as a way of forcing cultural pressure on the political system. Second-wave-generation feminists also employed a variety of tactics from the more institutionalized efforts to change public policy and law (e.g., Title IX and antidiscrimination laws in employment) to the more direct-action, culturally focused tactics (i.e., guerilla theater and consciousness-raising). These tactics largely depend upon the political and social times and the avenues open to make social change. As social movement scholars David Meyer and Suzanne Staggenborg argue, "Activists assess their opportunities and competencies in various arenas and the impact that activities in the arenas will have on supporters and opponents."[28] Throughout its history, U.S. women's movement activists have assessed the environment and used both cultural and institutional tactics.

In the communities studied, feminists continue in the same tradition, drawing on a tactical repertoire by assessing the environment around them. Yet most of their tactics are largely cultural in nature except when faced by a crisis that demands interaction with policymakers. This is not to argue that young feminists are not engaged in changing public policy and laws. Young feminists come to organizations such as NOW, NARAL, the Feminist Majority and other established groups to work on issues like abortion rights, voter registration and education. In addition, young feminists create their own groups, using technologies such as the Internet to influence public policy. However, in these three communities, the focus ranges from education to personal empowerment to challenging cultural norms. I argue that the focus on the cultural is not as a result of a national discourse in magazines and the Internet or the result of a generation of apolitical feminists, but is instead the result of a political generation of feminists who have seen a myriad of policy and legislative backlashes and embrace a variety of tactics influenced by the social and political climate around them. Woodview focuses on promoting educational projects turned outward while Evers instead embraces more personalized, cultural tactics aimed at rectifying the omissions of the past. Green City has built a community of activist organizations that experienced activists enter into and find a home in the linked feminist and queer communities.

This move toward the cultural has become one of the cornerstones in the tension between feminist generations. Often second-wave-generation feminists characterize contemporary feminists as only "wanting to be able to bare their midriffs," a form of political navel gazing.[29] This skepticism of cultural tactics contributes to the notion that the women's movement is nowhere and is not making any sort of effective change. Yet, social movement scholars warn against focusing too much on institutionally focused tactics as bringing desired outcomes. In an examination of the environmental movement, Nelson Pichardo Almanzar and his co-authors argue that concentrating only on the institutionalized tactics ignores the ways in which activists seek to make change through everyday behaviors. They find that everyday behaviors such as recycling, buying "green" and focusing on saving natural resources are an indication of movement adherence and, when taken collectively, can be viewed as tactics of social movement activism.[30]

If cultural tactics can be effective, what does this mean to the study of social movements? Scholars tend to divide tactics into two categories: institutional (i.e., using means accepted within institutions for making change such as lobbying or letter writing) and direct-action (i.e., going outside conventional channels of making change such as the Miss America pageant protest).[31] Large social movements may incorporate both tactics depending on the context of the struggle. For example, the contemporary U.S. LGBT movement in its fight for equality in marriage rights has employed the institutional tactics of lobbying and voter referendums as well as more cultural tactics such as symbolic weddings. While same-sex weddings in California, later overturned by court action, did not correspond to lasting political change in the state, Verta Taylor and her co-authors argue that the cultural ritual of weddings challenged the dominant power structure and culturally advanced activists' claim for equality.[32]

This study of contemporary feminism reinforces the idea that movements engage in tactics that are neither institutional nor direct-action but instead are cultural and often expressed in personal, situational and everyday actions. By not acknowledging the existence of cultural tactics, communities such as Evers only look active when organizations are formed, leading to skepticism about the continuity of the movement, increasing the sense of the movement's being nowhere. Turning attention to cultural tactics at the community level provides evidence of invigorated feminists from a political generation responding to the community around them, drawing on a tactical repertoire that makes sense in their lives and their times. If contemporary feminists are doing activism through cultural tactics, how are they talking about their activism? In the next two chapters I address two arenas where contemporary feminists puzzle out the legacy of issues of race, ethnicity, class, gender, sex and sexuality in their discourse and actions.

5

Grappling with Oppression and Privilege

We are the colored in a white feminist movement.
We are the feminist among the people of our culture.
—CHERRIE MORAGA AND GLORIA ANZALDUA, *This Bridge Called My Back, 1983*[1]

Is it possible to construct a feminist genealogy that maintains inclusivity? Does feminism still exist for women of color or is it just a "white thing"? Are generation X women of color participating in feminism?
—REBECCA HURDIS, *Colonize This!, 2002*[2]

PUBLISHED ABOUT TWENTY years apart, these two statements speak to the continuing need for U.S. feminism to acknowledge and address issues of racism, privilege, diversity and inclusivity in the movement. The first statement comes from the groundbreaking volume *This Bridge Called My Back: Writings of Radical Women of Color*, an anthology born out of a need to address racism and the marginalization of women of color in the second-wave generation. For contemporary feminists, this anthology is often their first introduction to the history of issues of feminism, race, class and ethnicity.[3] The second statement is from the anthology *Colonize This!* in which young women of color speak out about their struggles to identify with U.S. feminism and call for white, middle-class, Eurocentric feminists to recognize their biases and prejudice. Contemporary feminist Rebecca Walker, often credited with sparking a "third wave," argues that "capital *F* Feminism needs an overhaul" and that it is time to address racist feminists (among others) "who are so far removed from the street they can't organize their own wallets, let alone a rally."[4] The 1980s and 1990s saw the emergence of multiple anthologies and books that tried to do exactly that—overhaul feminism. *Colonize This!* responds to "the profound disappointment in white feminist theory to truly respond to the specific cultural and class-constructed conditions of women of color lives."[5] These repeated critiques shaped a generation of feminists who see inclusivity, diversity and the acknowledgement of race and class privilege as priorities. In 1997, scholars Leslie Heywood and Jennifer Drake wrote of the contemporary movement:

> A third wave goal that comes directly out of learning from these histories and working among these traditions is the development of modes of thinking that can come to terms with the multiple, constantly shifting bases of oppression in relation to the multiple, interpenetrating axes of identity, and the creation of a coalition politics based on these understandings—understandings that acknowledge the existence of oppression, even though it is not fashionable to say so.[6]

The call to "acknowledge the existence of oppression" continues. In 2009, a professor posted on a women and gender studies listserv, "Does a sense of empowerment/entitlement of young women replicate the whiteness of the movement? Ignore women who are marginalized? Does [women's studies] reinforce?"[7]

The concern over domination and unacknowledged privilege in feminism and the consequential need for diversity and inclusivity, often spurred on by writings of women of color, is the result of a history taught to contemporary feminists in which women of color, lesbians and poor women are left out of the movement, their concerns and issues ignored in favor of white, middle-class, heterosexual activists. Indeed, many accounts of the movement confirm these perceptions. For example, Paula Giddings writes of how women of color were forced to leave white feminist organizations, turned away by prejudice and discrimination in the movement.[8] Others, such as Michelle Wallace, write of the difficulty of being a feminist of color in the 1960s and 1970s.[9] However, some feminist scholars argue that while many white women did not acknowledge the intersections of race, class and gender, there were times when some white women and women of color did work together to fight racism and sexism.[10] A third narrative of race relations and feminism is that women of color organized in separate groups that are often left out of the history of feminism.[11] I would argue all three of these accounts are correct with the history of the movement being one of discrimination and exclusion, cooperation and mutually exclusive actions. Overall, it is evident that U.S. feminism has struggled to create an inclusive movement. Feminist historian Nancy Hartsock acknowledges that "white, middle-class feminists always knew there were race and class issues—I think there's been some revisionist history implying they didn't—but they didn't always know how to deal with them."[12] As I have argued, the commonly known historical record of U.S. feminism is flawed, resulting in a story of complete exclusion of women of color, poor women and lesbians, a dramatic overstatement of the actual dynamics, and a lack of acknowledgment of the work done by nonwhite, non-middle-class feminists. But drawing on the popular historical record, many contemporary feminists' goal is to make up for the past—in other words, to do better and create a movement that is neither racist nor classist but inclusive of all people.

In this chapter, I examine the goal of contemporary feminists to build a diverse movement and their discourse for dealing with issues of racism and classism. This analysis of the communities is shaped by two dynamics. First, I draw upon the broader discourse of contemporary feminism that a central goal of the movement is to address the inadequacy of past feminisms and renounce race and class privilege, attack racism in the movement, and create a truly inclusive movement. I then use this broader discourse to examine the actual talk and tactics of the different feminist communities. I draw upon the terminology and language of the communities in this analysis as a way of illustrating how these issues are understood and articulated. Therefore, my analysis focuses on issues of race-ethnicity and, to a lesser extent, social class, which was rarely mentioned by the interviewees.[13] While racism, white privilege and inclusivity generated much discussion, only the Evers feminists mentioned the issue of social class diversity and often only in passing.[14] I return to discuss issues of social class (and the lack of discussion about it) at the end of the chapter. My goal here is to not judge either generation on their ability to address these issues but to show the variation in the discourse and actions of contemporary feminists.

As I have illustrated, how contemporary feminists approach social issues (and the tactics for making change) depends largely on the community context. The feminists of Woodview, Green City and Evers all acknowledge the importance of addressing these issues. In all the communities, rectifying the lack of diversity was seen as an ongoing project, and most of the white community members pointed to a lack of people of color in their networks and communities as a problem. Despite these overall similarities, there were significant differences between the communities in how they addressed race and making an inclusive movement. In Woodview and Green City, the concerns were voiced from the perspective of white, middle-class women. As a result, the efforts to address racism were often framed as tokenizing, effectively immobilizing their efforts. Evers, the community with the largest population of feminists of color, had the most developed tactics and discourse. However, their tactics largely emerged only after there was a hate crime incident on campus. I begin with the predominantly white network of feminists at Woodview and their discourse on racism, ethnocentrism and the need for inclusivity.

Woodview—Searching for a Vocabulary. In Woodview, there was no racial-ethnic diversity among the respondents, with all of the interviewees identifying as white and middle class. This, I argue, played a significant role in why efforts to address racism and classism and increase diversity did not emerge as some of the group's major issues. While the Woodview feminists were aware of the problems of racism, classism in feminism and the emphasis placed on inclusivity in contemporary feminism, their community environment did not encourage them to tackle these issues or help them build a vocabulary to address these issues. For example, Sally said:

> I think third wave is very inclusive, but at the same time it's so exclusive. I think women of color and poor women are still excluded from third-wave feminism . . . I don't think I've come into contact with a lot of lower-class women or women of color or those types of organizations, and I haven't really seen a lot of participation or been part of a diverse group.

While Woodview feminists may be aware of the larger rhetoric, there was not much conversation happening within FFW. For example, some of the women involved in FFW could not remember ever having addressed the question of involving more women of color or women from different social classes in their group. For example, Emily, who had been involved for several years, could not remember ever having heard the issue come up during her time with the organization. Leslie had a similar experience.

JO: Do you feel issues about race and ethnicity and inclusivity are addressed?
LESLIE: I think they're something that we all—that we all care about—so that we're all pretty much more willing to make it a part of [the group's focus]. Or maybe we see it as all connected; sexism, racism and homophobia are all the same basic thing. . . . I think as a group we would welcome that. I'd be hesitant to say that [we would not] fight for something specifically racist related because it is a similar sort of fight, but I don't know. Definitely women who are subjected to racism would absolutely be something that we'd be all about. So I think we see it as all related. That's not something that we would shut the door to but maybe not something that we've addressed really yet specifically. I'd certainly be interested and I think the other girls would.

Leslie's comments indicate that Woodview feminists are aware of the history of the movement and issues of racism and inclusivity; however, they did not specifically address increasing their group's racial-ethnic diversity as a feminist issue overall. Their lack of contact with people of color created a hesitancy—a lack of vocabulary—on how to deal with the issue. This hesitancy in addressing racism was evident in Zoe's discussion of making Woodview, and FFW in particular, more diverse. She said:

ZOE: Just because someone else is black is [not] going to make them have a different perspective, but sometimes, someone who is not white will bring a totally different perspective to it, you know what I'm saying? I don't know if that makes any sense *or if I'm even allowed to say that* [emphasis added], but—it's just—right now it's [FFW is] not diverse. It's a feminist organization, but it's like—I don't know. It's more kind of—I don't know what I would label it.

JO: So why do you think it's so white?

ZOE: I think it started that way and it's easy to continue on the same path. It's easier. It's easier.[15]

Zoe's sense that even talking about race and racism directly may not be allowed was a common theme in Woodview. Feminists knew that they should be concerned about racism, but did not know how to address it in a manner that was informed and respectful. This lack of vocabulary and direction was evident when race did become an issue. When the group had to cast a black woman for one of the roles in the *Vagina Monologues*, Zoe described the resulting tension:

OK, for example, this year at the monologues, we're casting and we're sitting there and we're looking around, and there's a part that specifically says this should be performed by an African-American woman and we're like, "What are we supposed to do?" Like go up to someone and be like, "Hey you're black, want to be in the monologues?" How do you even approach that? Just because someone is black doesn't mean they're necessarily going to want that part, you know what I'm saying? And how we approach it is we just started asking people and I was really honest with people. I was really like, "You know our group is so white it's out of control." ... I knew that that part had to be done by someone because that's a really important part of the monologues. It's one of the only monologues about a lesbian. I didn't want it to be like last year. Kamesha [the black woman who did the part] was tokenized.[16]

The idea that the group was so "white it's out of control" also concerned Ben. While he wanted a more diverse group, he worried about tokenizing the students of color who joined FFW. He said:

[The women's movement is] definitely too white for me. I can even say with Forum for Women, we struggle so much. How do we get diversity to the group? I mean, because you get to this point where you don't want to tokenize people, and you don't want to pull [aside] a black woman and say come to our group because you're a black woman. . . . The [racial] segregation is just so structured. I mean, just walking through [Woodview's student center] you see that. . . . You can't claim to be all-inclusive when you're leaving out black women and black men.

From Zoe's and Ben's comments, it is clear that they identify and struggle with the idea of feminism and FFW as primarily white. Yet it is also clear that Woodview feminists have not developed a strategy on how to make the network an inclusive one, and that having people of color join their group is the only identified strategy. Ben points to the racially segregated campus as one reason for the group's whiteness. Indeed, I noted that the student center, one of the main gathering spots for commuting students between classes, often had tables separated by race and ethnicity, and this separation continued beyond this building. In conversations with students at Woodview, I was repeatedly told that that there was little intermingling of races and ethnicities. I argue that this overall lack of racial integration at the university made coming up with strategies beyond recruiting members for the group and the *Vagina Monologues* difficult to imagine.

Although Zoe, like many of the Woodview feminists, was not sure how to talk about race, she did want to try to make FFW less white. She talked about working with other student organizations and trying to have conversations with people of color about the need for diversity. As a member of the university student governing board, she was involved in bringing a speaker to campus for a diversity training. Despite these conversations and efforts, she still felt stymied by her lack of strategies. She concluded:

I don't know. I'm kind of like scared like EEEEE [she makes a scared noise]. I want it to be diverse. I want to just snap my fingers and be like, "Okay, our organization has a bunch of different interesting people in it," but it doesn't unfortunately.

Part of this hesitancy to deal with race was a result of the focus of the leaders. To Laura, the first president of FFW, feminism was still primarily about being women and focusing on that as a commonality. She said:

I think a lot of girls are really focusing in on those issues that have to do with embodying women as a whole and not segregating as women have done in the past based on ethnicity, class, race and all that. . . . They're not just zoning in on this one particular thing like we're zoning in on reproductive rights. Or we're zoning in on inequality or on race relations. . . . We want to see a day when those things just don't even matter. We want to be a part of a movement where something happens where we can bring women together and just say we all have something in common. Those things are so minor in the big scale of things and in the big picture of things we don't need to focus on that. We need to focus on us as being women and what we can do for the women's issues, no matter what.

Intersectionality is the concept that argues that our social lives are an integrated matrix of race, class, gender and sexuality and we cannot separate one issue from the other—they mutually influence our interactions, opportunities and access to resources.[17] While Laura is advocating an intersectional approach to feminism in her discussion of not segregating women by a single issue, she reifies the idea that race can divide the movement and that gender and sex are the most important.

The lack of a focused antiracist discourse by white feminists in an environment with racially segregated networks resulted in a group that talked about the importance of diversity but had no real direction in how to achieve it. Take, for example, a notice that appeared in the FFW newsletter under the headline "Mission Diversity," written by Jaclyn:

> Another ambition I consider crucial is expanding the group; not only increasing membership, but opening our doors to new faces of every race, sex, sexual orientation, religion, age and background. This will not only add to the quality of dialogue exchange [and] the forum's members' experience, it has the ability to bring new issues to the table. A diverse group of enlightened persons is essential for unlocking the full potential of FFW.[18]

While Jaclyn, a white woman who was one of the only members to grow up in an inner-city environment that was predominantly black, obviously cares about making the group more diverse, she outlines no specific plan of action other than having "new faces" come to FFW. As a result, the group stayed predominantly white during the time I was observing. Occasionally women of color would join the group, often on their own initiative because they identified as feminists and/or were women's studies majors.

Overall, at Woodview a strategy for dealing with inclusivity as an issue has not been fully developed. The amount of attention paid to making a more diverse group varies by leadership and often stalls out by lacking a coherent strategy on ways to proceed. I argue these dynamics emerge from the community environment. The racial-ethnic dynamics of the overall community, one of segregation, as evidenced by the student center, tends to isolate whites from people of color. In addition, Woodview's feminist community depends upon personal networks, which also exacerbate the issue. In an environment hostile to feminism, the group strategizes around well-developed mainstream issues such as educational efforts on domestic violence, breast cancer and reproductive rights. Racism and inclusivity in the movement only come to the forefront for the group when they are specifically called upon to address it, such as in the case of casting the *Vagina Monologues,* but even then there is no clear strategy in place. I argue that the absence of a developed strategy is not because Woodview feminists are intentionally ignoring race, but because of a variety of factors that make the issue difficult for them to articulate in a meaningful way. I now turn to examine the dynamics in a community with a more developed vocabulary—Green City.

Green City—Awareness and Separation. In Green City, the interviewees' racial-ethnic and class demographics were similar to Woodview, with almost all identifying as white and middle class, and they also lived in neighborhoods that had distinct racial-ethnic compositions.[19] Overall, they believed that contemporary feminism needs to address racism, classism and white privilege, but the community segregation made this difficult to do. They also shared the belief that people of color organized in communities separate from the predominantly white feminist, lesbian and queer communities. For example, Marley noted:

> I think that the community of colors separate [from the white community]. It is here. I think it is pretty much everywhere. And I do believe that there are genuine efforts especially, by the third wave, to be inclusive, but I think you can't do that until you understand and validate a unique experience, which I don't think happens on any level. It's hard because, especially in [Green City], because we don't have a very large minority community, and the minority community is very segregated to one part of town.

My observations align with Marley's that the area was segregated by race-ethnicity. When asked to describe the larger community, interviewees often broke the area into neighborhoods designated by social class or race-ethnicity. In addition, I noted that when attending events and hanging out at the feminist bookstore and local coffee shops (often located in white neighborhoods), there were few, if any, people of color present.

Despite this segregation, Green City feminists had a more developed vocabulary to talk about racism and discrimination. This was evident in a variety of conversations where feminists talked about issues such as neighborhood displacement and gentrification. From her position in the bookstore, Kelly was privy to conversations about these issues. For example, she said, "There's talk of the gentrification and therefore, the displacement of poor people, which often means people of color, specifically in [Green City]. And I know that that's a debate that's been going on outside and within the feminist community for a long time." Green City feminists also had a language to discuss the need to acknowledge white privilege within the movement and Green City networks. For example, Steve writes in her zine:

> Unless white, western feminists take action and admit their privileges and their own oppressive behavior, our place in the national and transnational arena as activist[s] will continue to be threatened. Everything that we might intend to accomplish could be disregarded and unsuccessful because of continual, damaging attitudes, beliefs and values.[20]

Gone here is the hesitancy seen in the remarks of Woodview feminists and instead, Steve draws on terms such as "privilege" and "oppressive behavior." This more sophisticated vocabulary was in part due to the fact that Green City feminists were often transplants who had a wider view of communities and the possibilities of racial and ethnic integration. This made them different from Woodview feminists who, with the exception of Jaclyn, had not experienced much outside of a predominantly white world. For example, Kelly talked about her past experiences in a different activist community. She said:

> I came from Austin [Texas], which is you would think a way more racist town being in a way more racist state, but the truth is that it wasn't. There was a variety of colors of faces in every room at every time—if you were in the kitchen restaurant cleaning or if you were in the boardroom talking politics. And that was something I guess I took for granted unfortunately because it doesn't happen here.

Part of seeing the problem of racial-ethnic and class segregation was working to rectify it. Even with a more developed vocabulary, Green City feminists still struggled with how to make contemporary feminism in their community more diverse. Samantha analyzed the community efforts this way:

> I think [she pauses] our intentions are good and we are more aware. So I don't know if we necessarily are hugely diverse, but we're definitely trying to make space and make pains to be—so to make people feel more comfortable—to make people of color feel more comfortable in the spaces that are maybe predominantly white. So people know that they have allies and advocates and it's not just some people that are like, "I think about my own issues!" "Girl power!" Blah, blah, blah.

While Samantha acknowledges racial segregation, the strategy does not move beyond inviting people of color into white spaces, what some have called "the add color and stir" tactic. Just as they did in Woodview, concerns about tokenizing arose. Marley noted that white feminist groups do try and reach out to communities of color, but it is often unsuccessful because the interaction is often initiated from a white perspective. She said:

> How much did any of these groups reach out? How much did they understand that they couldn't use their normal message and have it be effective? And I think that that's been and will continue to be [the way things are]. Not understanding that you have to incorporate economic issues. . . . There's a lot of tokenism, which I think a lot of people find offensive. A woman of color might find it offensive that, "Oh god, we really need to have that token whatever at the table so that we have all perspectives." Well, you don't if you're not adopting their experience as valid. If you're just looking at them as somebody at a table for a picture [it] is really offensive.

As a result, progress felt slow in coming. Susan, who had taken part in conversations on racism and inclusivity in various groups, was not optimistic. She said:

> I see people get frustrated. I get frustrated sometimes, and I've heard other people say, "Why do we keep talking about this when we keep spinning in circles?" But I think those are just moments of frustration because I also think, in general, that people understand the importance and are willing to keep it in there and keep that circle going in hopes that it will slowly move forward.

Kelly, from her vantage point at the feminist bookstore, thought that a conversation about race was still ongoing, even though she was not sure about that. She did note that there were several women of color organizations in town and the relationship between those groups and the white activist community could be "way more fluid—way more collaborative." Her comment confirms that segregation continues to be an issue for feminism with groups and networks separated by race, ethnicity and class. And again, as it was in Woodview, part of Green City's problem in addressing racism and racial-ethnic segregation is the lack of strategies, or as Susan indicates, even a defined direction. She said:

> The next step is to take this [conversation] further. Bridging what has happened in the generations before and what do we do with that now. How do we take it further because we all know racism still exists and we

see it and experience it in different ways whether you're in the dominant white group or not? It affects us. Where do we go from here with it?

By stating "where do we go from here?" the white Green City feminists clearly recognize and acknowledge the problems with racism in the movement, drawing on their past experiences to give them a broader vocabulary. In a social context with multiple communities, Green City feminists are aware of issues of space and separation and are somewhat optimistic that progress is slowly being made. Yet, they continue to construct a largely white network with no specific strategies for making feminism more inclusive other than the integration of white groups by people of color. I now turn to an extended discussion of Evers, the community with the most feminists of color.

Evers—Struggling with Privilege. Evers was the most diverse community of the three, with almost 30 percent of the feminists identifying in a racial-ethnic category other than white. However, similar to Woodview and Green City, the majority of interviewees were middle class. I find that race-ethnicity played a role in how issues of racism, diversity and inclusivity were constructed. While the Evers white feminists mainly addressed racism as an overall societal problem, women of color were more likely to address racism in feminism. Because of their social location, feminists of color often had the most sophisticated vocabulary, and they moved from dialogue to practice when racist and homophobic graffiti appeared on campus. To explore this dynamic, I begin by discussing how white feminists talked about race and diversity.

White Women Speak. In Evers, gone were the feelings of hesitancy and instead, the white feminists talked about racism and oppression with more awareness and depth than in Woodview. Similar to Green City, some Evers feminists drew on previous experiences in their discussions. Lila, a white woman who had attended a racially inclusive private high school, shared her perception of why Evers was not a more racially diverse college. She said:

Race at Evers is in a bad situation because I think being an all-women's college that is known for being to the radical left and [on the East Coast] does not make it very conducive to students of color coming here. [She sighs.] I mean, just being at [my private high school], it was much, much more diverse than Evers. And I don't blame people . . . if they're a student of color who wants to go to another school where they're in a supportive community—like Columbia. A lot of my black friends in high school wanted to go to a school like Columbia or Bryn Mawr or somewhere that was in a more supportive environment where they wouldn't be the only black person for who knows [how far]. I don't blame them. [She laughs.] I definitely think Evers is kind of grappling with those issues and it's definitely reaching out to more minority communities, but I still think . . . we're not addressing it as well as we could—definitely.

However, for Lila, the issue was not just the demographics of Evers as a college and community, but also the response of whites who exacerbated issues of race, often in well intentioned but misguided ways:

I don't think a lot of people at Evers know about or come from a background like [mine]. I think those people are from very white, progressive towns on the East Coast. And I think their approach then to fighting racism or whatever is different from black students who grew up in an all-black environment. . . . And then for me, who just grew up in a diverse background that wasn't necessarily very progressive at all, but I was certainly exposed to a lot of different cultures and a lot of different racial groups. So I think that—I think that there's an obvious sense of awkwardness when [she trails off]. A lot of things that happen here at Evers are that wealthy white girls from the East Coast who are from very wealthy, progressive communities try to come here and fight racism. [She laughs.] . . . Which you know isn't necessarily a bad thing, but it [she trails off].

While Lila stops short of labeling the actions of the "wealthy white girls" of Evers as misguided or problematic, she points to how dealing with racism is made more difficult by the lack of acknowledgment of white privilege.

Although lacking in their hometown experiences as identified by Lila, some of the white Evers feminists did come to understand issues of race and ethnicity through the writings of feminists of color. For example, Skye discussed a class on womanist thought she was taking with a well-known black feminist scholar and how that changed her perceptions. Because of this course, she changed her identification from feminist, with its racially exclusive connotations, to womanist. Her experience was similar to other white women who had come to writings of feminists of color through women's studies courses. Terri reflected on her women's studies class where she read *This Bridge Called My Back* among other works:

I think that [racial-ethnic oppression] is definitely something that is coming into discussion, and it's really, really important because I know one of the things that I did learn in women's studies last year that I hadn't really been exposed to was the fact that women of color had been, if not actively excluded from women's groups, sort of excluded just by virtue of the fact that this was feminism that was helpful to women who were a particular class and white. Therefore, there was no reason for women of other racial groups to be involved in it because they weren't representing the rights that they needed. It wasn't something that was really about equal access for all. It was just like, "Hey, come on and be feminist with us and help us fight for our rights and later on we'll deal with your rights." . . . I definitely think today it's becoming more understood that we need to include people, all different [people] whether it's different sexual orientations, different gender, I mean, even men can be involved in feminism. . . . I think it's really, really important to have a forum when women of all different races and classes can come together and share their experiences because I also think the commonalities between women of different classifications aren't talked about that much either.

Despite the fact that some women came to understand racism through women's studies, some at Evers believed that women's studies courses could do more. According to Bailey, part of the assumption that white feminism was still the norm was due to the structure of women's studies courses, a viewpoint echoed by the Evers feminists of color. Bailey said:

I think that when I hear a woman of color [say], "I'm not taking women's studies. That's for white women," then we have to say, "Okay, feminism, even it's still exclusive. It's implicitly excluding people." I mean, then you look at [a women's studies] syllabus and . . . we've got Audre Lorde and Sojourner Truth. [She laughs.] That's not very representative of women's studies and women's experiences.

Bailey continued describing the dynamics in a women's studies classroom:

I guess racism is probably the easiest one to talk about especially because [Evers] is so white and women's studies majors are predominantly white here because women of color don't see women's studies as being open to them, and I think that has in part to do with the Intro to Women's Studies [course] that we took. Even the stuff that you read from women of color, a lot of white women were able to make it about themselves and if they weren't, they were making it about themselves either saying how it related to their experience even if it didn't because they're white or upper class. Or they would turn it into how bad they felt about it. White guilt is something that I've seen a lot here, and it's just another way, I think, for white women to make the issue about themselves. . . . I do have a lot of guilt and sometimes you want to indulge in how bad you feel, but then you talk to people who are of color and [they] say, "You really don't need to feel bad. It's not about you." And you're like, "Oh, it's not about me." We're used to things being about us and about our experiences, and so I think the way the classes are conducted and the way discussions are had amongst a lot of white feminists still assume that white feminism is the norm.

However, despite the classroom dynamics and the unacknowledged privilege of the white women, Bailey came to see the problem as really based in the past efforts of feminists, fitting with the critiques made at Evers of the second-wave feminist generation. She said:

> I think a problem with the second wave—it's telling women to get out of the home and into the workplace—the issue is well, who is going to clean the house and take care of the kids? And that is usually a lower class of women of color. And that's still not something that we're talking about. . . .

The result of this combination of coming from predominantly white towns and cities, unacknowledged white privilege, and blaming the second-wave generation (and women's studies) for problems of the past and present was an environment where white, middle-class feminists were highly aware of the need to address racism, classism and segregation but were not always able to articulate workable strategies for change. Deborah, a white woman, reflected on this disconnect between discourse and accomplishment. She said:

> It's really interesting because when I started at Evers, there was a very particular group of people who were doing basically all of [the organizing] and they were women's studies majors. In that group of people [were] the head of Feminists Together and the head of the Student Labor Action Coalition. They were the heads of antiglobalization groups [and] the peace groups. They really came from a very theory-based place. . . . I remember the first Feminists Together meeting I ever went to. They were talking about how their theme for that year was interlocking systems of oppression, and there were no people of color in that room. So it was this really weird thing about people having theory that was antiracist, very class conscious, but the people who were still in the group were still the same people who get tagged to mainstream feminism all the time—the white, middle-class students.

So despite their more sophisticated vocabulary for talking about race, white feminists from Evers still struggled with how to address racism and create viable strategies for change. In addition, their lack of acknowledgment of white privilege and the claim to "also be a victim" were two of the issues identified as problematic by the Evers feminists of color.

Women of Color Speak. With a third of the Evers feminists identifying as women of color, their voices are a vital part of the discussion on racism in the community. Overall, they were critical of the way in which white feminists dealt with race. Julia, who identifies as a Colombian Latina, noted that instead of working to build a more integrated society, she saw many white Evers feminists dealing with race or class guilt by denying their own privilege. She said:

> I feel like feminism here . . . is very focused on [people saying,] "I'm a victim," "I've been oppressed" regardless or not whether that's true. People are very, very—it's very difficult to get people to accept that they have some sort of power in anything whether it's race or orientation or even gender identity.

Julia termed this denial of privilege "appropriation" and found it common among white Evers feminists. She said:

> There's the issue of appropriation, which is sometimes masked as feminism. . . . It's very paternalistic or maternalistic except that there aren't any men, you see. . . . It's like, "Since I'm feminist, I'm going to take these people's problems or this foreign concept and I'm going to make it my struggle." . . . I've really noticed so many people—and it's something that I obviously can't understand, but so many people struggle with the idea of being white and upper class, and just feel so guilty about that. And instead of maybe recognizing how they're privileged and how that's good and how they can use that privilege to do what they want to do—make society fair, whatever—people will just—for lack of a better word—people just freak out. . . . There's this whole downward mobility and appropriation trend that really, really bothers me.

As a Latina who has experienced discrimination, she found the idea of white feminists seeking out ways to label themselves as oppressed trivializing her experiences:

> People here will just be like, "Your Oppression. Oppression. Oppression," and look down on someone who's trying to get out of [oppression] whether it's financially or whatever. I don't want to be oppressed because I've already been oppressed for nineteen years. It's been subtle, but

working in a food place in the summer and having people talk to me slowly because they think I don't speak English is a form of oppression. That wasn't really that fun. I don't really want to do it again. . . . And I think that's a lot of what the third wave is doing to itself, is that in order to feel more alive or more with a purpose, we have to find something wrong [with ourselves] or some sort of oppression. . . . And I just think that we have all trivialized oppression because even when I hear myself talk about it . . . people have been racist and sexist to me, but it's never been a matter of life and death and it's only made me stronger. And when people were rude to me at [my work], it wasn't like they were going to kill me. It hurt my feelings and I didn't understand it, but I was still making money and what do I care? That person isn't paying my bills.

The result of this appropriation of oppression and lack of acknowledgment of privilege was an environment where women of color often did not engage in feminism, even though they were in a "feminist bubble." Deborah, a white woman, recalls encouraging a friend, a woman of color, to participate in feminist events on campus to see what was going on. Her friend replied that she would not get involved in "all that" because she would be "totally marginalized." However, some of the women of color at Evers did engage in feminism, despite their concern that racism and white privilege had not been addressed. Julia did come to identify as a feminist, but she noted she was an exception. She said:

And especially here I've realized the resistance that people have to labeling themselves feminist. And I've noticed it and through research and just talking to people, I've noticed that the resistance is very—usually very specific along racial lines, that women that aren't white . . . Latinas and black women are very hesitant to say that they're feminist.

Stella, a biracial woman, agreed that feminism as she knew it did not seem welcoming to women of color. She said, "I think race is still definitely a really big issue and white privilege. And yeah, I think we need to make, in a lot of ways, this concept of feminism more inclusive." This distancing from feminism by women of color was exacerbated by women's studies courses. As discussed in chapter 2, Evers feminists often saw women's studies as a representation of a racially exclusive second-wave feminist generation and were critical of it. Julia recalled one such course in feminist theory she had taken at Evers College:

I fought with the syllabus so much. . . . It wasn't structured the way that I would have expected. It was sort of chronological, sort of thematically, whatever, and we'd just go back and forth, and there were just lots of things that were absent like feminism abroad.

It was basically U.S. feminism or a white, middle-class feminism with [a] few pockets of—you know, we read the Combahee [River] Collective or something. So there were [a] few pockets of black U.S. feminism and maybe one or two pieces by Latinas and Asian Americans, but it was definitely one-sided.

She argued that the result of such classes and reading lists is that women of color don't see themselves as a part of feminism. She said, "Things like that I feel help perpetuate the myth that black women and Latino women and Asian American women can't be feminists. That culturally it's impossible for us to be so . . . you know?"

Another factor Julia found alienating was the language of Evers, particularly the term "woman of color." This was a new way of being identified when she came to Evers from Miami. She explained:

I'd never heard the term really before I came to [Evers] because I don't really consider myself a woman of color in Miami. It's very mixed, you know? And even racial ideas in Latin America and amongst Latinos are very different, even though I'm relatively brown, not really that much. By way of class status or education or last name even, I could be white even if I was darker. It doesn't matter that I have curly hair.

Although she did not identify as a woman of color at home, Julia soon realized that at Evers she would be labeled as such.

And the phrase is just very weird and the first time I heard it was because Evers has a program . . . they invite students of color to come visit this school. And they kept saying it, "women of color," "women of color." And I was like, "What is that?" I don't know what that is.

She continued:

And it's just a term I don't like. I understand it's used in *This Bridge Called My Back* in the 1980s. It had—it's highly political and it was a way of uniting people, but I think it's kind of obsolete now. And I also don't think that the term itself reflects the way that people are "raced" by others. So I prefer to say "colored" because it's active and even though it has a history. . . . [The term women of color] reflects the idea that says women from Argentina who come here are automatically women of color, but they're blonde and blue eyed. It just reflects the idea that the U.S. is so obsessed with race whereas, for example, [in] Latin America, really we're all one cosmic race and even though it's not necessarily true ideologically, everyone is more concerned with nationality than color. So I don't like "women of color."

In part, Julia's resistance to the term "women of color" was due to the fact that it did not make racial oppression less present at Evers. It was a course with a professor with a similar background that made her realize that she wanted evidence, not just vocabulary. She remembered:

In my sociology class last semester—we had this fabulous sociology class with . . . she's my current advisor now. She's great. She's the first Latina professor, and quite possibly the first Latina teacher I've ever had. So she's the physical representation of what I want to be—a professor, yeah. So she's my goal personified. And I've never had that before. And can you imagine what it's like to never have had—we don't even look alike physically. She's lighter skinned and from a different country. She's from the Dominican Republic. But just the idea that this woman has the same cultural background as I do and has had the same struggles that my family has had and she's, like, made it, you know?

And I've never seen that before. I've never been exposed to that before. And that was really powerful for me.

In addition to being grateful for the chance to see another Latina at Evers and one that represented her possible future, Julia also found a form of feminism she was not aware of before at Evers. Through the works of Cherrie Moraga and Gloria Anzaldua and *This Bridge*, she found a feminism that was relevant to her and "more compatible" with her culture. This was a feminism that she had not been exposed to before and she "didn't necessarily see reflected physically in the people that go to [Evers]."

In sum, Evers is a place where white feminists and feminists of color talk differently from each other. White feminists focused on racism in society and feminists of color focused on white feminists' lack of acknowledgment of privilege. Julia's story is particularly informative about the dynamics at Evers. She seeks evidence of equality and the owning up of white privilege and not just "better" terminology and white guilt. So while overall there is more dialogue at Evers than at Woodview or Green City, the task of becoming a more inclusive movement remains difficult. However, Evers feminists had a chance to put their theory and language into practice when the college was the site of racial and homophobic graffiti.

The Incident at Evers. In 2002, on the walls of two student houses graffiti messages appeared, reading, "Die nigger, die" and "Die, dykes, die." Upon discovery of the graffiti, the college was in an uproar. Professor Andrews said of the incident, "It was pretty extreme. . . . It was these students' homes where this was happening." According to Andrews, the college investigated to find out who had written the graffiti, referring the incident to the local police force, which brought in a handwriting expert. In response to the graffiti, the students immediately sprang into action and formed a group called The Student Coalition (TSC), which drafted a list of demands and held a series of marches, walkouts and a sit-in at the administration building. The demands included creating a task force of race consultants to serve as a liaison between students of color and the administration, antiracism training and mandatory diversity workshops for all houses, sanctions against campus public safety, and an implemented policy of procedures to deal with hate crimes. The students requested residence housing for only students of color, and that pictures of students of color not to be used in a tokenizing way in college catalogs. In addition, they asked that faculty of color continue to be recruited and retained. The demands also included issues of gender identity and expression. Many of these largely student-driven demands were eventually met, including a student government committee charged with monitoring the 2002 demands and a task force to consider identity-based housing for students of color.

As discussed in chapter 4, TSC was able to achieve a number of demands by using institutionally focused tactics. The incident brought together a coalition of groups able to mobilize large numbers of students and press the administration with their demands. Their success was due, in part, to their ability to articulate issues of racism and solutions. Many of the feminists of color became involved in the organizing efforts. Stella, who identifies as Chinese and white, described her involvement in TSC:

> I was involved in The Student Coalition last spring, and it was an organization that just existed for a couple months. It had a very specific goal after the hate crimes that I was talking about—dealing with that. We submitted a list of like ninety demands to the administration and went into negotiations with the administration and had brown-outs, which is where all of the students of color get together for dinner in one house or another, especially a house in which nothing has occurred. We had a kiss-in in the place where the homophobic thing happened. A lot of it was about addressing, or a lot of the visible part of that, was about addressing institutionalized racism, classism and homophobia at Evers, but what really went into the demands was about support—supporting students, all different kinds of students—support for trans students, support for students

of color, support for low income students, just what they could do better to support us as students and make the community safer. And I think that through all of that just because of who was working on it; it was really feminist and . . . we defined what we needed and we are entitled to.

White feminists also joined in on the struggle. Sandra, a white woman, saw the incident as arising from the institutionalized racism embedded at Evers College and the administration's lack of action. She emerged as one of the organizers of TSC. She said:

It was a reaction to the immediate incidents, but also a long stemming tradition of the administration at this college ignoring the fact that it's an unhealthy environment for a lot of people. And they, a lot of minority students, see that there will be houses [where the administration] will put one token minority student in the house and [didn't] understand that people feel uncomfortable with that. There's a lot of animosity on campus, and the administration didn't do anything about it. Then there were a lot of details about stuff, like a couple of people who worked for the college got in trouble because one of them made a remark about the sanitation in one house being less than pleasant because there were international students and "niggers" in the house, and they got in trouble. There was one house [with the graffiti] "Die, dyke, die," and "Die, nigger."[21] And the administration did nothing, and public safety remarks were, "Okay, you women, calm down." Basically in just one surge, this campus was torn apart. There was [*sic*] screaming matches and all-college forums. . . . We formed a group who would break into rooms in the middle of the night and have four-hour [-long] meetings which turned into sobbing [sessions]. [We were] planning what we would do in response to the college and we came up with a list of demands and then gave them to administration. It was also open house weekend with all of the prospective students and stuff and we flooded the whole campus with banners saying this is still a racist, homophobic, classist institution and handed out pamphlets on what had gone on to all of the prospective students.

Sabrina, who identifies as a black Latina, was one of the prospective students who learned about the incident when she came to Evers on a college recruitment trip. She remembers:

When I came here, there were race issues going on and students were so active about telling the prospective [students]. I had people come to me and be like, "Don't worry, we're working on it," and I had people come to me with flyers, wearing shirts and pins, and being like, "You don't want to be here."

While it is clear that the incident sparked organizing on campus around race, taking a closer look at the incident also reveals what it meant to activists and community members. For some white feminists, the racist graffiti showed them a new and puzzling side of their environment. For example, Terri, a white woman, said:

It's a very tense environment in terms of racial issues to some extent, which surprised me. I wasn't really aware of it until last spring there was—there were a lot of racial incidents on campus and this big source of tension, and it really felt like students were reverting into their general classifications and sort of withdrawing from those who were different from them. There was the sort of atmosphere of distrust and it was kind of scary to me because I had no idea where it was coming from and a lot of it, it was difficult because certain events had happened and the college didn't really publicize them. Toward the end of the year, they made an effort to let the students know what was going on, but there was this whole tense situation.

Even with its success with negotiation with the administration, TSC still struggled with issues of race and white privilege internally. The coalition also had the added complication of other groups using the incident to press for their agendas. While TSC and the groups it worked with were relatively successful, the coalition was fragile and began to splinter within a few months. One group that was unhappy working with TSC was CROW, a creative writing group for women of color, started by friends Gabriella and Melita. Gabriella, one of CROW's organizers and a self-identified black Hispanic, related the history of the two groups. She said:

CROW actually began the semester before the hate crimes. Over the summer, me and another woman [sic] had been talking about how there wasn't really a forum for creative writing for women of color. Specifically in the sense that most of the time when women of color produce creative work, it's taken to be political, regardless of what it's actually about.

She continued:

So, what ended up happening after the hate crimes ... Melita and I both had a lot of experience as organizers by then. We ended up sending out e-mails and stuff like that in trying to garner grassroots support. What ended up happening is as much, and TSC emerged. At first, they approached CROW for an antiracism campaign. . . . We cosponsored events with them. And then what happened was that TSC was having a lot of issues internally, and CROW was having a lot of issues in terms of gatherings because a lot of people were like, "We're really confused about what CROW is doing," because it had originally emerged as an open mic night. So it was like, "What is CROW doing?" So CROW and TSC put together a really massive rally, which is credited to TSC to my eternal bitterness. But it was a really huge rally. And Melita tried to keep true to CROW's original statement, which was—that unlike a lot of more confrontational student organizations . . . we do want to acknowledge that there is a place for our allies to speak out and have feelings in the fight against racism.

For Gabriella, the coalition between the groups began to fall apart because of the environment at Evers, where white privilege was not always acknowledged. She said:

Yeah, so the thing about Evers and racism and activism is that it's still Evers. You know, it was really funny to me. So, apparently there were all these anti-TSC people who infiltrated TSC and started spreading rumors to each of the members of the [TSC's] executive board about what the other members of the executive board were doing. So that ended up fracturing TSC still further, and then some of the women of color felt like they weren't allowed to have a voice. And then some of the white women felt like they were allowed to have a voice, but their voice was cut off because sometimes during their meetings, there'd be a woman of color speaking or about to speak and someone would raise their hand and would interrupt her and one of the women of color board members would be like, "You know, that was really inappropriate." . . . At one meeting [a woman of color said,] "I don't want to offend my white allies or anything like that, but I do want you to understand this is not your show. So please be quiet." So . . . and stuff like that would happen a lot.

According to Gabriella, as the problems at the meetings intensified, the coalition faced other issues. One issue was when a group emerged that focused on anticorporate activism and the rights of transgender students. This group began to organize against TSC and its allies. When CROW managed to get free lemonade for one of the rallies, the anti-TSC group began to "chalk" that the rally was really about taking corporate money. According to Gabriella, the anti-TSC group was led by a group of transgender activists who were known as "agitators" on campus. In retrospect, Gabriella concluded that all of the group dynamics were nothing new in the history of feminism. She said the whole experience contributed to "my sense of what feminism would have been like in the sixties and seventies."

Gabriella's conclusion about the internal group dynamics may ring true for many second-wave-generation feminists who found organizing within the movement difficult. Evers students were able to mobilize immediately once the incidents were made public, holding several successful demonstrations, and creating and obtaining a list of demands from the administration. However, the coalition of TSC, CROW and other groups began to splinter as issues of voice, authority, race and gender emerged in the meetings. While TSC accomplished many of its demands, we cannot know how much more could have been accomplished if the organizations could have retained a cohesive coalition. Even with the ideology that antiracism and diversity are important to feminism, Evers feminists still had trouble building a truly inclusive coalition even when sparked by overt racism on campus. While some white feminists saw the need to get involved, they struggled to find a way to participate without dominating. Feminists of color mobilized to address race but found that issues of gender diversity, in the form of transgender activists, undermined their coalition. The outcome of these dynamics was a short-lived and tumultuous campaign that achieved many policies but left the culture of racism and white privilege largely in place. I observed firsthand how these dynamics lingered at Evers even after the administration granted many of the TSC demands. As described at the beginning of chapter 1, organizers continue to discuss the events on campus a year later by holding meetings in dormitory parlors. At the event I observed, women of color facilitated the discussion with little input from the white women in the room; instead, many of the young white women cried quietly during the presentations and discussion but did not speak out, leaving much of the racial dynamics in place.

Grappling with Oppression and Privilege

After examining the three communities, I return to the question: How is contemporary feminism dealing with oppression and privilege? Despite the focus on diversity and inclusivity, the answer is that feminism in the three communities still has far to go. In Woodview, there was an awareness that issues of racial-ethnic and class inclusion were important; however, feminists were hesitant to address these issues and unsure as to how to proceed. As a result, in Woodview, tokenizing people of color was one of the only strategies that activists knew, a strategy they were very uncomfortable pursuing. Green City feminists came with a greater understanding of what an inclusive community should be, but because of the separation of communities they were unable to accomplish it. Evers, unlike the other communities, was presented with an opportunity to build a truly diverse coalition of groups to deal with racism. While the coalition did succeed in changing policy, it did little to influence the overall community culture.

If contemporary feminists care so much about inclusivity, why, then, are these three communities still struggling? One reason, I argue, is the result of communities still largely segregated by race-ethnicity. Predominantly white communities continue to build a still largely white feminist movement. Only in Evers do we see women of color and white women working together. Woodview and Green City feminists continue to live in predominantly white worlds and this influences the networks and organizations they build. This failure at racial-ethnic diversity can be seen in other areas of the women's movement. For instance, in 1998, New York City NOW President Galen Sherwin wrote a letter to members in the NOW newsletter reflecting on the NOW Northeast Young Feminist Summit:

> ... We had high hopes for a summit focusing on young feminists: unity, diversity, a bridging of gaps, a coming together. We have strong convictions concerning our generation and an optimistic view about what we can accomplish as the next wave to pick up the cause and fight hard. However, some things unsettled me. .... The issue of race, for instance, could not be avoided in an auditorium where the vast majority of participants were affluent white students. By my count, there was a small number of Latinas, a smaller number of African-Americans, and one Asian participant. This was upsetting. What does this say about us as a group? It's true that there were people who wanted to attend but could not.... Are we not reaching out in the right way to these communities? Or, is it a case of preaching to the pre-converted?[22]

As a result, inclusivity becomes a concept in feminist discourse and not a practice. By this, I mean there are discussions of diversity in all the communities, but not much movement past dialogue into practice.[23] Contemporary feminists work to create what they perceive to be lacking in the feminisms of the past—inclusivity. But instead the call for diversity becomes just that—a call without substance. Without an acknowledgment of privilege and a strategy based on an understanding of the issues, diversity is difficult to achieve. Feminism is not the only social movement to struggle with these issues. This focus on the concept of diversity without a plan of implementation is evident in other social movements. For example, scholar Jane Ward in her study of diversity practices in gay and lesbian organizations found a similar dynamic—consciousness without true application. She writes:

While race, class and gender inequality and segregation are not new to the movement, the current era is witness to new institutional and ideological tools that hide or naturalize these outcomes and lead lesbian and gay activists to believe they have succeeded at creating an inclusive, multi-issue movement. "Celebrating diversity" and the ideas and practices it represents is one such tool; it is a smoke and mirrors trick that distracts us while "diverse" people and ideas leave the movement.[24]

Without a serious attempt to move antiracist dialogue into practice, the dilemma of diversity in the U.S. women's movement will continue. As long as feminists continue to organize in communities that are segregated by race, the important dialogue about what race and ethnicity mean in social movement communities will not happen.

While it is evident that the communities struggle with race, missing in this chapter is a discussion of social class. As mentioned earlier, Evers feminists were the only ones to address social class in a more meaningful manner. For example, Ava from Evers argued that there has been some progress on race, but issues of class were still not being acknowledged. She said:

I say when it comes to white women recognizing their privilege; I think we have gotten a lot farther than we were back in the day . . . You are not going to necessarily have an upper-class woman who is going to advocate for the lower-class women's rights . . . And that's a problem in itself that you are not going to have Mary Jane . . . advocating for a black poor woman. . . . [She takes a long pause.] I think people of color have gained more tolerance—women of color. I think that class is an issue that is still not being addressed.

Lila agreed that Evers had not started a meaningful dialogue on social class, but she was hopeful that it would start. She said:

I don't think that class is brought up at all at Evers, which is unfortunate, and I think they are working on it. We had an open forum recently at the [college] senate, which [student's name] chairs, and it was great. . . . People brought up a lot of class issues. I think that it's going to be looked at more.

Part of the reason for this lack of discussion was the culture of "victimhood" or appropriation as Julia labeled it. Lila continued:

But I think it's . . . another interesting thing about Evers versus a lot of other schools that I know, is that here, because of this PC-ism on campus,

I really don't think it's cool to be wealthy as it is if you go to [private college] and they're all driving BMWs and [wearing] their Burberries and whatever and whatnot. But here, I think it's very a unique situation because the people want to seem like they're more progressive than the next person or less materialistic or, "I only eat vegan food," or whatever and "I have a solar-powered car," that means you can't look like you drive a fancy car or whatever. So I think that if class were to be brought up here . . . it would be brought up in an interesting perspective because people certainly aren't flashy about what they own here at all or who comes from where.

Julia echoed Lila's thoughts on the subject. She said, "People are still reluctant to talk about class. People are more okay with race and sexual orientation, but class is still very . . . because this society is not supposed to have classes." Julia traced part of this inability to talk about class back to second-wave-generation feminism, in particular Betty Friedan, author of the landmark book *The Feminist Mystique* that brought many women into feminism in the 1960s:

Betty Friedan . . . she started the feminist mystique because she was a white, middle-class woman. She didn't have things to do. She had someone cleaning her house while she wrote that book and that doesn't devalue her book or her feminism at all. What it comes down to is she was very, very privileged. She had an education. . . . She had a good husband. . . . . She had a housekeeper. She had a nice house. She had time to think about how she was being oppressed . . . which a lot of people don't necessarily have. Whereas I think, "That's great. What about her housekeeper?"

Julia and Lila highlight several reasons for the lack of discussion of class in contemporary feminism. First, U.S. citizens often find discussions of class difficult, and when asked to identify their social class, most claim a middle-class lifestyle whether or not this is accurate. As Lila points out, in some contexts, no one wants to identify as "wealthy" and at Evers, class privilege remains unnamed along with white privilege. Secondly, new social movement scholars argue that there has been a shift from working- class movements to lifestyle movements, such as the women's, LGBT and environmental movements, which draw on actors interested in promoting or protecting their quality of life. This leaves contemporary movements often populated by those in the middle class who have leisure time and resources.[25] Consequently, middle-class activists may be less tuned into issues of classism. Finally, I would argue that although feminist activists and scholars state that social class is as important as race, overall, there is not the same broad focus on social class in analyses of the U.S. women's movement as there has been on race and ethnicity.[26] Much of the analysis of poor and working-class women is examined through the lens of union or neighborhood organizing and not specifically feminism.[27] In her analysis of social class and feminism, bell hooks argues this is largely because of the media's focus on the concerns of privileged white women.[28] This lack of attention results in contemporary feminists learning a simplified history that focuses more on racial exclusion and often excludes groups of feminists who specifically critiqued issues of social class as an issue or as a matter of diversity.[29] However, social class does emerge in some settings. In a 2000 meeting of several prominent feminist scholars, including Evelyn Nakano Glenn and Barbara Ehrenreich, the overall conclusion was that the movement had gained much for women but had not addressed the widening gap between social classes and the exploitation of poor and immigrant women by privileged women.[30] Based on their conclusion, contemporary feminism has far to go with addressing classism within the movement. If contemporary feminists are still struggling with race-ethnicity and class, how then are they addressing sex, gender and sexuality? It is that question that I address in chapter 6.

6

It's a Brave, New Gendered and Sexed World

WE, THE QUEER, TRANS, LESBIAN, GAY, BISEXUAL, TWO SPIRIT, GENDER NONCON-
FORMING PEOPLE gathered together at the United States Social Forum, to continue to
build a national movement of our people to fight state sponsored destruction of our
communities. We do hereby establish our interdependence to one another to ensure
our people's Safe Self-Determination . . . [and] to respect and celebrate our varied
gender and sexual identities. . . . Our identities are not our possessions; we do not own
them, and we are more than any one label. . . .
—The Roots Coalition United States Social Forum June 25, 2010

THE 2010 U.S. Social Forum was a gathering of a diverse group of activists with the intention of building "a powerful multi-racial, multi-sectoral, inter-generational, diverse, inclusive, internationalist movement that transforms this country and changes history."[1] One of the groups participating, The Roots Coalition, serves as an example of how activists, including feminists, are talking about the changing gendered and sexed world of the twenty-first century. We live in a time where gender (i.e., our social beliefs about masculinity and femininity) and sex (i.e., our ideas about our biological sex and sexuality) are being redefined in political ways. Instead of adhering to the conventional categories such as male and female, masculine or feminine, gay or straight, there is a trend across social movements to adopt more fluid categories of identity; in other words, there is a development to deconstruct static ideas about gender, sex and sexuality into more fluid understandings. The contemporary feminist movement is no exception to this trend. The Internet teems with articles, blogs and Web sites on feminism and transgender, sexuality and gender. Academic studies follow suit with studies of drag kings, transgender transitions, and assertions of a sexual self. In feminist anthologies, activist Emi Koyama argues for a "Transfeminist Manifesto," and "queergirlofcolor" is the preferred identification of writer Leah Lakshmi Piepzna-Samarasinha.[2] The terminology of "trans," "queer" and "genderqueer" have entered into the discourse of contemporary feminism, and in this chapter, I question how identity fluidity is being done and talked about in the communities studied. The answer lies, as I have argued throughout this book, in the community environment and its influence on discourse. In particular, I examine three aspects of identity fluidity: gender and the embracing of a "genderqueer" identity, sexual orientation and the adoption of a "queer" identity, and transgender. To do so, I first briefly define and outline each of these identity terms.

Queer and Genderqueer. The concept of genderqueer draws on queer theory, coming from a postmodern approach, which rejects traditional sexual orientation categories of heterosexual, lesbian, gay, bisexual or asexual.[3] Instead, "queer" is a fluid identity that rejects the confines of sexual orientation categories. In this view, sexuality is not innate and instead is the result of socialization and cultural conventions. According to queer theorists, having to choose a sexual identity category is a form of oppression that locks people into classifications that sustain discrimination and prejudice along with preserving heterosexual privilege. By choosing to deconstruct sexuality categories, queer is a new category of identity, free from reinforcing heterosexual and patriarchal privilege.

The term "genderqueer" then builds on the definition of queer. One of the achievements of the second-wave feminist generation was the introduction of women's studies into the university curriculum and the conceptualization of gender as different from sex. Feminist scholars argued that sex is something determined both biologically through hormones, chromosomes and genitalia, and socially in that these biological markers are found significant in a society (i.e., how much of a penis or vagina does a person need to be considered a man or a woman). Gender, on the other hand, is culturally determined and socially learned. Gender is a set of behaviors and expectations that go along with a particular sex category. Whereas sex is assigned as either female or male, gender is socially and culturally determined as feminine (or womanly) and masculine (or manly). Since gender is not fixed biologically, it is fluid, with most people having both feminine and masculine attributes, and fluctuating between those gender identities during their lives. One outcome of the idea of fluid masculinity and femininity is the notion of genderqueerness. By rejecting the sex dichotomy of maleness and femaleness, genderqueers are people who choose to identify as both masculine and feminine or neither, rejecting any sort of gender categorization and presenting a persona that is not obviously male or female, masculine or feminine. By claiming this identity, genderqueers often do not align themselves with any sort of sexual identity or orientation. Genderqueers dismantle notions of categorizing people based on sex, a notion I will discuss later that has ramifications for the women's movement.

Transgender. Transgender is an umbrella term for people who "do not conform to gender stereotypes, roles and expectations."[4] The term "transgender" is often defined to include identities such as gender bender (does not conform to societal gender expectations), genderqueer, intersexual (born with ambiguous or both female and male sex organs), transsexual (identifies as the sex opposite of one assigned at birth), male-to-female transgender or MtF (males who transition to female) and female-to-male transgender or FtM (females who transition to male). Although transgender is seen as a term that covers both queer and genderqueer identification, in this analysis, I separate out these three terms based on their usage in the communities studied. In the case of transgender, I refer to MtF and FtM individuals who change their sex and/or gender in a variety of ways ranging from pronoun usage and names (e.g., Steve and Tadeo who chose more masculine names), dress and appearance and physical alteration of the body through hormones and surgery. Despite the existence of transgender people throughout history,[5] there has only recently been a flurry of articles examining the adoption of transgender identities. These articles have often focused on FtM transitions happening on college campuses similar to Evers, that is, private colleges on the East Coast. In a 2001 article entitled "Girls Will Be Boys" about these colleges, the author writes, "Transgender organizing is picking up steam and trans alliances are far more vocal than they were five years ago."[6]

With the growing focus on identity fluidity and an increase in FtM transgender people on college campuses, I turn my attention to the three communities to see how issues of queer, genderqueer and transgender have influenced contemporary feminism as a discourse shaping activist identities. I find that the adoption and incorporation of these ideas into communities varies by environment, history and the relationship to second-wave-generation feminism. Woodview, with its hostile environment, is the most conservative in its approach to identity fluidity. Many of the Woodview feminists continue to identify in conventional ways (e.g., man or woman, gay, straight or bisexual) with little to no discussion of transgender.[7] As for sexual orientation, a large number of Woodview feminists identified as lesbian; however, they were hesitant to make it a major part of their focused feminist identity. Evers feminists continue to respond to a more open environment by viewing identity fluidity positively and, at the same time, basing some of their responses on their perceptions of second-wave-generation feminism around gender, sex and sexuality. At Evers, lesbian becomes an old-school form of identification, with "queer" being the preferred term, and transgender issues are integrated (and sometimes in conflict as illustrated in chapter 5) with other social issues in the community. Green City feminists exist in a different environment with a vibrant, separate and yet linked queer community. As a result, they create a form of feminism that embraces genderqueer, queer and trans identities. However, when feminism is not evident in those identities, Green City feminists (as well as Evers feminists) become critical. I examine each community in turn to elaborate how contemporary feminists talk and do this brave, new gendered and sexed world.

Woodview—"It's Personal, not Political." Woodview was the community least likely to discuss queer, genderqueer and trans as issues influencing their feminist identity and activism. Instead, feminists were more likely to stick to conventional ways of identifying themselves. These views of identity are not surprising in a community where the focus is on educating a hostile community and working to build group solidarity as well as recruiting potential allies. As a result, the feminists identified as either female or male, with no one adopting the idea of queer or genderqueer. Only one respondent varied by writing that her sex was "womyn," a second-wave-generation redefinition of woman to not include the word "man," indicating more of openness to the past rather than a rejection of gender and sex categories. In the same vein, Woodview feminists defined themselves in conventional sexual orientation categories, such as gay, straight or bisexual, with almost half identifying as lesbian. It was the number of lesbians in the group that shaped the community's notions of gender equality, not issues of identity fluidity. According to Ben, the presence of lesbians merged ideas of gay rights with feminism.

JO: In terms of what FFW has done, do you feel like the group as a whole is onboard with women's issues and gay and lesbian issues merged together?
BEN: I definitely see it as everybody being onboard. . . . I mean, if I look at our [executive board], four of the five officers consider themselves to be LGBT citizens, so, I mean, it's definitely something people are onboard with for sure.[8]

While Woodview feminists did not adopt the idea of sexuality as fluid, they did see it as a continuum where people could change their sexual identities over time. Whereas queer is not choosing a specific category, sexuality as a continuum allows for one to change categories over time or combine them. For example, in the demographic form given to the interviews, one Woodview woman responded, "I am currently in a heterosexual relationship, but open-minded." Another identified as a "bisexual lesbian," giving some evidence that the community did not see sexuality categories as forever fixed but instead flexible and capable of transitions. Indeed, Laura argued that the idea of sexuality as a continuum is a common contemporary feminist belief. She said:

> I think there is a very large amount [of feminists] in the third wave who are becoming very sexually liberated and not only as far as having sex but

experimenting sexually and becoming very much more open to homosexuality, open to bisexuality. . . . I think a lot of them are realizing that there is a continuum somewhere.

The focus on sexuality as a continuum did not mean that everyone felt comfortable articulating how they saw themselves. This was true for Paulina. She remarked that while at Woodview she wanted to identify as a "lesbian with a boyfriend" to indicate her lack of attachment to a heterosexual identity, but she did not think the group would understand.

Despite the stereotype that all feminists are lesbians, the reality at Woodview is that many are lesbians.[9] However, the link between lesbianism and feminism was something several of the FFW members found difficult to articulate. For some, it was people around them that made the connection. For example, Judith recalled her coming out as a lesbian and a feminist to her mom. She said:

It took [my mom] a really long time to get over the fact that I was doing things because I want to be doing them. So I think maybe she thought for a second I was becoming a feminist because all the people I was hanging out with were feminists and then she—the same kind of thing happened when I came out too. She's like, "Well, you are hanging out with these new people." [I replied] "No, mom, I'm really gay, it's the way it goes."

While Judith did not see her feminism or lesbianism as linked (even though her mom did), Sally did see a powerful connection between her sexual life and her coming to adopt a feminist identity. She recalled:

I became involved with this woman who was in women's studies and I started dating her, and she encouraged me. . . . and that was when I got more concrete ideas about what I thought feminism was, and during that time, I think I defined it more. What made me so angry was my fear and . . . [she takes a long pause]—it [was] a power issue with men and feeling that they had the power to instill this fear in me, and I think that I was so angry about that, and I just wanted to reclaim a lot of things

For Sally, lesbianism was linked with feminism and the rejection of patriarchal power. Others saw a similar connection. For example, Emily viewed her lesbianism through the lens of patriarchy. She said, "I'm not sure that I can explain exactly why, but I think that I just feel like I can relate to other women better and sharing similar experiences makes intimate relationships that much more powerful for me, and . . . without feminism, it just couldn't happen." In the same vein, Anna was more comfortable in linking feminism with lesbianism. For her, lesbianism embodied a deep sense of connection she saw as integral to feminism. She said:

> When I look at myself, I think there is a connect. Because the very thing that attracts me to lesbian relationships are the things that I see absent in heterosexual relationships. For instance, the emotional, not that there is not an emotional bond between a man and a woman, but there is an intense, at least in my experience, there is a more intense, a deeper, more emotional connection between two women. And there is a strong, a stronger sense of egalitarianism and I don't—I have never experienced that egalitarianism with a man or in a relationship with a man. . . .

But even with this linking, Anna was hesitant to overstate the connection. She continued:

> I don't think that sexuality is a big issue with feminism. I really don't think right now that there's a tie. There might be a tie to it there, but I don't think that it is required that you be sexual, be a lesbian, to be a feminist, that you need to love sexually women to be a feminist. I don't think so. But I think you are more inclined to be a feminist if you do love women.

Overall, the common sentiment at Woodview was that there was a personal connection between lesbianism and feminism, but Woodview feminists were hesitant to claim a political connection. This is the result of Woodview's focused feminist identity that seeks to bring all allies into the community; to claim one had to be a lesbian would alienate potential allies and make negotiating a hostile environment even more difficult. In a time when most feminists are stereotyped as man-hating lesbians, Woodview lesbians had a difficult tightrope of identity to negotiate.[10] Although many saw a personal connection with sexuality, they could not articulate that connection without feeling like they were feeding into stereotypes about lesbians and gay men. This was evident in Ben's comments on his sexuality, gender and feminism:

> I see a linkage between sexuality and gender. There definitely is a linkage and I'm still struggling with that, but at the same time, there's definitely a separation. . . . I separated my sexuality from my gender in a way. I don't know if that makes sense. I separated it, and I didn't see the fact that I was acting—that I felt more—I guess you could say feminine. I'll use the word

"feminine." I didn't see that as the reason for me having conflict with myself. I actually was having conflict with my sexuality—I guess that's what I'm trying to say is I didn't see that [my femininity] as being the reason that I was gay. Like that wasn't the problem. . . . I guess, in a way, I think what maybe drew me to feminism in a sense . . .

What Ben articulates for all Woodview feminists is that feminism allows them the personal freedom to define themselves as more than stereotypes and to claim a meaningful identity, yet they hesitate to make their personal identities political statements. Feminism at Woodview then becomes the home place in which identities can be articulated and expanded beyond the stereotype of the feminazi or the effeminate gay male, but it is it their identities as feminists that are political. For Ben, being feminine and being gay, when situated in feminism, became a source of personal strength to work for political and social equality.

While Woodview feminists did not embrace identity fluidity, they did see issues of sexuality as important to feminism. However, this was largely articulated as a series of issues meant to educate the overall community. For example, questions about sexuality and feminism quickly turned to discussions of AIDS, HIV and STDs (sexually transmitted diseases) in my conversation with Sally. Along with issues of sexual health, another key issue addressed by Woodview feminists was that of promiscuity and the double standard that women face. For example, Jane recalled a program she had recently watched on sexuality and the need for girls to remain virgins and reflected, "Why are girls growing up fed this idea?" In sum, Woodview feminists did not engage in discussions of gender or sexual fluidity. Instead they focused on how their sexual identities were personally but not politically linked to feminism. Consequently, their focus on issues of sexuality centered on the need to undo stereotypes (i.e., the sexually active slut) and educational efforts on sexual health. It is not surprising, then, that Woodview feminists also entered into few discussions about transgender.

During the first years of FFW, discussions of transgender arose infrequently. However, over time, transgender became more a part of the discourse at Woodview, but never to the same extent it is apparent in Evers or Green City. The increase was due, in part, to the visible presence of a transgender student on campus, and in 2008, students, staff and faculty began a campaign to include gender identity and expression in the university's nondiscrimination policy. However, the most common way in which transgender was discussed was as the "T" in the acronym LGBTQA, which is used when discussing the gay, lesbian, bisexual, questioning and ally community at the university. As community members got more exposure to transgender issues, it did become a part of their consciousness but was not embraced by all. Zoe described how FFW reacted to transgender issues:

JO: What about trans issues, does that ever come up?

ZOE: Oh, we don't talk about that! [She laughs ironically.] . . . We've gotten into discussions . . . with some people from the group, people who don't really understand. They're like, . . . is someone who does drag always transgendered? . . . I don't know where to start. I don't even know a whole lot about the issue. . . . There's not a whole lot of understanding with stuff like that at all within our group. Maybe two or three people, including me, even have a little understanding. I don't even claim to have a huge understanding, but I'm learning. Especially being at [the local gay, lesbian, bisexual, transgender resource center] and talking to people. . . . At first I was like—Michigan Womyn's Music Festival? Oh yeah, it's a women-only space and then I'm— [she asks herself] "How do I feel about that? Yeah, transgender people should probably be included in that." I never thought about that because it didn't involve me directly, you know. . . . I want to know more about stuff like that, but then there are some people within the group who are like, "Eeeee, we don't want to talk about it. We don't want anything to do with any of that stuff."

Zoe is referring to the annual Michigan Womyn's Music Festival, which enacted a policy in 1992 to exclude women who were not women-born-women, a policy that has led to debate and division in the women's movement. In 1994, transgender activists started Camp Trans, a space for transgender women to protest the festival and provide an alternative camping space. It was through Zoe's exposure to the festival that she began to think about trans issues. Ben saw the community's dealing with transgender more as an issue of denial in the overall LGBT movement as opposed to an issue of community ignorance. He said, "I think transgendered issues are definitely something that's extremely important and it's definitely ignored. I mean, I think it's ignored in the feminist community, it's ignored . . . in the LGBT rights movement." Through either lack of education or denial, transgender was largely a nonissue for Woodview feminists. As I will discuss, this varies considerably from Evers and Green City. Instead, the most problematic issue related to gender, sex and sexuality was the division between lesbian and straight members that emerged in the group.

Although the lesbian and gay members of FFW were hesitant to claim that one had to be gay to be a feminist, heterosexual feminists found that they struggled to feel a part of the group at times. The most troubling times were when the group had social interactions that were populated by mostly lesbians. Kyra was one of the straight women who struggled with connecting with the other feminists. She recalled several incidents where she felt left out, including having to listen to a group of FFW members talk about going to a gay bar. She said, "But it was just like they were already friends and I'm just having to sit there [listening to] how they went to the gay bar, and I'm not gay and I'm just like, 'Okay, this sucks.'" Her sense of alienation from the group increased after attending a party where she felt misunderstood and left out. She recalled one incident where she laughed at something a lesbian FFW member had said and was called a homophobe. She said, "And I was thinking about it afterward. I don't feel right with her putting me on the spot like that—trying to call me out when I'm not homophobic. . . . That was shitty." Maura, in a heterosexual relationship, also felt uncomfortable at some of the group's social gatherings. She said, "I just couldn't go to [a lesbian member's] baking party . . . from what I hear, it was a lot of cuddling, and since the four of them are there [names two lesbian couples in the group] it's weird going into situations like that." She continued describing how it felt to be a part of the group at times:

> I feel for once, I feel like the minority because I eat meat and I like boys and I don't know. . . . I don't feel like I'm a lesbian. I could, I guess, if I wanted to, but it would be more of a forced thing, but I've had a lot of friends that are gay, a lot of close friends that were girls and my mom for a while thought that [I was]. I was under suspicion for a while because I broke up with my boyfriend and hung out with these two girls that were, they weren't even friends, it was two different lesbians that had nothing to do with each other and she's [my mom's] like, "I knew they were lesbians because she wore a bandanna."

In describing her discomfort, Maura identifies three important aspects of being a feminist at Woodview. First, as attested by Kyra, it is an environment where lesbians are in the majority and can be alienating to heterosexual women. Secondly, even though the group does not draw a strong connection between lesbianism and feminism, the fact that Maura seriously considers if she should identify as a lesbian indicates the way sexuality and feminism merged personally at Woodview. Finally, the comment by her mother that she knew the woman was a lesbian because she wore a bandanna also illustrates the level of stereotypes about sexuality in the Woodview community, attesting to the hostile nature of the environment not only to lesbianism, but to anything that seems out of the norm in that culture.

The result of this environment is a feminist community that addresses sex, gender and sexuality in conventional ways. People largely fit into expected categories of sex, gender and sexuality. Feminism has the ability to expand and enhance people's understandings of themselves, but it does not push the boundaries of identity. In sum, Woodview feminists talk about gender, sex and sexuality in a similar way to how they talk about race and ethnicity. While there is some consciousness of the issues, there is no resulting action such as the adoption of identity fluidity—queer, genderqueer or trans—as a course of action. Instead, the group focuses more on educating the external community. Sexuality has a personal link to feminism but is not seen as a political statement. While the group depends upon its tight internal bonds for survival, those bonds manifest at times as cliquishness that threatens those bonds, making the group more vulnerable to the antifeminist culture around them. So how do ideas of gender, sex and sexual fluidity influence the feminists in a different environment, one of a feminist bubble?

Evers—Boundaries as Old School. Compared to Woodview, the community at Evers is a very different place. Not only is feminism accepted (and somewhat expected), the area surrounding the community was very open to gays, lesbians and bisexuals and was known for its accepting atmosphere. As a testament to this cultural state, Sandra chose to attend Evers College because of the overall community tone. She said:

> I used to come up here all the time when I was younger because I live a half hour away from here. So, me and my friends [sic] would come up and would just hang out and meet people. In regards to being queer, I knew at the age of thirteen I could come up and hang out with people and look around and see rainbows everywhere and it was just really accepting and it was very attractive. It's nice to know I can walk down the street dressed like how I wanted to dress and not have somebody stop their car and start yelling at me. So, it was more the environment that helped, not so much the school.

This focus on openness to sexual difference was a key aspect of the community. For example, Ava noted that the discourse on other issues in the community was still problematic. She said, "I think that we've definitely gotten much further in sexuality than we have in anywhere else—well, even with race and class. I'd say sexuality we have gotten the farthest in."

Just as the critique of the second-wave feminist generation was the foundation about ideas of antiracism and inclusivity, (as in chapter 5), so it was with sexuality. These critiques of second-wave feminism and sexuality at Evers reflected the conversations happening in other milieu, including academia. For example, scholar Merri Lisa Johnson writes that a contemporary feminist goal is to press forward "sex-positive in a culture that demonizes sexuality, and sex-radical in a political movement that has been known to choose moral high grounds over low guttural sounds."[11] As a response to the perceived antisex ethos, Evers feminists created a community focused on celebrating their sexuality and sexual encounters. While Evers feminists did not always see themselves reflected in media reports about contemporary feminism, they did acknowledge that there was a focus on "reclaiming" sexuality. For example, Becca argued:

> [Sexual freedom] is another thing that media latches onto. You think you are a feminist if you sleep with eight trillion people, like somehow this is empowering, [but] I do believe that there is sort of an opening up. We acknowledge that women like sex too. . . . being sexy. We can deal with that. . . . Second-wave feminists made it sound like women have lost their desires except what has been imposed by men. And today [contemporary feminists] are saying, "Screw that." [She laughs.] We love sex as much as men do.

This idea of reclaiming sexual desire, however overstated it is in the media, was a central aspect of Evers feminism. Becca continued:

> I think a part of this is good. [Contemporary feminism's] not afraid of sex. . . . The second wave was, "Pornography is evil." Then the third wave was, "Nah, man, we like pornography too. Don't act we're not into that stuff and everything." I think that is really valuable because we have to acknowledge that we're not being—Andrea Dworkin's whole thing was all sex is rape, and that is just crazy.[12]

Just as Evers feminists defined themselves, their tactics and issues in opposition to their perceptions of the second-wave feminist generation, they also drew on these perceptions to create a community that was "pro-sex." One manifestation of this pro-sex culture was creating an environment where people are aware of other's sexual intimacies. For Sabrina, this was the cause of some discomfort. She said, "We joke about it all the time in the dining room like, 'Oh, I heard so and so' or 'The walls here are so thin.' We joke about it, but I get a serious anxiety about people hearing me." While celebrating sexual activity was seen as positive, Deborah had concerns that part of this pro-sex culture was reinforcing patriarchy. She said:

> A lot of the feminism I see at Evers—that is, a really big part of it—we've gone towards a very pro-sex, pro talking about sex, making sex okay—acknowledging and validating other kinds of sexuality, other kinds of sexual expression and promoting women's sexual identity. . . . Sometimes I want to say, "Hold on, just because we don't want to objectify women should that mean that we should just objectify everybody? . . . Is there something in particular about women and sex and oppression that has

gotten totally obscured by the totally valid desire to have women's sexuality be recognized and positive and free and without restrictions based
on gender or sex?"

This fear of going too far with a pro-sex culture was a part of the ongoing debate
about sexuality at Evers. Deborah continued, "I have a lot of arguments at school
with people about this and I have mixed feelings about this."

In addition to celebrating themselves as pro-sex (despite the qualms of some),
Evers feminists continued their critique of second-wave-generation sexuality
through the rejection of the identity of lesbian. According to several feminists in
the community, lesbian was "old school." This came as a surprise to Paulina, who
came to Evers from Woodview where she had been afraid to identify as a "lesbian
with a boyfriend" and being a lesbian caused dissension between feminists. After
moving to Evers, she recalled having an argument with a friend that revealed
some of the Evers stereotypes of lesbians as "too second wave." In the midst of the
argument, her friend asked:

> He said, "Well, is she a lesbian?" And I said, "No, actually she's not.
> Why would you even ask?" And he said, "Well, lesbians analyze every-
> thing and they're really crunchy granola . . . " blah blah blah. . . . [Lesbian
> is] almost a stigmatized word just like "feminist" is a stigmatized word
> for some people. Yeah, it's just interesting how the stigmatized word of
> "lesbian" or "feminist" at Woodview would [make feminists] liberal,
> crazy, bra-burning, nutty, man-hating, witchcraft-practicing women,
> and here it's touchy, feely, granola, vegetarian, Birkenstock-wearing, Ani
> DiFranco–listening.[13]

The labeling of lesbians as "old school" is the result of an environment where
identity categories are seen as restrictive, and, in the case of "lesbian," too second-
wave generation. Instead, Evers feminists embraced the idea of being queer and
genderqueer. Lila saw this move to queer as a result of a new movement "that's
going to revitalize people." While Lila sees this movement as having a larger effect,
it also influenced the way that Evers feminists identified themselves. At Evers,
most of the respondents answered the question about their sex with "female" but
added qualifiers such as genderqueer, or "trans, sex-female." One respondent
wrote: "Sex: female, gender: undecided—use female pronouns." This way of identifying was in a response to how Evers feminists saw second-wave-generation
feminism as locking them into identity categories that needed revision. For example, Bailey recalled a conversation with her mother on how her feminism and
sexuality differed:

JO: Do you see yourself as having a different kind of feminism [than your mother]?

BAILEY: Absolutely. My mom asked me after a year and a half at Evers, "Bailey, we need to talk. Are you gay or straight?" And I was like, "Mom that's so second-wave. You don't have to be either one." And we ended up having a really fabulous conversation about sexual fluidity and a spectrum and how I identify myself and how I don't identify with that binary. And that's something that she really hadn't heard before.

Bailey's sexual identification went beyond the personal and instead was something she saw reflected in her generation and community. She continued:

So, I think the sexual fluidity of our culture and our generation is absolutely third-wave. . . . But that's definitely a difference that I've seen that our parents and our professors expect a certain sexual and identity rigidity that a lot of people just don't understand.

The result of this critique is the creation of an environment where gender, sex and sexuality fluidity is embraced and identifying as a woman (in the perceived second-wave-generation sense) is seen as inhibiting that fluidity. This could even go beyond how some of the Evers feminists identified, hinting at the ideologies of the next cohort of feminists. For example, Gabriella recalled meeting a student during her employment in residential life. She said:

One of my first years [student] I was talking to her and she was like, "I don't see myself as a feminist because I don't define myself by my gender." And I was like, "Well, feminism isn't necessarily about you defining yourself by your gender. It's recognizing that other people define you by your gender." And she was like . . . "I self-identify as being neither [man nor woman] because I self-identify as being me."

For Bailey, the idea that identity fluidity was a generational issue was confirmed by the responses of the professors at the all-women Evers College who she saw as not being open to the idea of queer and genderqueer. She credited this to their embracing womanhood and the category of female as the basis for their feminism:

That's definitely a tension I've seen with professors and students, especially at Evers, because last spring we voted to take the pronoun "she" out of the student constitution. . . . I don't think that's something that a lot of professors really expected. [Removing gendered pronouns] is a very third-wave, more contemporary movement to move away from the butch-femme, gay-straight sort of binaries that infuse or that we associate with the second wave.

While this critique of the second-wave feminist generation moved Evers feminists to adopt the politicized identities of queer and genderqueer, it also opened the way for an exploration of transgender. Tadeo argued this was in part due to the second-wave generation resistance to transgender, particularly FtM people:

> I have talked to a lot of older friends who identify as lesbians and traditional feminists and they think that a transgender person is a violation—a traitor. Why [would you not] want to not identify as a woman? . . . Why do you have to identify as something else? Worst of all, why do you want to identify as a guy?

What Tadeo is describing is the premise of one of the most well-known feminist texts rejecting transgender—Janice Raymond's 1979 *The Transsexual Empire*. In Raymond's critique, both trans men and women fare badly. Transsexuals are rejected as either power-hungry women who want male privilege (FtM) or confused men who reinforce women's oppression (MtF).[14] Scholar Sally Hines argues that second-wave radical feminist theory, as articulated by Raymond, emphasizes women's essential natures and constructs a barrier to trans men and women who seek feminist support and community.[15]

While Evers feminists may not be familiar with Raymond's work, they were aware of her argument and found it problematic. For example, Abby found this legacy of exclusion an obstacle to her identification as a feminist. She said:

> I personally have problems with [identifying as a feminist] sometimes because the feminist intelligentsia and feminist ideology [are] really exclusive a lot of the time. I was actually having a discussion with the trans activist group the other night, and it's problematic because feminism. . . often excludes trans people and people of color and people who aren't U.S citizens and the list just goes on and on.

She continued:

> You know, feminism should be looser. So, I guess I'm arguing more for what feminism shouldn't be than what it is. And it should be in support of people who are female, female-identified or [have] female experience[s] or ever have been any of those three.

Sandra saw the second-wave feminist generation in a similar light, as excluding transgender people and narrowing feminism too much. She said:

> I think feminism right now is women realizing that they are part of a larger community, that their interests are important . . . like transgender issues in particular. . . . What do you do with the people who are the sex of a woman but their genitals are male, can they still be feminists? . . . I've started to think that maybe feminism is just people who are just reflecting on what it is to be female, what it is to be a woman and how difficult that is in society, and how feminism changes your perspective.

She continued:

> And I think that old feminism was very much a political response that didn't do anything socially or culturally, and I think now a lot of feminism has to [focus on] queer advocacy because that's challenging the heterosexual normative, which I think feminism wanted to do a lot of it, but was scared to take that step and say, "Why are we ashamed to just be how we are?" "Why do we have to have these labels?" . . . We don't have to fit into this normal society, which is still based on men.,

Issues of transgender took center stage with race at Evers at the time of the hate crime incident in 2002. Sandra saw the incident as a chance to address issues of gender and sexual identity, particularly around transgender, and educate administrators and students. She said:

> A big thing that came out of [the turmoil over the graffiti] was that a lot of people said, "I don't feel comfortable on this campus because every time I go to an assembly, it's like we are [all] women." . . . We had panelists going into every house—our housing system is basically small community living—where at the beginning of the year, the people within the house get together and talk about sexuality. It is mandatory for the underclassmen, so you have eight people talking about their sexual orientation, their identities and stuff because sometimes we have people who are transgender who come into the house because there turns out to be one in every house, and talk about it and just start educating people about it. There are a lot of questions, but it's definitely hard for a lot of first-year [students] to sit there and to hear someone [say], "You know what? I don't identify myself as being a woman. Don't refer to me as a 'she.' "

The result of the visibility of FtM transgender was that at Evers, with its submerged feminist identity, the focus on trans rights often easily combined with feminism, creating what writer Emi Koyama calls "transfeminism."[16] For Lila, the relationship between feminism and trans activism was clear. She said:

> I think that definitely transgender people are part of the feminist movement because I just think that [the] feminist movement [is] standing up and doing something about being discriminated against. And I don't think that transgender people should be discriminated against at all and the [hate crime] statistics are horrible.

Ava saw the increase in the number of trans students as a reason to incorporate trans issues and feminism. She said, "Right now, we have a lot of students on campus who identify as transgender and who identify as a man. . . . [Feminism should] understand the oppression of people who identify as [trans]gendered." For Deborah, the merging of feminist and transgender issues was a new, "more radical" development of feminism. She noted she could particularly see this in her younger sister and her friends who are still in high school. She said:

> Maybe it's just my sister, but [she and her friends] think about racism, they think about classism, they think about sex oppression and gender oppression and sexuality. They think a lot about sexuality, gay/lesbian/bisexual/transgender issues. I mean, the fact that my sister and her friends in high school are talking about transgender issues is exciting. It's really exciting, and I think that it presents so many opportunities.

Overall, Evers, with its critique of the second-wave feminist generation and its submerged feminist identity, is a community that embraces the idea of sex, gender and sexuality fluidity. Picking a sexual category such as lesbian is old school, and the perception is that the second-wave feminist generation was antisex and antitransgender. While the openness of the community and the strength of the critiques against past feminisms may have promoted identity fluidity, not all Evers feminists were comfortable with all aspects of these ideas. For many, the impact of taking away the category of "woman" from the women's movement concerned them. For example, Deborah said:

> I'm really drawn to the idea of deconstructing gender; I think a lot of people are especially in the academic community or doing feminist theory . . . but then I wonder how are we going to advocate on behalf of what we still think of as feminist issues if we don't have gender? I mean, how are we

going to fight for equal pay for equal work when you would have to say "women"? You would have to say still, "Women don't get paid as much as men in society," but if you don't have women and men anymore ...

Becca continued in the same vein but found the deconstruction of gender even more problematic than Deborah. For her, it was out of touch with the reality of the world around her. Becca said:

> I hear a lot of the conversations about, "Let's decategorize the category of woman." ... I do not get this. I will never get this. Let's act like we can erase gender? I do not believe that is possible in the world that we live in and in the world where we have brains that are programmed to categorize people. And I don't even necessarily see gender itself as a problem, but rather the way the larger systems impose disenfranchisement along gender lines. So I am not down with it. I feel like that is my major complaint of my understanding of third-wave feminism because [of the] whole "let's be genderless" point.

While the community was an environment open to identity exploration, moving outside this "bubble," as indicated by Becca, concerned some feminists. Skye noted that at Evers it made sense to deconstruct gender, but she questioned it in other contexts. She said:

> But in general, in the world, I mean, if I am talking about FGM [female genital mutilation] in Sudan, for example, gender is incredibly important. And so I think identifying women's human rights, putting *women* on the label is really important because you need to take account of the historical oppression and the historical contexts. (Emphasis added.)

Because they identified as feminists, Evers activists held onto the central concerns about the status of women in society and had some ambivalence with aspects of gender fluidity.

The case of Evers illustrates that in certain accepting environments, social movement actors can explore a variety of ways to address oppression and discrimination. However, those tactics, such as promoting identity fluidity, do not transfer to all other contexts.

While Evers feminists fought for trans student rights, such as the removal of pronouns from the student constitution, they are also not completely comfortable with FtM transgender activists on campus. One concern with transmasculinity was that it could become rigid in its own way. Deborah recalled a conversation she had with a friend about the type of trans activism done at Evers, even when it was identified as feminist. She said:

> I was talking to someone yesterday about transfeminism at [Evers] and how in a lot of ways, the trans community at [Evers] is transmasculine and kind of rigid in its own special way and how a lot of that identity and sexuality and gender gets policed in new ways. [My friend] was saying that . . . it's just the same binary as you had before in a lot of ways, and she was lamenting the fact that there really isn't that much space for gender fluidity at [Evers].

For Paulina, it was that privilege that made her uncomfortable. She initially joined a trans activism group because she wanted to be an ally and explore her own feelings about gender. However, she eventually left the group because she was disturbed by some of the dynamics. She recalled one meeting where people were asked to identify where they were on a gender continuum by placing themselves in a line. She recalled:

> So I placed myself somewhere in the middle. Because I was appearance-wise, I'd say I'm pretty feminine, but I feel masculine too, so I put myself in the center. And then members of the organization are, "Okay, now here's the game," and they put you where they think you belong. And people were going all over the place and that's really funny and it seems like a great game, but the people that were placing you were the really masculine-type trans people, and I thought that's just like in the world where these hypermasculine hegemonic males structure [the world].

Although Paulina continues to support trans people, she did note that at Evers, the more masculine a trans person was, the more power they seemed to have. For her, this was just reproducing masculine privilege in a new way. In a similar vein, scholar Kristin Schilt provides a nuanced examination of transgender men and privilege. She finds that transmen who cannot pass as "men" at work experience ostracism, while others who can pass, experience respect as men. She argues that this dynamic illustrates the persistence of gender inequality in society.[17]

The ambivalence expressed about transmasculinity at Evers serves as a testament to the submerged nature of feminism in the community. The concerns with both genderlessness (or gender fluidity) and transgender (as manifested in transmasculinity) come from a feminist understanding of the world situated in ideas of oppression and discrimination. Evers feminists build their identity in a community of acceptance using second-wave-generation feminists as the oppositional foundation of their beliefs about sexuality, sex and gender. Yet Evers feminists return to core feminist ideals of the importance of the category of woman and the owning of masculine privilege—ideas that do not sound dissimilar to those articulated in the second-wave generation.

Green City—Troubled with Drag. When examining how contemporary feminists talk and do gender, sex and sexuality, Green City presents a different sort of environment—a place where there are distinct communities focused on sexual identity. As I have discussed, Green City feminists are linked with the queer community, evidenced by the number of queer-identifying feminists. Issues of queer mix easily with feminism. For example, Green City is the home to a well-known author who writes extensively on "queer" parenting for feminist parents who do not fit a traditional heterosexual model. Green City is also a site where queer and trans issues are beginning to distinguish themselves with more articulation of differences.[18] Overall, Green City is the site where gender, sex and sexuality are constructed differently than in Woodview's Midwest or Evers's East Coast.

Yet, despite this very different environment, Green City feminists struggled with some of the same generational issues with sexuality seen in Evers. The second-wave feminist generation is also seen as antisex and antisexuality here. However, Susan, an older women's studies student, did not place the blame solely on older feminists. She said:

> Feminists in the seventies [were] really fighting to break gender roles and get out of those boxes that they were placed in and having to be sexual objects for men and that kind of thing. And then seeing younger women today wanting to be sexual objects at times and that that is a choice that they make, or not viewing it as placing themselves as sexual objects but expressing their sexuality and being proud of that and wanting to be able to express it in any way that they desire. And that those sexual desires they have [are] political. Expressing those in a different way is a political action. And I sense that older women see it as a step back.... I think they view it as sexual promiscuity when that's not necessarily how the younger generation is feeling about it. And so not really understanding what that difference is.

Susan's discussion of the intergenerational tension around sexuality is a much gentler critique than those made by Evers feminists. Yet implicit is the same idea—that ideas of sexuality are different for each generation. For Green City feminists, it is not only generational but also cultural, identifying differences between regions of the country. According to Marley, understandings of gender fluidity were a part of the progressive culture of the "Left Coast" that she did not see on the East Coast. She said:

I spent three years on the East Coast, and I try to explain the difference between here and there when it comes to gender identity. It's like two totally different languages. . . . I subscribe very much more to the West Coast gender identity or transgender identity. Here you'll see a lot more fluidity in gender expression, a lot less adherence to identifying, not using a pronoun at all or switching pronoun use or just choosing not to identify with a culturally established gender. Period. I happen to really support that, although I gender identify female, I very much can understand because there are things about my life that don't fit that label and so it's such a limiting thing. So I think a lot of the experience here is within the transgender community or the gender variant community—there's a lot of fluidity. It's not like okay, and now "I'm a man."

What Marley identifies as the difference between the coasts is the idea of playing with gender and not necessarily presenting a sexed and gendered appearance. Steve's decision to rename herself is an example of that gender play. She described how she came to identify as a genderqueer and select her new (masculine) name. She said:

I just love the name Steve and I'm actually thinking about changing my name legally to Steven. . . . I would challenge people's [ideas] because my gender is primarily [feminine.] It would challenge people that I have a masculine name and it really has. People have asked me lot of questions about it. . . . I was trying on different, several different names before I figured out I wanted to do Steve. I just also think there is incredible power in naming and renaming yourself.

Steve is an example of what Marley calls "Left Coast" gender expression. Steve is not doing transgender; she is doing genderqueer. She creates an ambiguous gender identity by renaming herself but continues to describe her gender as feminine. The importance of distinguishing between these identities is evident in one of Steve's zines where she created a reproducible form for health care providers in order to increase sensitivity to different sexual and gender identities including (to be checked off) the identities of Queer, Trans, Gay, Lesbian and Bisexual.[19]

As apparent in the story of Steve, the linking of a queer and feminist identity was not problematic. Indeed, for some, the linking of these communities could provoke an exploration of their identities. For example, Susan talked in detail about how being a feminist in women's studies classes brought her to question how she should identify in a community like Green City. She said:

I mean, it was funny just starting in the women's studies department and being[she pauses] very strongly pushed to identify myself as far as sexual orientation goes and justify my marriage and why I'm part of that institution and that kind of thing. . . . So it was pretty—it was actually a pretty intense situation.

Although married to a man, Susan chooses not to identify as heterosexual, a decision she explained:

JO: So you talk about not identifying as a heterosexual—can I ask how you do identify?

SUSAN: [She pauses.] Sexual identification is really tricky for me . . . I am a really strong believer of the fluidity of sexuality, and I think that the words and the context that we use right now to define sexuality goes against what sexuality truly is—it's boxes—it's lines. And also, as someone living a heterosexual life, to then identify myself as queer or whatever doesn't acknowledge the life experience that I have right now and so I try not to identify. I mean, why should I? Unless I have a chance to kind of say all that [she laughs], then it's not going to be true.

JO: So you don't find "queer" open enough to fit into?

SUSAN: I think if I wasn't married I might, but even "queer" if you say "queer" to someone generally, we all kind of think of the same things and I still don't fit into that "same thing," you know what I mean? I've been with a straight man for eleven years. I've never been with anyone else. So what does that mean to the queer movement and to identify as queer? So, it just doesn't fit exactly. I mean, I would say it fits closer than anything else.

Susan struggles with the identification of queer because queer to her is living a life of playing with gender, or gender bending, and having a variety of sexual partners. As a woman married to the same man for eleven years who has only had him as a sexual partner, the idea of queer does not fit, yet she lives in a queer and feminist linked world and consequentially chooses not to identify as any sexuality.

One result of the acceptance of a queer identity was that there was an openness to understanding what it meant to identify as trans. This openness was uneven at times, with schisms emerging in the different activist communities. While queer and feminist communities linked together in Green City, the lesbian community was less integrated. The boundaries between the lesbian and the queer/feminist communities were often the result of generational ideas about identity fluidity. For example, Steve recalled having a conversation about the Michigan Womyn's Music Festival with a middle-aged Green City lesbian. She remembered:

I met a woman at a party, she's probably in her mid forties, this was around Christmas. And she was talking to me about [how] she's part of the Michigan Womyn's Festival.... And she's been a person who's been planning this festival for ten years and been part of it for a really long time. And she was talking to me about her issue with trans female-to-male (FtM) people. She feels like they're taking on masculinity and gaining male privilege. And where I certainly think that is a possibility for some people, to me it sounded like she was implying—and she's like a butch dyke, that's how she identifies—to me, it's like she was implying that it's much easier to be a trans person than a butch dyke in this world, and I disagree because I think that ... it's more acceptable to be a butch lesbian than to change your gender. That's crazy to some people. They don't understand it. They don't even know the first thing about it. They don't get it. And so saying ... framing things in a dualistic manner is not constructive, you miss the whole hierarchy of masculinities.

The woman Steve talked to was again relating the ideas of feminists such as Janice Raymond who saw transgender and transsexualism as a way for women to obtain male privilege without changing women's status in society.[20] The division between the lesbian and the trans community was also noted by Kelly. She recounted how the feminist bookstore became trans friendly as a reaction to a women-born-women-only policy. She said:

The Lesbian Community Project started its mission as being woman-born-only-women's space and inevitably, more than a couple of years ago, the trans community was like, "What?" [She laughs] and they held to their woman-born-women-only space for a number of years and it definitely was divisive in that community. [The bookstore] saw that happen and said, "No way, we won't let that happen here," and immediately created [a] trans inclusive policy and has been trans friendly ever since. We have both trans women and trans men that work here and that (sic) have served on the board.

While some in the lesbian community rejected transgender, another issue was how transgender fit with the feminist community. Lana remarked that she found many in the trans community not supportive of feminist ideas or women in general. She said:

People aren't as worried about [she pauses] certain issues until it affects them, but, I mean, there's also—and this is very un-PC of me—but the trans community, I have friends of mine that are trans and they're just like, "Down with the pussy," and . . . I completely support people who are going through that, but [she pauses] it almost hurts to hear someone say that.

While transgender and drag are not synonymous, performances of cross-dressing highlighted many of the issues that troubled feminists about the trans community. For example, Steve, who often performed as a drag king and adopted a genderqueer identity, was often bothered by some of what she saw portrayed in performances. In her words, "I've seen some drag stuff that was really messed up in my opinion." She elaborated:

I'm a drag king, and a lot of times what ends up happening is this sort of cultural appropriation of masculinity by women who are pretending to be men and they're acting sexist and macho and that really sends a message that that's what you have to be like to represent yourself with a gender identity of a male. And so, it's been really profound, and so I look at all of this and it always comes back to my being a feminist and the way that I view things.

Just as Steve had a feminist view of drag, her journey to become a drag king was prompted by a feminist desire to explore gender privilege. She recalls:

I had dressed in drag a few times for like parties or something. I did it one time for a gender bender I went to. . . . It's just like a variety show. And I really liked it and . . . I liked that people didn't recognize me at all, that I would go up to my friends and be like, "What's going on?" and they're like, "Eh . . . creepy guy." And that I really look like a dude. And then I started taking this gender critical inquiry class and really examining my own gender privilege. And gender privilege a lot of times—it's just sort of this blanket statement that women are oppressed. But if you're born into a gender role—if you're given a gender role—assigned a gender role that you're comfortable with—you have gender privilege. If you look like a woman and feel like a woman and people tell you you're a woman and you have a female biological system, then you are privileged because there are people that don't have that privilege. . . . So just understanding I should challenge my perceptions of my gender identity more and why am I so comfortable with just being a woman.

For Steve then, doing drag was more than performing; it was a chance to explore her feminism and ideas of privilege and oppression, something she saw lacking in some drag performances. As she summed it up, "It's the dressing up and it's theater and it's a personal revolution." Steve's desire to explore the gender dynamics of drag carried over into the community, and along with Kelly, she organized a panel on drag at the feminist bookstore. One aspect of the panel was to examine some of the sexist messages embedded in drag performances. She described the panel discussion:

> We had a discussion of gender and drag and doing drag responsibly [and] we talked about white privilege—being a white person doing a number by a person of color and cultural appropriations and appropriation of masculinity and misogyny. A lot of what I observed were women being— we call it bio-queens because they like dress up in whatever but they're biologically women and they're dressing like women. But a lot of the bio-queens [are] being really sort of objects in the numbers and seeing that that's problematic when we're supposed to be a progressive political sort of thing and drag is really radical and queer and out there and queer, not in the sense of sexuality queer, but queer as in outside of the norm. So there was a need to talk about some of these things. I saw a show where there was a drag king and he was doing Prince and he did "Darling Nikki," which is a really, really sexual song. There's a big [amount] of the sexual content in a lot of drag, which is totally fine because sex is something that translates really well universally as comedy. So, he did the thing where he had a blow-up doll in his number and she had a banana [shoved] in her mouth at the end of the thing and I was really offended. I thought that was really disrespectful. I have no problem with people playing with blow-up dolls, I'm not judging that. But it was the fact that we have this whole audience of people and they are looking at us and we're explaining to them what drag is through our actions and it's not cool to me to translate that drag means taking on this masculine culture and being an asshole.

My observations confirm Steve's statements. In the drag king show I attended, most of the performances had an evident sexual content in which the performance of "woman" was sexually objectified and heterosexuality was reproduced as normative. For example, in a performance to the song "She Blinded Me With Science," a drag king playing a male scientist has his "female" assistant strip to her panties and bra and gives her tips, stripper style, tucked into her clothes.[21] A result of the bookstore's panel on drag was a commitment by the speakers to keep doing educational panels and according to Steve, "Keep working on how really politics are a big part of [drag]."

It is important to note that observations by Steve and myself of drag king performances as misogynistic in content and ideology are confined only to the performances we viewed (or participated in, as in Steve's case) in Green City. Sociologist Eve Shapiro finds that drag has the power to "destabilize hegemonic gender, sex and sexuality" when done in a feminist ideological and organizational context.[22] Similarly, Lelia Rupp and Verta Taylor in their study of drag queens find that these gender transformative performances can be oppositional in nature and "unpack" versus reify gender norms.[23] These variations in drag also indicate the importance of community-level analysis with a focus on feminism.

Overall, in Green City, talking about feminism also meant talking about queer and trans identities. The link between feminist and queer activists made the deconstruction of sex (in the form of transgender), gender (through the adoption of genderqueer and drag king identities) and sexuality (through the identification as queer) relatively common and without much controversy. While Green City feminists did see the adoption of these identities as a progression from second-wave-generation feminism, this was not a major source of debate or tension in the community. Instead, the progressive environment of Green City where feminism was accepted led to a critique of trans masculinity and drag king performances. The existence of these critiques illustrates a critical, ongoing feminist discourse and not a wholesale acceptance of gender deconstruction and identity fluidity.

It is clear that while Woodview struggles to talk about gender, sex and sexual fluidity in identity, Evers and Green City are more comfortable with these ideas and have incorporated them into their identities. Compared to the discourse on race-ethnicity and class, it appears that contemporary feminists are not only talking more about the deconstruction of sexed and gendered identities but they are creating communities where theory (through discourse) and practice (through action) merge. The community differences illustrate how contemporary feminists can explore a variety of ideas and identities when the community is not under attack for being openly feminist. In Woodview, the focus remains on articulating feminism in a way that is palatable to the larger community around it. Adopting oppositional gender, sex and sexual identities does not fit with Woodview feminists' need to be seen as not so different from the rest of the community. Woodview feminists largely struggle with the dilemma of creating tight networks among straight and lesbian feminists without developing cliques and focus on education versus deconstruction and identity fluidity. In Evers, feminists continue to define themselves strongly against the second-wave generation and their perceptions of it as antisex and not truly progressive. Green City feminists do not fight so much against the second-wave generation, but instead the linking of queer and feminist communities creates an environment of acceptance where, as Susan's comments attest, being feminist comes with the assumption of being queer.

"Woman" in Feminism

In all the communities, though, the discourse of deconstruction and identity fluidity is dynamic. The feminists of Evers and Green City launch strong critiques against the sexism and misogyny they see evident in the trans and queer communities, while Woodview struggles to find the vocabulary that will allow these conversations to commence. One central aspect of these conversations is the importance of the category of woman to feminism. Evers feminists, in particular, are troubled by the idea of removing "woman" completely from feminism and the implications for policy applications. Also evident in these conversations are the voices of heterosexual feminists who struggle to fit into the community discourse of sexuality, and in the case of Woodview, a largely lesbian network.

A common thread in their talk is how without feminism as a part of redefining sex, gender and sexual identities, patriarchal ideas of sexism and sexual oppression can flourish. Returning to the notion of contemporary feminism being so everywhere it is no longer relevant, the continued critique of feminists of trans and drag is a testament that this is not so. Even with the diffusion of feminism into our culture, the feminists of Woodview, Evers and Green City retain their core beliefs, sustained by the environment around them. The complexity of gender, sex and sexual fluidity in these three communities illustrates how feminists are still negotiating the boundaries of a feminist identity. While contemporary feminism advocates choice in how one chooses to name oneself, it does not do it at the peril of feminist beliefs, as many critics claim. Those beliefs are intact, negating the view that contemporary feminists have entered into an "anything goes" free-for-all of sex, gender and sexuality. Questions such as does the women's movement need the category of woman in order to organize for equality are important ones in considering the future of feminism. In a world of gender fluidity in which sex is not the point of departure for understanding social circumstances and lives, does feminism become irrelevant or does it transform the movement and its ideologies? The continued feminism of Woodview, Evers and Green City point to the latter—that feminism does continue. It is this idea of continuity in a new social world where conceptions of feminism change and yet remain the same that I address in the conclusion.

Conclusion

SITTING WITH MY family on the deck of a rented vacation home in the midst of rural Ohio, my sister-in-law turned to me and asked, "What is your book about?" She followed that question by asking, "So, what *is* going on with feminism today?" In that moment she asked two of the questions I have wrestled with over the last several years while writing this book. Sitting in the sunshine, I began to talk. I told her that feminism is not dead and that communities shape how contemporary feminism is done. After several minutes of my explanations, she then asked, "So, what *are* feminists doing today?" It was here that I stumbled. I know what contemporary feminists are doing. I have spent years talking and being with them, but I wanted to list tangible accomplishments—demonstrations, policy changes and legislative outcomes—so she understood the importance of my research and the continued relevance of feminism. I wanted to show her (using the framework of conventional social movement theory and the language of outcomes) that contemporary feminism was making her life better. But we were having this conversation situated in a place where Rush Limbaugh and Glenn Beck inform most political opinions, a place where the Confederate flag continues to be displayed on bumper stickers and ball caps. While I believe that contemporary feminism continues to make a difference, at that moment, the feminist communities of Woodview, Evers and Green City seemed a world away. Looking back on this conversation, I can see that here is another example of how feminism is nowhere (i.e., not an identifiable voice in the political discourse of this place), and yet, as I sat on the porch with my family, I could also see how all of us have been touched by the everywhere of feminism. We expect our daughters and sons to have equal opportunities in the world around us. My sisters and I have made a variety of life choices made possible by the efforts of feminists. We have attended college in a variety of disciplines and fields. My sisters have entered and exited the workplace based on the needs of their families, and not the dictates of societal gender norms or corporate policy. We all carry credit cards in our own names and can apply for bank loans as individuals. We are married, divorced, partnered. We are two-parent, single-parent and stepparent families. Just the simple diversity of our family lives is evidence of the importance of feminism; as women, we have never had to stay dependent on men for our survival; there have always been options. These are all evidence of the success of second-wave-generation feminists who succeeded in changing the world from that of my grandmother and my mother to the world of my sisters. So, thinking about my family sitting on this deck, I am struck again by the paradox of the nowhere and the everywhere of feminism.

In retrospect, I also realize that I stumbled on my sister-in-law's question on what are feminists doing because I too often align movement efficacy with visible institutional challenges (or at least draw on them to prove the continued existence of the movement). What I have sought to make clear in this book by integrating a history of the movement and unpacking generational similarities is that feminists have always worked in both the institutional and cultural arenas. The more cultural focus of contemporary feminism is not a retreat from the political (and politics) but is instead a strategy shaped the experience of coming to feminism in a political generation where institutional gains faced often immediate and continued backlash, and cultural challenges gain both positive and negative attention from the larger society and other generations of feminists. It is this focus on culture that often makes contemporary feminism appear everywhere and nowhere.

I am not the first writer or scholar to puzzle over these ideas of culture and politics, and movement decline versus movement diffusion. This paradox is represented in one of my favorite articles on contemporary feminism from the satirical "newspaper" *The Onion*. In an article entitled "Women Now Empowered by Everything a Woman Does," the writer quotes a fictional source as claiming, "From what she eats for breakfast to the way she cleans her home, today's woman lives in a state of near-constant empowerment." The source continues, "Shopping for shoes has emerged as a powerful means by which women assert their autonomy."[1] Here, I see the primary idea of the paradox of contemporary feminism. It is so everywhere in our culture that it appears to be apolitical and meaningless. While I appreciate the satirical wit of *The Onion*, I would argue that contemporary feminism is the result of the diffusion of past feminist ideology and efforts, creating a different kind of feminism in a very different time. Other writers, both popular and scholarly, have addressed this sense that contemporary feminism exists in a different social context. Ariel Levy calls this the generation of "girls gone wild," her way of identifying a social context filled with what Susan Douglas calls "enlightened sexism" and Angela McRobbie terms "faux feminism."[2] All share in the idea that feminism has seeped into the popular culture to such an extent that women (and men) are often told that girls (and women) can be anything and the "can do" messages are repackaged in the form of commodities for us to purchase and consequently experience empowerment. Yet also in these writings and others is the idea that feminism is everywhere, meaning that it continues to exist and to make social and political change. Pamela Aronson labels it "living feminism"; Susan Douglas calls it "embedded feminism"; and Jessica Valenti sees it as "full frontal feminism."[3] No matter the terms, the ideas are the same—there is a new feminist political generation operating in an environment that draws on the past but takes a different form from the feminism of forty years ago. However, these writings largely present this political generation in broad strokes; missing in these analyses is the nuanced picture that emerges from an examination of social movement communities.

In this book, it is the feminist communities of Woodview, Evers and Green City that allow me to investigate more deeply the status of feminism in this paradoxical world. It is in these communities that feminist identities are constructed, forged from a political generation that lives in a very different world from the ones of their forefeminists, and set in a particular social and political context. It is this community context that shapes many aspects of the contemporary feminism they do. How feminists interpret and incorporate the past and the second-wave feminist generation often depends on their environment. It shapes how they create tactics for social change; it forges an ongoing struggle in their discourse of antiracism and inclusivity, and shapes the fluidity of their identities as gendered and sexed people. And—unless you look—these communities are largely invisible. However, just because we cannot always see them does not mean they aren't there. It was as a result of my "looking" that I stood in the freezing rain with the feminists of Woodview as they "aired" the dirty laundry of sexual abuse with the Clothesline Project and marveled at their courage in a place that obviously did not welcome them. It was because I "looked" that I saw the complexity of ways in which the Evers feminists were struggling to deal with issues of race and transgender as I sat and listened to speakers inform first-year students about the hate crime incidents the year before. In that room, I heard anger, confusion, sadness and shame, and marveled at their courage to explore such tough topics emotionally, intellectually and politically. It was because I "looked" that I saw the celebration along with the misogyny of a drag king show in Green City. I laughed and danced along with the rest of the audience but also could sense the women around me reacting when the performers went too far in reenacting tired old sexual scenarios, and I marveled at how they kept true to their feminist ideologies in a shifting (sometimes confusing) world of gender, sex and sexuality.

Each of the communities studied presents a different kind of feminism— from the focused feminism of Woodview, to the submerged feminism of Evers, and the linked queer feminism of Green City. While I present these as case studies set in particular regional contexts, I argue that these communities have the ability to reveal larger patterns shaping the overall movement, patterns that have relevance to all social movement scholars. A central part of my argument has been that social movement scholarship needs a more expansive way of viewing the role of community interactions in movement continuity. I have argued that long-lasting movements are shaped by political generations, which in turn are reflections not only of the broader political and social dynamics but also are influenced by the way in which individual social factors (such as gender, sex, race, age and so forth) are constructed in this time. If we conceive of a political generation as the context of social movement, then the interactions at various societal levels from the micro to the meso to the macro within a generation will shape the way in which activism is done and perceived.

Traditionally, levels of social movement interaction have been conceptualized in a sort of hierarchy, with a focus on the international or national level for broad conclusions or the interpersonal level for understanding individual identity or ideology construction. I argue that instead of a hierarchy, we need to see an overlapping of national, local and grassroots/individual/network levels.

At the intersection of these three is the social movement community. It is this intersection that forms the place of movements, something Katja Guenther identifies as the location where everyday life, geographic location and a sense of identity and belonging emerge.[4] Central to this intersection are the concepts of political and cultural opportunity structures. In places hostile to feminism, feminism looks significantly different than in places where feminism is accepted.

These overlapping levels of analysis are set in the context of a particular political generation, and as social and political conditions shift, more than one movement generation can exist at the same time. The relation between these generations

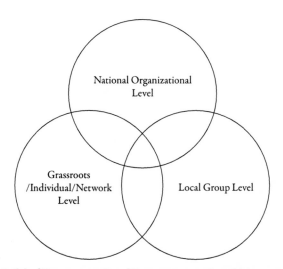

FIGURE 7.1 Model of Community Level Interactions in Social Movements.

depends on the amount of acceptance in changes in activism and ideology, creating identity boundaries. That is, who is "us" and who is "they." Communities struggling to articulate feminism welcome all potential allies, including those from the second-wave feminist generation. In communities expected to embrace feminism, those relations are more problematic, with second-wave-generation feminists often rejected as a "straw man" device, a misrepresentation of much of 1960s and 1970s feminism. Woodview feminists honor the second-wave generation but lack a complete understanding of that generation's accomplishments. Evers feminists build their identity against the second-wave generation, creating a foundation that relies upon their perceptions of their mothers' (and others') feminism. In Green City, contemporary feminists distance themselves from the past but still build upon it in a much gentler critique. In sum, contemporary feminists, depending on the community context, honor, build upon and reject the past.

Just as generational identities and collective identities shift in their constructions, so do social movement communities. The activist centers vary from community to community and change as political generations and the social context change. Yet the communities are all doing a form of feminist activism, ranging from the educational efforts of Woodview, the emotional and political exploration of identities in Evers or the redefining of feminism with queer feminists of Green City. It is clear that contemporary feminists, despite their differences, continue to try to change the world around them. To borrow a phrase from Chris Bobel, "it is time to call off the autopsy"; these communities show that contemporary feminism continues to be a force for social change.[5]

Understanding movement continuity then needs a meso-level examination to reveal its complexity. This means that movements are made up of shifting activist centers, constantly reconfigured collective identities, and are subject to the emergence of new political generations. This does not mean that social movements build on unstable foundations, making case studies of communities a hazardous place to look for patterns in the overall movement. Instead, as Dorothy Smith argues, case studies based on an understanding of societal power dynamics (or "relations of ruling") have the ability to reveal broader patterns at play. In other words, Woodview, Evers and Green City are not representative of all feminist communities; however, they do reveal the common factors influencing all feminist communities.

While these communities present patterns of similarities, they also present the question of difference. A common way of looking at social movements is that they must be unified, meaning all participants working for the same goals under the same ideologies and strategies, as a determinant for obtaining their goals. The differences between the communities offer an example of the complexity, multiplicity and contradiction of contemporary feminism. In Woodview, the feminists repeatedly see their goal as offering a feminist-friendly space for free thinking and a place to fight expectations. As a result, they create a group where education is a focus and social networks are primary. In Evers, the key word is "choice." Their goals are to create a world where there is no shame for whoever they choose to be, a world where they are visible and analyzing the power dynamics around them. Green City feminists work to end gendered and sexed expectations, creating a new feminist identify that links to other social issues. These approaches range from focusing on the external world to an introspection of self. They are political and personal at the same time. And none of these communities are doing the contemporary feminism often lambasted in the public sphere, yet all are doing the contemporary feminism that makes sense in their communities. As feminist scholar Cathryn Bailey argues, "Another important lesson to be learned may be just this; that complexity, multiplicity, and contradiction can enrich our identities as individual feminists and the movement as a whole."[6] Taking the case of contemporary feminism as evidence, I would argue that most social movements are built on complexity, multiplicity and contradiction, and it is only through simplistic representation and/or times of extreme crisis or opportunity that movements look like they are made up of unified members all working for the same goals with the same beliefs.

Staying with the theme of difference, much of this book has illustrated the gap between the widespread perception and representation of contemporary feminism and the reality found in the communities. While much of my broader analysis has come from writings in the popular press and on the Internet in the form of listservs and blogs, there is another level to contemporary feminism that is not necessarily represented in the popular press or embedded at the local level—that of the feminism happening in national organizations. While NOW is not synonymous with all national feminist organizations, it is one of the most visible. In July 2010, I attended the national NOW conference in Boston to see how this organization was dealing with the generational strife so often noted in the media. In order to see what was going on, I attended workshops such as Young Feminist Leaders—Effectively Engaging and Organizing Young Adults and plenaries such as State of the Women's Movement: Feminism Today and Tomorrow and Lift Every Voice: Women of Color and Empowerment. At the conference of approximately 350 people (noted by the organizers), in all the sessions the rooms were filled predominantly with older white women. However, approximately 20 to 25 percent were young women and many of those were interns highly engaged in the business of NOW. In the workshop on young feminist leaders, four young white women and one young woman of color spoke passionately about feminist organizing on their college campuses, sharing techniques and ideas with the seventy- plus members in the audience (predominantly older white women). Well steeped in the discourse of generational tension, I expected to hear at some point the older women's disappointment with the activism or level of engagement by the young feminists. Instead, the women in the audience asked questions on specific techniques, thoroughly engaged in the discussion. The only sense of generational separation came when one of the young organizers announced that she had been tweeting throughout the workshop as a tactic to bring the organization more visibility. After her announcement, I heard the two older white women behind me note that using this as a tactic had never occurred to them. Throughout the conference, there was no focus on feminist generations or generational issues. In fact, seldom were generations specifically addressed. Kim Bottomly, president of Wellesley College and a conference speaker, was the only one to specifically address the needs of young women, and her argument ran counter to much of the popular media. She argued that young feminists are aware of the past, concerned with the future and will fight to preserve the rights so hard won by older generations. The discussion of women of color and empowerment followed the same route with the focus on the issues, none of which included the need to address issues of racism and inclusivity within the women's movement and the current generations of feminists. My observation that feminist generational division was not a focus of this NOW conference was confirmed when, following the event, one young woman wrote on NOW's Blog for Equality:

> As I am all too aware, young women are particularly likely to be written off for perceived vapidity or naïveté. However, I found with every workshop, plenary and issue hearing that I attended that young people—young women—were being heard. In fact, they were taking on leadership roles within the conference and within their activist circles . . . And when I spoke, I felt respected.

She concluded:

> At the NOW conference, older feminists let young feminists voice our experiences rather than have our experiences dictated to us. After years of feeling silenced, I find that sort of openness precious. Thank you, NOW, for making me feel like a part of the movement rather than a hanger-on. Thank you for valuing not only the past and the present, but also the future.[7]

NOW's 2010 national conference confirms many of the ideas that emerge from this study of feminist communities. First, it questions whether intergenerational tension is overstated. As Chris Bobel points out in her examination of menstrual activists, there is tension but often that tension gets exaggerated in the media.[8] The mother-daughter divide in feminism is a good story and in some places it is the reality of feminism, for example, at Evers. But it is not the primary narrative of feminism in other communities and, as the NOW conference illustrates, at the national level. In the case of the 2010 NOW conference, I also would argue that the mood of generational unity and cooperation was the result of the very divisive conference held the year before. At the 2009 conference, the long-standing president was stepping down and the two contenders were pitted against each other in terms of generation: the young black woman who wanted to bring another (younger) generation into NOW and the older white woman who represented NOW's status quo.[9] When Terry O'Neill (the older white woman) was elected, the intergenerational debates and criticisms raged on, with both sides feeling disrespected and misunderstood.[10] I speculate that NOW, sensitive to membership numbers and internal debates, made a particular effort to incorporate young women into the organization, hence the number of interns. By putting these young women into positions of authority in the organization and the conference, they level the playing field and allow young women to emerge as skilled organizers with something to teach older feminists. This does not mean that generational dissension is gone; instead, like most aspects of contemporary feminism, these tensions often depend on context. It also illustrates how intergenerational tension is not a given in all interactions between generations; NOW is apparently working to decrease some of this tension and, according to the young women present in 2010, this effort is succeeding.

A second issue that the 2010 NOW conference raises is the focus of the young women on local, campus organizing. I hypothesize that one reason for the respect these young organizers received in the workshop was the fact that they were doing a form of organizing on their campuses that is not always the case in all NOW chapters. Indeed, the organizers at the Young Feminist Leaders panel focused on their local communities, mainly their campuses. The campaigns led by many of these young women would sound familiar to the feminists in this study. They worked to educate their campuses through the Clothesline Project, the *Vagina Monologues*, antirape and sexual assault organizations, women-centered film festivals, and protesting at crisis pregnancy centers. All of these locally focused actions are aimed at changing the policies and the culture of the communities around them. Like the feminists in this study, the young NOW leaders engaged in feminist action using tried and true techniques (e.g., encouraging goal setting, establishing timelines for actions, and doing chalking, tabling and flyers) as well as drawing on new technologies such as tweeting to inform others of their protests. They worked within the institutions by creating "power maps" of the administration for effective communication as well as urging activists to approach the media "to make feminism sexy and wonderful." They focused collectively on building community networks and groups but also engaged in national-level organizations such as NOW, the Feminist Majority and the Third Wave Foundation. In sum, the young leaders on this panel look a lot like the feminists in the communities studied. They draw on many of the same tactics, working to educate their communities and build networks, wanting to re-envision a "sexier" feminism while at the same time drawing and elaborating on the efforts of past feminists. I would argue that each of the women on the panel would agree that the feminism done in their communities was shaped by the environment, even when they worked with a national-level organization. Their efforts confirm the importance of community-level examinations of feminism to understand both its direction and its continuity.

As I focus on these young leaders, I return to a reoccurring thought of mine while writing this book. How do women who identify as second-wave feminists respond to some of the criticisms made of them? Particularly in the community of Evers, those criticisms seem harsh and embedded in a lack of understanding of the complexity of the work of older feminists. As unfair as some of these comments may seem, I argue that they are in fact an indicator of the movement's success. Journalist Rebecca Traister, in an article entitled "Are Younger Women Trying to Trash Feminism?" writes, "This is what victory looks like. Victory looks like young women who don't understand the coat hanger symbol."[11] In multigenerational movements, the criticisms of the next generation can be viewed as accomplishments; the second-wave feminist generation has shaped the society and the discourse, giving young women something to build upon and to reject. Their lack of understanding (for example, what a coat hanger symbolizes) speaks to the accomplishments of the second-wave generation and a change in the overall culture and structure of society. This indicates the vitality and continuity of feminism and should not be viewed as defeat or a change in the wrong direction. This is not to argue that an ahistorical approach to U.S. feminism is beneficial; however, as a number of feminist historians have argued, the history of the U.S. women's movement, as popularly understood, is problematic and contributes to contemporary feminists' lack of historical dimension and understanding. A common theme in this book has been that the wave metaphor exacerbates the generational divide that has been identified as one of the major characteristics of contemporary feminism and overstates the movement's decline. When we conceptualize feminism, or any social movement activism, as occurring in waves, we create a rise and decline that does not necessarily capture the community-level mobilization of a movement. I have worked to carefully identify the work of contemporary feminists as the result of a political generation situated in the accomplishments of older feminists. By identifying them as a contemporary feminist generation as well as a second-wave generation, I open up our conceptions to allow both political generations to overlap, influencing each other. Neither generation signals an end or beginning of feminism, but instead indicates a change in the social context in which these feminisms are articulated. By moving away from the wave metaphor and embracing the idea of overlapping, coexisting generations, the relations between activist generations are made more complex and their intertwining is revealed. Leandra Zarnow makes a similar argument that when we step away from the wave metaphor, feminist history is more complex and rich than when we rely on it.[12]

Taking into consideration the contemporary feminism illustrated in these communities, what then is the future of feminism in the United States? This book presents a snapshot in time in the communities studied. By doing so, I reveal that contemporary feminists are continuing the work of the first- and second-wave feminist generations but they are doing it in a different space and time. As they work to change the world around them through a variety of tactics, by embracing the identity of feminist and by gauging the work to be done in their communities, they are creating, just like the generations before them, a different social and political world. Until gender equality is reached in all its dimensions, feminism will continue to be a force everywhere in society, shaped by community context and changing the world in inherited generational spaces. That is its legacy.

Interviewee Demographics

Table A.1: Average Age and Student Status by Community

	Woodview	Evers	Green City
Average Age	21	20	26.5
Student Status	100%	100%	20%

Table A.2: Race-Ethnicity by Community

Race-Ethnicity	Woodview	Evers	Green City
Caucasian/White	12 (92%)	11 (65%)	9 (90%)
Black	0	0	0
Biracial	0	3[1]	0
Chicana/Latina	0	2	0
N/A	1	1	1
Total	13	17	10

[1]The specifically named biracial combinations were "Biracial: Asian (Chinese)/White," "Black Hispanic" and "Black Latina".

Table A.3: Gender/Sex Breakdown by Community

Gender/Sex	Woodview	Evers	Green City
Woman	12 (92%)	14 (82%)	9 (90%)
Man	1	0	0
Gender Queer	0	1	1
Trans	0	1	0
Undecided	0	1	0
Total	13	17	10

Table A.4: Sexuality Breakdown by Community

Sexuality	Woodview	Evers	Green City
Heterosexual	3	3	1
Lesbian	6 (46%)	2	1
Bisexual	1	1	0
Queer	1	7 (41%)	5 (50%)
Combination	1	3	1
Other/NA	1	1	2
Total	13	17	10

Table A.5: Social Class Breakdown by Community

Social Class	Woodview	Evers	Green City
Poor	1	1	0
Working Poor	0	0	0
Working Class	2	2	0
Lower Middle Class	5 (38%)	2	5 (50%)
Upper Middle Class	4 (31%)	9 (52%)	2
Upper Class	0	0	0
Combinations	0	2	2
NA	1	1	1
Total	13	17	10

Case Study Comparisons

Table B.1: Snapshots of Area Factors

Community	Population	Average Income	Percentage White	Percentage –Nonwhite (with largest minority)	Housing Costs	Majority Political Party Affiliation
Woodview	1.2 million (county)	$100,000	88%	12% (7% Asian)	$260,000	67% Republican
Evers	29,000 (town)	$42,000	88%	12% (5% Hispanic)	$225,000	49% Democrats
Green City	1.3 million (metro area)	$64,000	78%	22% (7% Hispanic, 7% Black, 6 % Asian)	$225,000	76% Democrats

Notes

INTRODUCTION

1. Leila J. Rupp and Verta Taylor, *Survival in the Doldrums: The American Women's Rights Movement, 1945 to 1960s* (New York: Oxford University Press, 1987).
2. Ginia Bellafante, "Is Feminism Dead?" *Time* 151 (1998): 25, http://www.time.com/time/magazine/article/0,9171,988616-2,00.html/.
3. Riot Grrrl is a feminist punk music scene that developed in the early 1990s in the Northwest. It got national attention as a form of social movement activism by the mainstream press. Riot Grrrl organizing continues in the twenty-first century with online sites such as http://riotgrrrlonline.ning.com/. Marisa Meltzer, "Quiet Riot," *Bust Magazine* (June/July 2010):71. For a history, see Sara Marcus, *Girls to the Front: The True Story of the Riot Grrrl Revolution* (New York: HarperCollins, 2010).
4. For example, Ariel Levy's *Female Chauvinist Pigs: Women and the Rise of Raunch Culture* (New York: Free Press, 2005).
5. Michael Winerip, "Where to Pass the Torch," *New York Times*, March 8, 2009, http://nytimes.com/2009/03/08/fashion/08generationb.html/. Courtney Martin, "The End of the Women's Movement," *The American Prospect*, March 30, 2009, http://prospect.org/cs/articles/.
6. Mary Hawkesworth, "The Semiotics of Premature Burial: Feminism in a Post-feminist Age," *Signs* 29 (2004):961–986.
7. Myra Marx Ferree, "Soft Repression: Ridicule, Stigma, and Silencing in Gender-Based Movements," in *Authority in Contention, Research in Social Movements, Conflicts and Change,* Daniel J. Myers and Daniel M. Cress, eds., 25 (2004): 85–101.
8. As cited in Stephanie Gilmore, "Bridging the Waves: Sex and Sexuality in a Second Wave Organization," in *Different Wavelengths: Studies of the Contemporary Women's Movement,* Jo Reger, ed. (New York: Routledge, 2005), 97.

9. Phyllis Chesler, "The Failure of Feminism," February 24, 2006. http://www.phyllis-chesler.com/163/the-failure-of-feminism/.

10. Michael Messner, *Taking the Field: Women, Men and Sports* (Minneapolis: University of Minnesota Press, 2002).

11. An example of this can be seen in the environmental movement. Careful consumption, home gardens and recycling (being "green") are now adopted by many as everyday actions, not seen as political outcomes of the movement.

12. Jennifer Baumgardner and Amy Richards, *Manifesta: Young Women, Feminism and the Future* (New York: Farrar, Straus and Giroux, 2000), 17.

13. Ednie Kaeh Garrison, "Are We on a Wavelength Yet? On Feminist Oceanography, Radios and Third Wave Feminism," in *Different Wavelengths: Studies of the Contemporary Women's Movement*, Jo Reger, ed. (New York: Routledge, 2005), 237–256.

14. J. Craig Jenkins, "Resource Mobilization Theory and the Study of Social Movements," *Annual Review of Sociology* 9 (1983):527–553; John McCarthy and Mayer Zald, "Resource Mobilization and Social Movements: A Partial Theory," *American Journal of Sociology* 82 (1977):1212–1241; Sidney Tarrow, *Struggle, Politics and Reform: Collective Action, Social Movements and Cycles of Protest* (Ithaca, NY: Cornell University Press, 1989).

15. Kimberly Dugan. *The Struggle Over Gay, Lesbian, and Bisexual Rights: Facing Off in Cincinnati* (New York: Routledge, 2005); Stephen Engel, *The Unfinished Revolution: Social Movement Theory and the Gay and Lesbian Movement* (Cambridge: Cambridge University Press, 2001).

16. Kimberly Dugan, "Just Like You: The Dimensions of Identity Presentations in an Antigay Contested Context," in *Identity Work in Social Movements*, Jo Reger, Dan Myers, and Rachel Einwohner, eds. (Minneapolis: University of Minnesota Press, 2008), 21–46.

17. Holly J. McCammon, Courtney Sanders Muse, Harmony D. Newman, and Teresa M. Terrell, "Movement Framing and Discursive Opportunity Structures: The Political Successes of the U.S. Women's Jury Movements," *American Sociological Review* 72, 5 (2007): 725–749.

18. Jo Reger, "Drawing Identity Boundaries: The Creation of Contemporary Feminism," in *Identity Work in Social Movements*, Jo Reger, Dan Myers, and Rachel Einwohner, eds. (Minneapolis: University of Minnesota Press, 2008), 101–120.

19. Raka Ray, *Fields of Protest: Women's Movements in India* (Minnesota: University of Minnesota Press, 1999); Steven Buechler, *Women's Movements in the United States* (New Brunswick, NJ: Rutgers University Press, 1990); Leila J. Rupp and Verta Taylor, "Forging Feminist Identity in an International Movement: A Collective Identity Approach to Twentieth Century Feminism," *Signs* 24, 2 (1999):363–386; Suzanne Staggenborg, "Social Movement Communities and Cycles of Protest: The Emergence and Maintenance of a Local Women's Movement," *Social Problems* 45, 2 (1998): 180–204.

20. Ray, *Fields of Protest,* 6.

21. Suzanne Staggenborg and Verta Taylor, "Whatever Happened to the Women's Movement?" *Mobilization: The International Journal of Research and Theory about Social Movements, Protest and Collective Behavior* 10, 1 (2005): 41.

22. See, for example, some of the best known: Rory Dicker and Alison Piepmeier eds., *Catching a Wave: Reclaiming Feminism for the 21st Century* (Boston, MA: Northeastern University Press, 2003); Sara M. Evans, *Tidal Wave: How Women Changed America at Century's End* (New York: Free Press, 2003); and Leslie Heywood and Jennifer Drake, eds., *Third Wave Agenda: Being Feminist, Doing Feminism* (Minneapolis: University of Minnesota Press, 1997). See also Kathryn Ziegler's in-depth discussion of the use of the metaphor in "'Formidable-Femininity': Performing Gender and Third Wave Feminism in a Women's Self Defense Class" (doctoral dissertation, Southern Illinois University—Carbondale, 2008).

23. Another issue of terminology is the use of "feminism" and "women's movement" as interchangeable. While there are persuasive arguments for why these terms are not interchangeable in a global sense, in the U.S. women's movement activists readily identify as feminists and in this study I rely on the meaning and the terms used by interviewees. See Myra Marx Ferree and Carol McClurg Mueller, "Feminism and the Women's Movement: A Global Perspective," in *The Blackwell Companion to Social Movements,* David Snow, Sarah A. Soule, and Hanspeter Kriesi, eds. (Oxford: Blackwell, 2004), 576–607.

24. For example see Ruud Koopmans, "Protest in Time and Space: The Evolution of Waves of Contention," in *The Blackwell Companion to Social Movements,* David Snow, Sarah A. Soule, and Hanspeter Kriesi, eds. (Oxford: Blackwell, 2004), 19–46, for his use of protest waves.

25. Kathleen A. Laughlin, Julie Gallagher, Dorothy Sue Cobble, Eileen Boris, Premilla Nadasen, Stephanie Gilmore, and Leandra Zarnow, "Is It Time to Jump Ship? Historians Rethink the Waves Metaphor," *Feminist Formations* 22, 1 (Spring 2010): 76–135.

26. Laughlin et al., "Is It Time to Jump Ship?" 78.

27. Garrison, "Are We on a Wavelength Yet?" ; Nancy Naples, "Confronting the Future, Learning from the Past: Feminist Praxis in the Twenty-First Century" in *Different Wavelengths: Studies of the Contemporary Women's Movement,* Jo Reger, ed. (New York: Routledge, 2005), 215–236; Benita Roth, *Separate Roads to Feminism: Black Chicana and White Feminist Movements in America's Second Wave* (New York: Cambridge, 2002); Kimberly Springer, "Strongblackwomen and Black Feminism: A Next Generation?" in *Different Wavelengths: Studies of the Contemporary Women's Movement,* Jo Reger, ed. (New York: Routledge, 2005), 3–21; Becky Thompson, "Multiracial Feminism: Recasting the Chronology of Second Wave Feminism," *Feminist Studies* 28 (2002): 337–663; see also Laughlin et al., "Is It Time to Jump Ship?"

28. Naples, "Confronting the Future"; Jo Reger, "Introduction" in *Different Wavelengths: Studies of the Contemporary Women's Movement,* Jo Reger, ed. (New York: Routledge, 2005), xv–xxx.

29. Suzanne Beechey, "When Feminism Is Your Job: Age and Power in Women's Policy Organizations," in *Different Wavelengths: Studies of the Contemporary Women's Movement,* Jo Reger, ed. (New York: Routledge, 2005), 117–136.

30. For example, Elizabeth Armstrong and Mary Bernstein, "Culture, Power and Institutions: A Multi-Institutional Politics Approach to Social Movements," *Sociological Theory* 26 (2008): 74–99; Suzanne Staggenborg, "Beyond Culture versus Politics: A Case Study of a Local Women's Movement," *Gender & Society* 15 (2001): 507–530; Verta Taylor, Nella Van Dyke, and Ellen Ann Andersen, "Culture and Mobilization: Tactical Repertoires, Same-Sex Weddings and the Impact on Gay Activism," *American Sociological Review* 74 (December 2009): 865–890; Nella Van Dyke, Sarah A. Soule, and Verta A. Taylor, "The Targets of Social Movements: Beyond a Focus on the State," in *Authority in Contention, Research in Social Movements, Conflicts and Change,* Daniel J. Myers and Daniel M. Cress, eds., 25 (2004): 25–51.

31. Even though most of the sample for these case studies were predominantly younger as I discuss later.

32. Susan Douglas refers to this feminist generation as the "millennials." Susan J. Douglas, *Enlightened Sexism: The Seductive Message That Feminism's Work Is Done* (New York: Times Books, 2010), 6.

33. Nancy Naples, "Confronting the Future" ; Jo Reger, "Introduction."

34. Chris Bobel finds a similar correlation with age in her study of menstrual activists. See Chris Bobel, *New Blood: Third-Wave and the Politics of Menstruation* (New Brunswick, NJ: Rutgers University Press, 2010), 3.

35. This also illustrates how community context shapes activist generations with college-based communities drawing slightly younger participants than communities not centered on a college or university.

36. Lelia Rupp and Verta Taylor, "Foreword," in *Different Wavelengths: Studies of the Contemporary Women's Movement,* Jo Reger, ed. (New York: Routledge, 2005), xi.

37. Nancy Hewitt, ed., *No Permanent Waves: Recasting Histories of U.S. Feminism* (New Brunswick, NJ: Rutgers University Press, 2010).

38. Jenkins, "Resource Mobilization Theory."

39. For the approaches critiqued by Staggenborg and Taylor ("Whatever Happened?"), see the contentious politics approach in Charles Tilly, *Social Movements, 1768–2004* (Boulder, CO: Paradigm Publishers, 2004); "collective action aggregates," in Gerald Marwell and Pamela Oliver, "Collective Action Theory and Social Movement Research," *Research in Social Movements, Conflicts and Change* 7 (1984): 1–27; "ideologically structured action," in Mayer Zald, "Ideologically Structured Action: An Enlarged Agenda for Social Movement Research," *Mobilization: An International Journal* 5, 1 (2000):1–16; "collective challenges,"

in David Snow, "Social Movements as Challenges to Authority: Resistance to an Emerging Conceptual Hegemony," *Research in Social Movements, Conflict and Change* 25 (2004): 3–25.

40. Janet Zollinger Giele, *Two Paths to Women's Equality: Temperance, Suffrage and the Origins of Modern Feminism* (New York: Twayne Publishers, 1995), 2.

41. Buechler, *Women's Movements in the United States*; Ellen Carol DuBois, *Feminism and Suffrage: The Emergence of an Independent Women's Movement in America 1848–1869* (Ithaca, NY: Cornell University Press, 1978); Giele, *Two Paths to Women's Equality*.

42. Buechler, *Women's Movements in the United States*; DuBois, *Feminism and Suffrage*.

43. Giele, *Two Paths to Women's Equality*.

44. Rupp and Taylor, *Survival in the Doldrums*.

45. Myra Marx Ferree and Beth B. Hess, *Controversy and Coalition: The New Feminist Movement Across Three Decades of Change* (New York: Twayne, 1994); Sara Evans, *Personal Politics: The Roots of Women's Liberation in the Civil Rights Movement & the New Left* (New York: Vintage Books, 1980).

46. Evans, *Personal Politics*.

47. Jo Freeman, *The Politics of Women's Liberation* (New York: Longman, 1975).

48. Verta Taylor and Nancy Whittier, "The New Feminist Movement," in *Feminist Frontiers IV*, Laurel Richardson, Verta Taylor and Nancy Whittier, eds. (New York: McGraw-Hill, 1997), 544–561.

49. Jane J. Mansbridge, *Why We Lost the ERA* (Chicago: University of Chicago Press, 1986).

50. See Mansbridge, *Why We Lost the ERA*. Becky Thompson argues differently with organizations by women of color experiencing a "heyday" when organizations of white women went into decline. Thompson, "Multiracial Feminism."

51. Susan Faludi, *Backlash: The Undeclared War Against American Women* (New York: Crown Publishers, 1991).

52. National Women's Studies Association, "NWSA/Ms. Magazine Guide to Women's Studies," http://www.nwsa.org/msmag/index.php, 2009/.

53. See examples of 1960s- and 1970s-era memoirs such as Karla Jay, *Tales of the Lavender Menace: A Memoir of Liberation* (New York: Basic Books, 1999), and Ann Snitow and Rachel Dupleissis, *The Feminist Memoir Project: Voices from Women's Liberation* (New York: Three Rivers Press, 1998).

54. Faludi, *Backlash*.

55. Heather Cassell, "Third Wave Foundation," in *Women's Movement Today: An Encyclopedia of Third-Wave Feminism*, Leslie L. Heywood, ed. (Westport, CT: Greenwood Press, 2006), 324–325.

56. Beechey "When Feminism Is Your Job."

57. Baumgardner and Richards, *Manifesta*, 278–280.

58. Verta Taylor and Nella Van Dyke, " 'Get Up, Stand Up': Tactical Repertoires of Social Movements," in *The Blackwell Companion to Social Movements*, David

Snow, Sarah Soule, and Hanspeter Kriesi, eds. (Malden, MA: Blackwell Publishing, 2004), 262–293.

59. Nella Van Dyke, Sarah A. Soule, and Verta A. Taylor, "The Targets of Social Movements: Beyond a Focus on the State," in *Authority in Contention, Research in Social Movements, Conflicts and Change,* Daniel J. Myers and Daniel M. Cress, eds. 25: 25–51. See also the discussion in Ferree, "Soft Repression."

60. David S. Meyer, "How Movements Matter," *Contexts* 2, 4(2003):30–35; Suzanne Staggenborg, "Can Feminist Organizations Be Effective?" in *Feminist Organizations: Harvest of the New Women's Movement,* Myra Marx Ferree and Patricia Yancey Martin, eds. (Philadelphia: Temple University Press, 1995), 339–355.

61. Hank Johnston, "Protest Cultures: Performances, Artifacts and Ideations, " in *Culture, Social Movements and Protest,* Hank Johnston, ed. (Burlington, VT: Ashgate Publishing Limited, 2009), 5.

62. Nancy Whittier, *The Politics of Child Sexual Abuse: Emotions, Social Movements and the State* (New York: Oxford University Press, 2009).

63. Linda M. Scott, *Fresh Lipstick: Redressing Fashion and Feminism* (New York: Palgrave Macmillan, 2005), 54–60.

64. See Pamela Aronson, "Feminists or 'Postfeminists'? Young Women's Attitudes toward Feminism and Gender Relations," *Gender & Society* 17,6 (2003): 903–922. See also Ferree, "Soft Repression," for a discussion on the term "feminazi" as a form of micro-level ridicule of the movement.

65. Patricia Hill Collins, *Black Feminist Thought: Knowledge, Consciousness, and the Politics of Empowerment.* (Boston: Unwin Hyman, 1991); bell hooks, *Feminist Theory: From Margin to Center* (Cambridge, MA: South End Press, 1984).

66. Leandra Zarnow, "From Sisterhood to Girlie Culture: Closing the Great Divide between Second and Third Wave Cultural Agenda," in *No Permanent Waves: Recasting Histories of U.S. Feminism,* Nancy A. Hewitt, ed. (New Brunswick, NJ: Rutgers University Press, 2010), 273–302.

67. Karl Mannheim, "The Problem with Generations," in *Essays on the Sociology of Knowledge,* Paul Keckemeti and Paul Keegan, eds. (London: Routledge, 1952), 276–320.

68. Richard Braungart and Margaret A. Braungart, "Life Course and Generational Politics," *Annual Review of Sociology* 12 (1984): 205–231; Mannheim, "The Problem with Generations"; Beth Schneider, "Political Generations in the Contemporary Women's Movement," *Sociological Inquiry* 58 (1988): 4–21.

69. Mannheim, "The Problem with Generations."

70. Braungart and Braungart, "Life Course and Generational Politics."

71. Astrid Henry, "Feminism's Family Problem," in *Catching a Wave: Reclaiming Feminism for the 21st Century,* Rory Dicker and Alison Piepmeier, eds. (Boston: Northeastern University Press, 2003), 209–231.

72. Schneider, "Political Generations in the Contemporary Women's Movement."

73. Rupp and Taylor, *Survival in the Doldrums,* 91–92.

74. Garrison, "Are We on a Wavelength Yet?" 241.

75. Astrid Henry, *Not My Mother's Sister: Generational Conflict and Third-Wave Feminism* (Bloomington: Indiana University Press, 2004), 55.

76. Alberto Melucci, *Nomads of the Present: Social Movements and Individual Needs in Contemporary Society* (Philadelphia: Temple University Press, 1989); Scott Hunt, Robert D. Benford, and David A. Snow, "Identity Fields: Framing Processes and the Social Construction of Movement Identities," in *New Social Movements: From Ideology to Identity*, Enrique Larana, Hank Johnston, and Joseph R. Gusfield, eds. (Philadelphia: Temple University Press, 1994), 186; Verta Taylor and Nancy Whittier, "Collective Identity in Social Movement Communities: Lesbian Feminist Mobilization," in *Frontiers in Social Movement Theory*, Aldon D. Morris and Carol McClurg Mueller, eds. (New Haven and London: Yale University Press, 1992), 104–129.

77. Kimberly Dugan and Jo Reger, "Voice and Agency in Social Movement Outcomes," *Qualitative Sociology* 29,4 (2006): 467–484.

78. Hunt et al., "Identity Fields."

79. Ibid.

80. Joshua Gamson, "Messages of Exclusion: Gender, Movements and Symbolic Boundaries," *Gender & Society* 11, 2 (1997): 204.

81. Buechler, *Women's Movements in the United States*, 57.

82. Nancy Whittier, "Political Generations, Micro-cohorts, and the Transformation of Social Movements," *American Sociological Review* 67 (1997): 760–778.

83. Sarah Kliff, *Newsweek*, April 16, 2010, 10, http://www.newsweek.com/2010/04/15/remember-roe.html/. For example, see the response on Feministing.com, "The Pro-Choice Movement Would Fail Without Young Women," http://www.feministing.com/archives/020818.html/.

84. Cheryl Corley, "Two Women Campaign for NOW Presidency," National Public Radio, June 19, 2009, http://www.npr.org/templates/story/story.php?storyId=10 5619536&ft=1&;f=1001/; Associated Press, "NOW Choose Next President in Close Election," June 21, 2009, http://www.msnbc.msn.com/id/31478632/. This win was despite the fact that Lyles was touted by Gandy as being able to provide a generational shift for the largely over-forty membership.

85. Rachel Einwohner, Jo Reger, and Daniel J. Myers, "Introduction: Identity Work, Sameness and Difference in Social Movements," in *Identity Work in Social Movements*, Jo Reger, Daniel J. Myers, and Rachel L. Einwohner, eds. (Minneapolis: University of Minnesota Press, 2008), 3.

86. See a critique of this idea in bell hooks, "Sisterhood: Political Solidarity between Women," in *Feminism and Community*, Penny A. Weiss and Marilyn Friedman, eds. (Philadelphia: Temple University Press, 1995), 293–316.

87. Collins, *Black Feminist Thought*, 221–238.

88. DuBois, *Feminism and Suffrage*.

89. Ibid.

90. Paula Giddings, *When and Where I Enter: The Impact of Black Women on Race and Sex in America* (New York: Bantam, 1984); Roth, *Separate Roads to Feminism*; Thompson, "Multiracial Feminism."

91. See Silke Roth, "Dealing with Diversity: The Coalition of Labor Union Women," in *Identity Work in Social Movements*, Jo Reger, Daniel J. Myers, and Rachel L. Einwohner, eds. (Minneapolis: University of Minnesota Press, 2008), 213–231.

92. The Mexican American Women's National Association is currently known as MANA, A National Latina Organization (see their Web site http://www.her-mana.org).

93. Nadasen, "Is It Time to Jump Ship?" 99.

94. Jay, *Tales of the Lavender Menace*. For more on lesbians and NOW, see Stephanie Gilmore and Elizabeth Kaminski, "A Part and Apart: Lesbian and Straight Feminist Activists Negotiate Identity in a Second-Wave Organization," *Journal of the History of Sexuality* 16,1 (January 2007): 95–113.

95. The Combahee River Collective, "The Combahee River Collective Statement," copyright © 1978 by Zillah Eisenstein, http://circuitous.org/scraps/combahee. html/; Deborah King, "Multiple Jeopardy, Multiple Consciousness: The Context of a Black Feminist Ideology," *Signs* 14 (1988): 142–172; Collins, *Black Feminist Thought*, 199.

96. Cherrie Moraga and Gloria Anzaldua, eds., *This Bridge Called My Back: Writings by Radical Women of Color* (New York: Kitchen Table Women of Color Press, 1981).

97. Roth, *Separate Roads to Feminism*; Thompson, "Multiracial Feminism."

98. Roth, *Separate Roads to Feminism*.

99. Nancy Hewitt, "From Seneca Falls to Suffrage: Reimagining a 'Master' Narrative in U.S. Women's History," in *No Permanent Waves: Recasting Histories of U.S. Feminism* Nancy A. Hewitt, ed. (New Brunswick, NJ: Rutgers University Press, 2010), 15–38.

100. See, for example, see Daisy Hernandez and Bushra Rehman, eds., *Colonize This! Young Women of Color on Today's Feminism* (New York: Seal Press, 2002).

101. Respondents were asked in an open-ended question to identify their race-ethnicity, allowing them to choose the categories they identified by instead of me providing set categories.

102. Kia Lilly Caldwell and Margaret Hunter, "Creating a Feminist Community on a Women of Color Campus," *Frontiers* 25, 1(2004):23–38.

103. Zarnow, "From Sisterhood to Girlie Culture," 294.

104. For examples of the theoretical importance of the women's movement, see Staggenborg and Taylor, "Whatever Happened?" ; Jo Reger and Verta Taylor, "Women's Movement Research and Social Movement Theory: A Symbiotic Relationship," *Research in Political Sociology* 10 (2002): 85–121; Ferree, "Soft Repression."

105. For example, Suzanne Staggenborg and I document how even when the national organization of NOW foundered, some chapters flourished. Jo Reger and Suzanne Staggenborg, "Patterns of Mobilization in Local Movement Organizations:

Leadership and Strategy in Four National Organization for Women Chapters," *Sociological Perspectives* 49, 3 (2006): 297–323.

106. This is not a new perspective; for example, see Ann Enke's analysis of second-wave-generation activists and their establishment of public space. Ann Enke, *Finding the Movement: Sexuality, Contested Space and Feminist Activism* (Durham, NC: Duke University Press, 2007).

107. Lesbian Avengers is a direct action group that emerged in the early 1990s on the East Coast. Zines are handmade magazines that are flourishing on the East and Northwest coasts.

108. See Judith Ezekiel's analysis of 1970s feminism in Dayton, Ohio, *Feminism in the Heartland* (Columbus: Ohio State University Press, 2002); Nancy Whittier's analysis of Columbus, Ohio, radical feminism, *Feminist Generations: The Persistence of the Radical Women's Movement* (Philadelphia: Temple University Press, 1995); and Ann Enke's analysis of activists in the Twin Cities, Detroit and Chicago, *Finding the Movement*.

109. See Michael Burawoy, "The Extended Case Method," *Sociological Theory* 16, 1 (1998):16.

110. The interviewees from Woodview and Evers were gathered through a snowball sampling method where each person suggested others I should talk to. In Green City, the initial group of interviews was gathered through Friendster.com and other Web sites that allowed me to explain my research and ask for volunteers. Once the initial group was gathered, interviewees suggested other names of potential respondents. What this method allows for is gathering a group of people who are in the same networks, providing a deeper and richer understanding of community feminism and allowing me to identify how different networks of feminists are shaped by social context.

111. My initial approach to this study was using a grounded approach; open to all potential research directions that may have included a need for anonymity and confidentiality. While aspects of this study do not need this layer of protection in retrospect, I honor the commitment made in the interviewee consent forms.

112. The *Vagina Monologues* are a series of monologues collecting personal narratives on women's anatomy and sexuality compiled by playwright Eve Ensler (New York: Villard, 2001).

CHAPTER I

1. Stephanie Gilmore argues similarly in her analysis of NOW chapters, calling it the "politics of location." See Gilmore, "Rethinking the Liberal/Radical Divide: The National Organizations for Women in Memphis, Columbus and San Francisco," (PhD dissertation, Ohio State University, 2005). See also Katja M. Guenther, *Making Their Place: Feminism After Socialism in Eastern Germany* (Palo Alto, CA: Stanford University Press, 2010).

2. Robert S. Erikson, Gerald C. Wright and John P. McIver, *Statehouse Democracy* (New York: Cambridge University Press, 1993), 245.

3. Katja M. Guenther, *Making Their Place.*

4. John McCarthy and Mayer Zald, "The Trend of Social Movements in America: Professionalization and Resource Mobilization," in *Social Movements in an Organizational Society: Collected Essays,* Mayer Zald and John D. McCarthy, eds. (New Brunswick, NJ: Transaction Books, 1987), 337–391.

5. Jo Reger, "More than One Feminism: Organizational Structure, Ideology and the Construction of Collective Identity," in *Social Movements: Identity, Culture and the State,* David S. Meyer, Nancy Whittier and Belinda Robnett, eds. (New York: Oxford University Press, 2002), 171–184.

6. Facts and statistics presented for each of the communities were obtained from city, state and federal documents. They are not identified here for the sake of anonymity.

7. In addition, it was not until 2004 that gay, lesbian, bisexual and transgender faculty and staff formed an employee resource group to address issues such as domestic partnership benefits. This was accomplished only after the faculty protested being left out of the "diversity" groups proposed by administrators.

8. The book by Inga Muscio, *Cunt: A Declaration of Independence,* 2d ed., Emeryville, CA: Seal Press, 2002, works to reclaim the word and foster a women-positive society.

9. Since its inception, depending on the leadership of the group and their ability to meet deadlines and file paperwork, FFW has struggled at times to maintain its presence on campus. These efforts have been aided by the existence of a gender and sexuality center and directors who seek out students to lead the group.

10. The group advertised themselves as "an on campus feminist organization" that was active "in dealing with body-image issues, reproductive rights, rape awareness, as well as performing the *Vagina Monologues*. . . ." Flyer entitled "Pro-Women, Pro-Men, Pro-Diversity, Pro-Self Love, Pro-Individuality," 2003, author's files.

11. FFW newsletter, "Let's Have Fun," September 18, 2003, 1, author's files.

12. The Gay-Straight Alliance formed in 2003 with some overlap in members.

13. Personal e-mail, October 9, 2003.

14. Flyer, "You Don't Look Like a Feminist!" 2003, author's files.

15. FFW newsletter, "Get in Da Mode," September 18, 2003, 1, author's files.

16. Personal e-mail, September, 23, 2002; personal e-mail, "FFW-Protest from NOW," November 15, 2002, author's files.

17. FFW minutes, October 10, 2002.

18. Flyer, "Wash Away the Hate," for demonstration December 22 and 23, 2002.

19. For example, personal e-mail, "FFW Help Save a Women's Life," November 6, 2002; personal e-mail, November 10, 2002.

20. Doug McAdam, *Freedom Summer* (New York: Oxford University Press, 1990). Verta Taylor and Leila Rupp also write extensively on the importance of personal

networks in their work together on the U.S. women's movement. See Rupp and Taylor, *Survival in the Doldrums*, and Verta Taylor, "Sources of Continuity in Social Movements: The Women's Movement in Abeyance," *American Sociological Review* 54 (1989): 761–775.

21. Laughlin et al., "Is It Time to Jump Ship?"

22. Mary Fainsod Katzenstein, "Feminism within American Institutions: Unobtrusive Mobilization in the 1980s," *Signs: Journal of Culture and Society* 16, 11(1990): 27–54.

23. Steve is a biological female genderqueer who goes by a masculine name but prefers feminine pronouns. I discuss more of Steve's story in chapter 6.

24. According to the DykeNight Web site the events are for social networking with like-minded women.

25. Personal e-mail correspondence, August 19, 2004, author's files.

26. Promotional postcard, DragUpKnockDown, June 18, 2004, author's files.

27. According to the Camp Trans organizational history it was in 1999 that "Son of Camp Trans" was initiated by Rikki Wilchins and the Transsexual Menace, with support from many members of the Boston and Chicago Lesbian Avengers. The events of 1999 drew much attention and controversy, culminating in heated tensions as a small group of transgender activists were admitted into the festival to dialogue with organizers and to negotiate a short-lived compromise allowing only postoperative transgender womyn on the festival land. While this event brought the issue to people's attention once again, the actions used were criticized by other trans women. http://www.camp-trans.org/pages/ct-history.html/.

28. David S. Meyer and Nancy Whittier, "Social Movement Spillover," *Social Problems* 41, 2(1994): 277. Taylor et al. found that the majority of activists for same-sex weddings were also activists at some time in the women's movement. This movement spillover is also found between other movements besides the LGBT and the women's movements. Verta Taylor, Nella Van Dyke, and Ellen Ann Andersen, "Culture and Mobilization: Tactical Repertoires, Same-Sex Weddings and the Impact on Gay Activism," *American Sociological Review* 74 (December 2009): 865–890. For example, see Larry Isaac and Lars Christiansen, "How the Civil Rights Movement Revitalized Labor Militancy," *American Sociological Review* 67 (2002): 722–746.

CHAPTER 2

1. Jane O'Reilly, "The Housewife's Moment of Truth," *Ms. Magazine*, Spring 1972, 54–59.

2. I explore the process in "Organizational 'Emotion Work' through Consciousness-Raising: An Analysis of a Feminist Organization," *Qualitative Sociology* 27, 2 (2004): 205–222.

3. E. Eskenazi, "Speak from the " 'I': I've done C-R in the 70s, 80s and 90s," *NOW News*, files of the New York City Chapter of the National Organization for Women (October/November 1994), 6. Emphasis is mine.

4. In the collected volume, *Letters to Ms.: 1972–1987,* writing about the "click" moment was so popular that the editor of the volume referred to them as the "classic 'click' letters," which appear throughout the book. See Mary Thom, ed., *Letters to Ms.: 1972–1987* (New York: Henry Holt Co., 1987), xvii.

5. For example, see J. Courtney Sullivan and Courtney E, Martin, *Click: When We Knew We Were Feminists* (New York: Avalon Publishing Group, 2010), which includes chapters from contemporary feminist authors such as Jennifer Baumgardner, Amy Richards and Deborah Siegel.

6. Cheryl Hercus, *Stepping Out of Line: Becoming and Being Feminist* (New York: Routledge, 2005), 10–11.

7. Rose Glickman, *Daughters of Feminists* (New York: St. Martin's Press, 1993), xiii.

8. For example, in 2004 the U.S. Census Bureau reported that women make 75.5 cents for every dollar a man earns. http://usgovinfo.about.com/od/censusandstatistics/a/paygapgrows.htm (accessed July 8, 2010).

9. I borrow this analogy from Judith Lorber who argues that thinking about gender is like fish thinking about water. Judith Lorber, *Paradox of Gender* (New Haven: Yale University Press, 1994).

10. David A. Snow, E. Burke Rochford, Jr., Steven K. Worden, and Robert D. Benford., "Frame Alignment, Micromobilization, and Movement Participation," *American Sociological Review* 51 (1986): 464–481.

11. Hercus, *Becoming a Feminist.*

12. In fact, in Woodview there was one particular young woman who influenced many of her friends and classmates. However, mothers were the most often discussed.

13. McAdam, *Freedom Summer.*

14. Gloria Steinem, "Why Young Women Are More Conservative," *Outrageous Acts and Everyday Rebellions* (New York: Holt, Rinehart and Winston, 1983), 211–218.

15. Abigail Halcli and Jo Reger, "Strangers in a Strange Land: The Gendered Experiences of Women Politicians in Britain and the United States," in *Feminist Frontiers*, 4th ed., Nancy Whittier, Verta Taylor, and Laurel Richardson, eds. (New York: McGraw-Hill, 1996), 457–471. These experiences do not always bring women into feminism. Kathy Blee writes about sexual assault as one avenue to becoming an activists in organized hate movements. Kathleen Blee, *Inside Organized Racism: Women in the Hate Movement* (Berkeley: University of California Press, 2002).

16. Aronson, "Feminists or 'Postfeminists' ? "

17. Meyer and Whittier, "Social Movement Spillover."

18. Evans, *Personal Politics.*

19. In fact Hercus finds that higher education is one of the three most important social settings in becoming a feminist.

20. In Evers, organizations could affect students' perception of activism in general. See chapter 1 for a discussion of the grassroots organization The Student Coalition.

While this group promoted activism and activist identities, it was not specifically feminist and led to a more submerged feminist identity.

21. Lila's mother is from the Midwest, which may play a factor in her moving away from identifying as a feminist over time because of the more conservative nature of the region, as illustrated by Woodview.

22. Glickman, *Daughters of Feminists.*

23. Others have also engaged in these analyses. See Henry for an extensive discussion of generational conflict and the metaphor of mother and daughter in feminism.

24. Majorie Jolles, "'Real Women' In Women's Studies: A Reflexive Look at the Theory/Practice Dilemma," *Feminist Teacher* 18, 1(2007):74–85.

25. Jolles, "Real Women," 74.

26. Some of the Green City residents moved more than once before settling in Green City.

27. Punk, a social movement expressed through appearance and music, is focused on rebellion against the dominant culture. Starting in the United Kingdom in the late 1960s, it carried over to the United States in the mid-1970s and early1980s.

28. McCarthy and Zald, "Resource Mobilization."

29. For examples, see McAdam, *Freedom Summer*; Rupp and Taylor, *Survival* ; Taylor, "Sources of Continuity."

CHAPTER 3

1. Susan Dominus, "Feminists Find Unity Elusive," *New York Times*, February 1, 2008, http://www.nytimes.com/2008/02/01/nyregions/01bigcity.html/.

2. Katha Pollit, "Amber Waves of Blame," *The Nation*, May 27, 2009, http://www.thenation.com/doc (retrieved June 3, 2009).

3. This description comes from Gloria's Steinem's blurb on the back cover of the book.

4. For example, Baumgardner and Richards address it in detail in *Manifesta,* and as does Astrid Henry in *Not My Mother's Sister.*

5. Phyllis Chesler, *Letters to a Young Feminist* (New York: Four Walls Eight Windows, 1997), 1–2.

6. Chesler, *Letters to a Young Feminist*, 43.

7. Gilmore "Bridging the Waves," Naples, "Confronting the Future."

8. Gilmore, "Bridging the Waves,"97.

9. Stephanie Herold, "Young Feminists to Old Feminists: If You Can't Find Us, It's Because We're Online," *Campus Progress* (July 19, 2010), http://www.campus-progress.org/opinions/5914/young-feminists-to-old-feminists-if-you-cant-find-us-its-because-were-online (retrieved July 20, 2010).

10. Astrid Henry, "Solitary Sisterhood: Individualism Meets Collectivity in Feminism's Third Wave" in *Different Wavelengths: Studies of the Contemporary Women's Movement*, Jo Reger, ed. (New York: Routledge, 2005), 82. Author's emphasis.

11. Catherine Orr, "Charting the Currents of the Third Wave," *Hypatia* 12,3 (1997): 32. Author's emphasis.

12. For feminist scholar Sara Evans this is somewhat forgivable. She offers that these historical simplifications in that [second-wave feminism] "was simply too complex to bear a single telling—or even several." Evans, *Tidal Wave*,259.

13. Merri Lisa Johnson, ed., *Jane Sexes It Up: True Confessions of Feminist Desire* (New York: Four Walls Eight Windows, 2002). This edited volume provoked debates on a variety of feminist Web sites when it was published.

14. See Taylor and Whittier, "Collective Identity in Social Movement Communities."

15. Hunt et al., "Identity Fields."

16. Sleater-Kinney is a three-woman band from the Pacific Northwest that emerged from the Riot Grrrl and punk scene. They have a large feminist following. The Donnas is a four-woman hard-core rock band formed in 1993.

17. Henry, *Not My Mother's Sister.*

18. "Womanist" is a term coined by Alice Walker that integrates race and ethnicity with feminism. Alice Walker, *In Search of Our Mother's Gardens: Womanist Prose* (New York: HBJ Publishing, 1983).

19. For example many transgender activists point to the popularity of Janice Raymond's 1979 book, *The Transsexual Empire: The Making of the She-Male,* which portrayed transsexuals as enemies to the women's movement. For a longer discussion, see Sally Hines, "'I am a Feminist but...' Transgender Men and Women and Feminism," in *Different Wavelengths: Studies of the Contemporary Women's Movement,* Jo Reger, ed. (New York: Routledge, 2005), 57–77.

20. Naomi Wolf, "Who Won Feminism? Hint: She's the Diva who Ran Cosmo," *Washington Post,* May 3, 2009, http://www.washingtonpost.com/ (retrieved May 6, 2009).

21. J. Craig Jenkins and Michael Wallace, "The Generalized Action Potential of Protest Movements: The New Class, Social Trends and Political Exclusion Explanations," *Sociological Forum* 11, 2 (June 1996): 183–207.

22. Robert D. Benford and David A. Snow, "Framing Processes and Social Movements: An Overview and Assessment," *Annual Review of Sociology* 26 (2000): 611–639.

23. In fact, new social movement theory is predicated on the idea that there has been a generational shift in movements, away from materialistic gains to pursuing goals based on lifestyle.

24. Ruth Cherrington, "Generational Issues in China: A Case Study of the 1980s Generation of Young Intellectuals," *The British Journal of Sociology* 48, 2 (June 1997): 302–320.

25. I make a similar argument about organizational dissension in my study of a NOW chapter in "More than One Feminism."

26. See Ednie Kaeh Garrison, "U.S. Feminism—Girl Style! Youth (Sub)Cultures and the Technologies of the Third Wave," *Feminist Studies* 26,1(2000): 141–170.

CHAPTER 4

1. Evans, *Personal Politics,* 214.

2. Taylor and Van Dyke, "Get Up, Stand Up." See also Charles Tilley, *From Mobilization to Revolution* (New York: Random House, 1978); Sarah Soule, "The Student Divestment Movement in the United States and Tactical Diffusion: The Shanty Town Protest," *Social Forces* 75 (1997): 855–883.

3. David S. Meyer and Suzanne Staggenborg, "Thinking about Strategy" Forthcoming in Making History: Movements, Strategy, and Social Change, edited by Jeff Goodwin, Rachel Kutz-Flamenbaum, Gregory Maney, and Deana Rohlinger. Minneapolis: University of Minnesota Press.

4. Not Martha, "To Make:Vegan Fox," http://www.notmartha.org/tomake/vegan-fox/.

5. *The Colbert Report,* December 3, 2008, http://www.colbertnation.com/the-colbert-report-videos/212027/december-03-2008/nailed—em—radical-knitting—em—radical-knitting/.

6. Rachel Fudge, "Shop * In the Name of Love," *Bitch* 32 (Summer 2006), 36–39, 94–95, and *Bust,* "Old's Cool: The Granny Peace Brigade Are Activists with a Senior Twist," and "Ready, Set, Toe! The Camel Toe Lady Steppers Shake Some Ass for Mardi Gras" (December/January 2009), 10 and 18 respectively.

7. For more on culture and feminist politics, see Suzanne Staggenborg's work, in particular Staggenborg and Amy Lang, "Culture and Ritual in the Montreal Women's Movement," *Social Movement Studies* 6 (2007):177–194; Suzanne Staggenborg, "Beyond Culture versus Politics: A Case Study of a Local Women's Movement," *Gender & Society* 15 (2001): 507–530; Suzanne Staggenborg, Donna Eder, and Lori Sudderth, "Women's Culture and Social Change: Evidence from the National Women's Music Festival," *Berkeley Journal of Sociology* 38 (1993/4): 31–55.

8. Meredith A. Evans and Chris Bobel, "'I am a Contradiction': Feminism and Feminist Identity in the Third Wave," *New England Journal of Public Policy* 1 and 2 (2007): 207–222; Natalie Fixmer and Julia T. Wood, "The Personal Is Still Political: Embodied Politics in Third Wave Feminism," *Women's Studies in Communication* 28, 2 (2005):235–257.

9. Judith Taylor, "The Problem of Women's Sociality in Contemporary North American Feminist Memoir," *Gender & Society* 22, 6 (2008): 705–727. See also Chris Bobel, "'Our Revolution Has Style': Contemporary Menstrual Product Activists 'Doing Feminism' in the Third Wave," *Sex Roles* 54 (2006): 331–345; Ricia Chansky, "A Stitch in Time: Reclaiming the Needle in Third Wave Feminist Visual Expression," paper presented at the National Women's Studies Association meetings(St. Charles, IL, 2007).

10. Baumgardner and Richards, "Feminism and Femininity," 59.

11. Collins, *Black Feminist Thought.*

12. Kate McCarthy, "Not Pretty Girls?: Sexuality, Spirituality, and Gender Construction in Women's Rock Music," *The Journal of Popular Culture* 39,1 (2006): 69–94, http://blackwell-synergy.com/doi/full/, 70 (retrieved May 31, 2007).

13. See Taylor and Whittier, "Collective Identity."

14. For example, see Verta Taylor, Nella Van Dyke, and Ellen Ann Andersen, "Culture and Mobilization: Tactical Repertoires, Same-Sex Weddings and the Impact on Gay Activism," *American Sociological Review* 74 (December 2009): 865–890.

15. In 2009, there were more than 4,200 V-Day benefit events and in ten years, the V-Day movement has raised over $70 million, http://www.vday.org/contents/vcampagins/indiancountry/join/. For more details, see Jo Reger and Lacey Story, "Talking about My Vagina: Two College Campuses and the Vagina Monologues," in *Different Wavelengths: Studies of the Contemporary Women's Movement*, Jo Reger, ed. (New York: Routledge, 2005), 139–160.

16. This dynamic repeated itself as evidenced in a campus newspaper article from March 27, 2010, which quoted the organizer as saying, "You see this word (vagina) and you're like 'Whoa' like 'what is this?' "

17. Verta Taylor, Leila J. Rupp, and Joshua Gamson, "Performing Protest: Drag Shows as Tactical Repertoire of the Gay and Lesbian Movement," *Authority in Contention, Research in Social Movements, Conflict and Change* 25 (2004):105–137. See also Rupp and Taylor, *Drag Queens at the 801 Cabaret* (Chicago: University of Chicago Press, 2003).

18. See R. Blau DuPlessis and A. Snitow, *The Feminist Memoir Project: Voices from Women's Liberation* (New York: Three Rivers Press, 1998); Karla Jay, *Tales of the Lavender Menace: A Memoir of Liberation* (New York: Basic Books, 1999); Linda Scott, *Fresh Lipstick: Redressing Fashion and Feminism* (New York: Palgrave Macmillan, 2005); Deborah Siegel, *Sisterhood Interrupted: From Radical Women To Grrls Gone Wild* (New York: Palgrave Macmillan, 2007). Friedan quote as cited in Siegel, 85.

19. Emphasis is mine.

20. Author's flyers. These are just a few of the activities, including the drag king show described in chapter 2.

21. Posted on the Web site (retrieved April 4, 2004).

22. Steve, "Say It! Fat! Fat! Fat!" in *Fatty, Fatty 2X4*, Issue 2, 2003. Author's files.

23. Chalking is a form of promoting groups, events or issues through writing in chalk on sidewalks and buildings. E-mail correspondence with Professor Andrews, September 22, 2004.

24. It is not clear here whether she is referring to contemporary feminist filmmakers or the second-wave feminist generation film company Women Make Movies founded in 1972.

25. *Bust* contains a multitude of advertisements and features on sex from being sex positive through the purchase of sex toys to columns that discuss sexual desire and dysfunction.

26. NYC Radical Cheerleaders, "No Justice," http://www.nycradicalcheerleaders.org/ (retrieved November 26, 2009).

27. Responding to criticism from the intersexual and transgender communities, Ensler added a transgender-themed monologue as an option in the 2005 script.

28. Meyer and Staggenborg, "Thinking About Strategy," 8.

29. As cited in Gilmore, "Bridging the Waves," 97.

30. Nelson A. Pichardo Almanzar, Heather Sullivan-Catlin, and Glenn Deane, "Is the Political Personal? Everyday Behaviors as Forms of Environmental Movement Participation," *Mobilization: An International Journal* 3,2 (1998): 185–205.

31. Taylor and Van Dyke, "Get Up, Stand Up."

32. Taylor et al., "Culture and Mobilization."

CHAPTER 5

1. Cherrie Moraga and Gloria Anzaldua, Introduction to section, "Entering the Lives of Others," in *This Bridge Called My Back: Writings by Radical Women of Color*, Cherrie Moraga and Gloria Anzaldua, eds. (New York: Kitchen Table, Women of Color Press, 1983), 23.

2. Rebecca Hurdis, "Heartbroken: Women of Color Feminism and the Third Wave," in *Colonize This! Young Women of Color on Today's Feminism*, Daisy Hernandez and Bushra Rehman, eds. (New York: Seal Press, 2002), 287.

3. In fact, many of the white feminists and feminists of color interviewed who had taken women's studies courses specifically referred to this anthology as a part of their racial awakening.

4. Rebecca Walker, "Foreword," in *The Fire This Time: Young Activists and the New Feminism*, Vivien Labaton and Dawn Lundy Martin, eds. (New York: Anchor Books, 2004), xiv. Emphasis by Walker.

5. Cherrie Moraga, "Foreword: The War Path of Greater Empowerment," in *Colonize This! Young Women of Color on Today's Feminism*, xiii. See also Rebecca Walker, ed., *To Be Real: Telling the Truth and Changing the Face of Feminism* (New York: Anchor Books, 1995), and Barbara Findlen, ed., *Listen Up: Voices from the Next Feminist Generation* (Seattle: Seal Press, 1995).

6. Leslie Heywood and Jennifer Drake, "Introduction," in *Third Wave Agenda: Being Feminist, Doing Feminism*, Leslie Heywood and Jennifer Drake, eds. (Minneapolis: University of Minnesota Press, 1997), 3.

7. Post to the SWS listserv [Sociologists for Women], April 5, 2009.

8. Giddings, *When and Where I Enter*, 1984.

9. Michelle Wallace, "To Hell and Back: On the Road with Black Feminism in the 1960s & 1970s," in *Feminist Memoir Project: Voices from Women's Liberation*, Rachel Blau DuPlessis and Ann Snitow, eds, (New York: Three Rivers Press, 1998), 426–442.

10. See Winifred Breines, *The Trouble Between Us: An Uneasy History of White and Black Women in the Feminist Movement* (New York: Oxford University Press, 2006).

11. Roth, *Separate Roads to Feminism*; Thompson, "Multi-Racial Feminism."

12. Traci Vogel, "Push Anywhere: An Interview with Nancy Hartsock," *The Stranger*, www.thestranger.com/, 10, 28, March 29–April 4, 2001.

13. In chapter 6, I examine how gender and sexual expression inclusivity is articulated by contemporary feminists.

14. Feminist scholar bell hooks argues, "Nowadays it is fashionable to talk about race or gender; the uncool subject is class." See hooks, *Where We Stand: Class Matters* (New York, Routledge, 2000), vii.

15. Emphasis is mine.

16. This role is one of the only monologues that specifies race.

17. See Collins, *Black Feminist Thought*; bell hooks, *Talking Back: Thinking Feminist, Thinking Black* (Boston: South End Press, 1989).

18. FFW newsletter, "Mission Diversity," September 18, 2003,author's files.

19. Only one feminist chose not to answer the question about her race-ethnicity.

20. Steve, "The White Face in the Mirror," in *Fatty Fatty 2X4: Adventures of and Social Commentary by a Queer Fat Chick,* Issue 3, 2003, author's files.

21. There are conflicting reports on whether it was one or two houses that had the graffiti.

22. Galen Sherwin, "Girls Are to Be Seen, Heard, and Believed," *NOW NYC Newsletter,* May/June 1998, www.nownyc.org/.

23. See also Kristen Schilt, "'The Punk White Privilege Scene:' Riot Grrrl, White Privilege, and Zines," in *Different Wavelengths: Studies of the Contemporary Women's Movement,* Jo Reger, ed. (New York: Routledge, 2005), 39–56.

24. Jane Ward, "Diversity Discourse and Multi-identity Work in Lesbian and Gay Organizations," in *Identity Work in Social Movements,* Jo Reger, Daniel J. Myers, and Rachel L. Einwohner, eds. (Minneapolis: University of Minnesota Press, 2008), 252.

25. For an extended discussion, see Fred Rose, "Toward a Class-Cultural Theory of Social Movements: Reinterpreting New Social Movements," *Sociological Forum* 12: 3 (1997): 461–494.

26. The lack of focus on social class in the National Women's Studies Association is the subject of Lois Helmbold's article "Classless and Clueless in NWSA: A History of the Poor and Working Class Caucus," *NWSA Journal* 14, 1(2002): 58–70.

27. See Roth, "Dealing with Diversity"; Nancy Naples, ed., *Community Activism and Feminist Politics: Organizing Across Race, Class and Gender* (New York: Routledge, 1998). An example of work that combines race, class and feminism is Premilla Nadasen, "Expanding the Boundaries of the Women's Movement: Black Feminism and the Struggle for Welfare Rights," *Feminist Studies* 28, 2(2002): 271–303.

28. hooks, *Where We Stand.*

29. For example, the work and theories of socialist and Marxist feminists is often not highlighted in the simplified historical record of U.S. feminism.

30. Tamara Straus, "Is Feminism Dead?" Alternet, February 11, 2000, www.alternet.org/.

CHAPTER 6

1. U.S. Social Forum, June 22–26, 2010, Detroit, Michigan, http://www.ussf2010. org/about/.

2. Emi Koyama, "The Transfeminist Manifesto," in *Catching a Wave: Reclaiming Feminism for the 21st Century*, Rory Dicker and Alison Piepmeier, eds. (Boston: Northeastern University Press, 2003), 244–259; Leah Lakshmi Piepzna-Samarasinha, "browngirlworld: queergirlofcolor organizing, sistahood, heartbreak," in *Catching a Wave*, 3–16.

3. Steven Seidman, "Deconstructing Queer Theory, or the Under-theorization of the Social and the Ethical," *Social Postmodernism: Beyond Identity Politics*, Linda Nicholson and Steven Seidman, eds. (Cambridge: Cambridge University Press, 1995), 116–141. See also Judith Butler, *Gender Trouble: Feminism and the Subversion of Identity* (New York: Routledge, 1990), which is often credited as the foundational text on the creation of queer theory.

4. TransGender Michigan, *TransGender Michigan: Basic Terms and Definitions* (Detroit, MI: TransGender Michigan, 2004).

5. Leslie Feinberg, *Transgender Warriors: Making History from Joan of Arc to Dennis Rodman* (Boston: Beacon Press, 1996).

6. T. Eve Greenaway, "Girls Will Be Boys," Alternet, June 6, 2001, http://www.alternet. org/print.html/ (retrieved March 22, 2004). There have also been similar articles in the *New York Times*: Alissa Quart, "When Girls Will Be Boys," March 16, 2008, and Fred A. Bernstein, "On Campus, Rethinking Biology 101," March 7, 2004 (both retrieved from http://www.nytimes.com/).

7. This conclusion is based on the interviews conducted in 2002 and 2003 at Woodview. Since that time, Woodview has had more exposure to transgender as an idea and an identity.

8. Here Ben uses the "T" in LGBT more as an acceptance of the convention of naming "gay" organizations than an acknowledgment of transgender.

9. Taylor and Whittier, "Lesbian Feminist Mobilization," 120–121, discuss the connection between feminism and lesbian in their analysis of dress and appearance.

10. For example, in the 2005 documentary, *I Was a Teen-age Feminist* (written and directed by Therese Shechter and distributed through Women Make Movies), the filmmaker interviews men on the street, who overwhelmingly associate being a feminist with being a lesbian.

11. Merri Lisa Johnson, "Jane Hocus, Jane Focus," in *Jane Sexes It Up: True Confessions of Feminist Desire* Merri Lisa Johnson, ed. (New York: Four Walls Eight Windows, 2002), 9.

12. Becca is referring to second-wave-generation feminist Andrea Dworkin's book *Intercourse* (New York: Free Press, 1988), where her argument is often seen as an indictment against heterosexual sex. There is a larger literature that argues she did not argue that all sex was rape and her views are often simplified. For example, see

Ariel Levy's profile of her, "The Prisoner of Sex," *New York Magazine*, May 29, 2005, http://nymag.com/nymetro/news/people/features/11907/.

13. Professor Andrews confirmed the idea that identifying as a lesbian was "old school" at Evers, recalling a classroom discussion in which "lesbian" was discarded as being situated in the past (e-mail correspondence, March 12, 2004).

14. Janice Raymond, *The Transsexual Empire: The Making of the She-Male* (New York: Teachers College Press, 1979/1994).

15. Hines, "'I Am a Feminist but . . .'".

16. Koyama, "The Transfeminist Manifesto."

17. Kristin Schilt, *Just One of the Guys: Transgender Men and the Persistence of Gender Inequality* (Chicago: University of Chicago Press, 2010).

18. Yet the communities remain linked in some matters. For example, in 2010 the feminist bookstore opened a transgender café inside the shop with the proceeds going to health care for the trans community, indicating the development of a separate trans identity in Green City and a continuing link to feminism.

19. Steve, "Dear Health Care Provider," in *Fatty Fatty 2X4: Adventures of and Social Commentary by a Queer Fat Chick,* Issue 3, 2003, author's files.

20. Raymond, *Transsexual Empire.*

21. Field notes, Green City, June 6, 2004.

22. Eve Shapiro, "Drag Kinging and the Transformation of Gender Identities," *Gender & Society* 21, 2 (April 2007): 250–271.

23. Rupp and Taylor, *Drag Queens of the 801 Cabaret.*

CONCLUSION

1. "Women Now Empowered by Everything a Woman Does," *The Onion* 39,6(2003), http://www.theonion.com/ (retrieved February 25, 2003).

2. Levy, *Female Chauvinist Pigs*; Douglas, *Enlightened Sexism*; Angela McRobbie, *The Aftermath of Feminism: Gender, Culture and Social Change* (Los Angeles, CA: Sage Publications, 2009).

3. Aronson, "Feminists or 'Postfeminists'?" ; Douglas, *Enlightened Sexism*; Jessica Valenti, *Full Frontal Feminism: A Young Woman's Guide to Why Feminism Matters* (Emeryville, CA: Seal Press, 2007).

4. Guenther, *Making Their Place.*

5. Bobel, *New Blood*, 173.

6. Cathryn Bailey, "Making Waves and Drawing Lines: The Politics of Defining the Vicissitudes of Feminism," *Hypatia* 12 (1997): 8.

7. Norma Nyhoff, "NOW Conference Gives Young Feminists a Voice," *Say It, Sister!, NOW's Blog for Equality*, July 13, 2010, http://www.now.org./news/blogs/ (retrieved August 5, 2010), http://www.now.org./news/blogs/ (retrieved August 5, 2010).

8. Bobel, *New Blood.*

9. I would argue that race also played a role in the election but was not openly discussed as was the issue of generations and age.

10. Susan Faludi, "American Electra: Feminism's Ritual Matricide," *Harper's*, October 2010, http://www.harpers.org/archive/2010/10/0083140/.

11. As quoted by Katherine Lanpher, "Are Younger Women Trying to Trash Feminism?" MSN Lifestyle, http://www.more.com/news/womens-issues/are-younger-women-trying-trash-feminism-0 (2008). The coat hanger symbolizes women who died trying to self-induce abortions before abortion was legalized.

12. Zarnow, "From Sisterhood to Girlie Culture."

Bibliography

Alfonso, Rita, and Jo Trigilio. "Surfing the Third Wave: A Dialogue between Two Third Wave Feminists." *Hypatia: A Journal of Feminist Philosophy* 12, 3(1997): 7–16.

Almanzar, Nelson A. Pichardo, Heather Sullivan-Catlin, and Glenn Deane. "Is the Political Personal? Everyday Behaviors as Forms of Environmental Movement Participation." *Mobilization: An International Journal* 3, 2(1998): 185–205.

Anzaldua, Gloria E. "(Un)natural bridge, (Un)safe Spaces." In *This Bridge We Call Home: Radical Visions for Transformation*, edited by Gloria E. Anzaldua and Analouise Keating, 1–5. New York: Routledge, 2002.

Aronson, Pamela. "Feminists or 'Postfeminists'? Young Women's Attitudes toward Feminism and Gender Relations." *Gender & Society* 17, 6(2003): 903–922.

Armstrong, Elizabeth, and Mary Bernstein. "Culture, Power and Institutions: A Multi-Institutional Politics Approach to Social Movements." *Sociological Theory* 26(2008): 74–99.

Associated Press. "NOW Choose Next President in Close Election." June 21, 2009. http://www.msnbc.msn.com/id/31478632/.

Bailey, Cathryn. "Making Waves and Drawing Lines: The Politics of Defining the Vicissitudes of Feminism." *Hypatia: A Journal of Feminist Philosophy* 12 (1997): 17–28.

Baumgardner, Jennifer, and Amy Richards. "Feminism and Femininity: Or How We Learned to Stop Worrying and Love the Thong." In *All About the Girl: Culture, Power and Identity*, edited by Anita Harris, 59–68. New York: Routledge, 2004.

———. *Manifesta: Young Women, Feminism and the Future.* New York: Farrar, Straus and Giroux, 2000.

Beechey, Suzanne. "When Feminism Is Your Job: Age and Power in Women's Policy Organizations." In *Different Wavelengths: Studies of the Contemporary Women's Movement*, edited by Jo Reger, 117–136. New York: Routledge, 2005.

Bellafante, Ginia. "Is Feminism Dead?" *Time* 151 (1998): 25. http://www.time.com/time/covers/0,16641,19980629,00.html/.

Benford, Robert D., and David A. Snow. "Framing Processes and Social Movements: An Overview and Assessment." *Annual Review of Sociology* 26 (2000): 611–639.

Bernstein, Fred A. "On Campus, Rethinking Biology 101." March 7, 2004. http://www.nytimes.com/2004/03/07/style/on-campus-rethinking-biology-101.html/.

Blee, Kathleen. *Inside Organized Racism: Women in the Hate Movement.* Berkeley: University of California Press, 2002.

Bobel, Chris. *New Blood: Third-Wave and the Politics of Menstruation.* New Brunswick, NJ: Rutgers University Press, 2010.

———. 'Our Revolution Has Style': Contemporary Menstrual Product Activists 'Doing Feminism' in the Third Wave." *Sex Roles* 54 (2006): 331–345.

Braungart, Richard, and Margaret A. Braungart. "Life Course and Generational Politics." *Annual Review of Sociology* 12 (1984): 205–31.

Breines, Winifred. *The Trouble Between Us: An Uneasy History of White and Black Women in the Feminist Movement.* New York: Oxford University Press, 2006.

Buechler, Steven. *Women's Movements in the United States.* New Brunswick, NJ: Rutgers University Press, 1990.

Burawoy, Michael. "The Extended Case Method." *Sociological Theory* 16, 1(1998): 4–33.

Butler, Judith. *Gender Trouble: Feminism and the Subversion of Identity.* New York: Routledge, 1990.

Caldwell, Kia Lilly, and Margaret Hunter. "Creating a Feminist Community on a Women of Color Campus." *Frontiers* 25, 1(2004): 23–38.

Cassell, Heather. "Third Wave Foundation." In *Women's Movement Today: An Encyclopedia of Third-Wave Feminism,* edited by Leslie L. Heywood, 324–325. Westport, CT: Greenwood Press, 2006.

Chansky, Ricia. "A Stitch in Time: Reclaiming the Needle in Third Wave Feminist Visual Expression." Paper presented at the National Women's Studies Association meetings, St. Charles, IL 2007.

Cherrington, Ruth. "Generational Issues in China: A Case Study of the 1980s Generation of Young Intellectuals." *The British Journal of Sociology* 48, 2(1997): 302–320.

Chesler, Phyllis. "The Failure of Feminism." February 24, 2006. http://www.phyllis-chesler.com/163/the-failure-of-feminism/.

———. *Letters to a Young Feminist.* New York: Four Walls Eight Windows, 1997.

Collins, Patricia Hill. *Black Feminist Thought: Knowledge, Consciousness, and the Politics of Empowerment.* Boston: Unwin Hyman, 1991.

The Combahee River Collective. "The Combahee River Collective Statement." Copyright © 1978 by Zillah Eisenstein. http://circuitous.org/scraps/combahee.html/.

Corley, Cheryl. "Two Women Campaign for NOW Presidency." National Public Radio, June 19, 2009. http://www.npr.org/templates/story/story.php?storyId=105619536

Dicker, Rory, and Alison Piepmeier, eds. *Catching a Wave: Reclaiming Feminism for the 21st Century.* Boston: Northeastern University Press, 2003.

Dominus, Susan. "Feminists Find Unity is Elusive." *New York Times*, February 1, 2008. http://www.nytimes.com/2008/02/01/nyregion/01bigcity.html.

Douglas, Susan J. *Enlightened Sexism: The Seductive Message That Feminism's Work Is Done*. New York: Times Books, 2010.

DuBois, Ellen Carol. *Feminism and Suffrage: The Emergence of an Independent Women's Movement in America, 1848–1869*. Ithaca, NY: Cornell University Press, 1978.

Dugan, Kimberly. "Just Like You: The Dimensions of Identity Presentations in an Antigay Contested Context." In *Identity Work in Social Movements,* edited by Jo Reger, Dan Myers, and Rachel Einwohner, 21–46. Minneapolis: University of Minnesota Press, 2008.

———. *The Struggle Over Gay, Lesbian, and Bisexual Rights: Facing Off in Cincinnati*. New York: Routledge Press, 2005.

Dugan, Kimberly, and Jo Reger. "Voice and Agency in Social Movement Outcomes." *Qualitative Sociology* 29, 4(2006): 467–484.

Dworkin, Andrea. *Intercourse*. New York: Free Press, 1988.

Einwohner, Rachel, Jo Reger, and Daniel J. Myers. "Introduction: Identity Work, Sameness and Difference in Social Movements." In *Identity Work in Social Movements,* edited by Jo Reger, Daniel J. Myers, and Rachel L. Einwohner, 1–13. Minneapolis: University of Minnesota Press, 2008.

Engel, Stephen. *The Unfinished Revolution: Social Movement Theory and the Gay and Lesbian Movement*. Cambridge: Cambridge University Press, 2001.

Enke, Ann. *Finding the Movement: Sexuality, Contested Space and Feminist Activism*. Durham, NC: Duke University Press, 2007.

Ensler, Eve. *The Vagina Monologues*. New York: Villard, 2001.

Erikson, Robert S., Gerald C. Wright, and John P. McIver. *Statehouse Democracy*. New York: Cambridge University Press, 1993.

Eskenazi, E. "Speak from the 'I': I've done C-R in the 70s, 80s and 90s." *NOW News*. Files of the New York City Chapter of the National Organization for Women, October/November 1994, 6.

Evans, Meredith A., and Chris Bobel. "'I Am a Contradiction': Feminism and Feminist Identity in the Third Wave." *New England Journal of Public Policy* 1 and 2 (2007): 207–222.

Evans, Sara M. *Tidal Wave: How Women Changed America at Century's End*. New York: The Free Press, 2003.

———. *Personal Politics: The Roots of Women's Liberation in the Civil Rights Movement & The New Left*. New York: Vintage Books, 1980.

Ezekiel, Judith. *Feminism in the Heartland*. Columbus: Ohio State University Press, 2003.

Faludi, Susan. "American Electra: Feminism's Ritual Matricide." *Harper's*, October 2010. http://www.harpers.org/archive/2010/10/0083140/.

———. *Backlash: The Undeclared War Against American Women*. New York: Crown Publishers, 1991.

Feinberg, Leslie. *Transgender Warriors: Making History from Joan of Arc to Dennis Rodman*. Boston: Beacon Press, 1996.

Ferree, Myra Marx. "Soft Repression: Ridicule, Stigma, and Silencing in Gender-Based Movements." In *Authority in Contention, Research in Social Movements, Conflict and Change*, edited by Daniel J. Myers and Daniel M. Cress 25 (2004): 85–101.

Ferree, Myra Marx, and Beth B. Hess. *Controversy and Coalition: The New Feminist Movement Across Three Decades of Change*. New York: Twayne, 1994.

Ferree, Myra Marx, and Carol McClurg Mueller. "Feminism and the Women's Movement: A Global Perspective." In *The Blackwell Companion to Social Movements*, edited by David Snow, Sarah A. Soule, and Hanspeter Kriesi, 576–607. Oxford, UK: Blackwell, 2004.

Findlen, Barbara, ed. *Listen Up: Voices from the Next Feminist Generation*. Seattle, WA: Seal Press, 1995.

Fixmer, Natalie, and Julia T. Wood. "The Personal Is Still Political: Embodied Politics in Third Wave Feminism." *Women's Studies in Communication* 28, 2(2005): 235–257.

Freeman, Jo. *The Politics of Women's Liberation*. New York: Longman, 1975.

Gamson, Joshua. "Messages of Exclusion: Gender, Movements and Symbolic Boundaries." *Gender & Society* 11, 2(1997): 178–199.

Garrison, Ednie Kaeh. "Are We on a Wavelength Yet? On Feminist Oceanography, Radios and Third Wave Feminism." In *Different Wavelengths: Studies of the Contemporary Women's Movement*, edited by Jo Reger, 237–256. New York: Routledge, 2005.

———. "U.S. Feminism—Girl Style! Youth (Sub)Cultures and the Technologies of the Third Wave." *Feminist Studies* 26, 1(2000): 141–170.

Zollinger Giele, Janet. *Two Paths to Women's Equality: Temperance, Suffrage and the Origins of Modern Feminism*. New York: Twayne Publishers, 1995.

Giddings, Paula. *When and Where I Enter: The Impact of Black Women on Race and Sex in America*. New York: Bantam, 1984.

Glickman, Rose L. *Daughters of Feminists*. New York: St. Martin's Press, 1993.

Gilmore, Stephanie. "Bridging the Waves: Sex and Sexuality in a Second Wave Organization." In *Different Wavelengths: Studies of the Contemporary Women's Movement*, edited by Jo Reger, 97–116. New York: Routledge, 2005.

———. "Rethinking the Liberal/Radical Divide: The National Organizations for Women in Memphis, Columbus and San Francisco." Ph.D. dissertation, Ohio State University, 2005.

Gilmore, Stephanie, and Elizabeth Kaminski. "A Part and Apart: Lesbian and Straight Feminist Activists Negotiate Identity in a Second-Wave Organization." *Journal of the History of Sexuality* 16, 1(January 2007): 95–113.

Greenaway, T. Eve. "Girls Will Be Boys." Alternet, June 6, 2001. http://www.alternet.org/story/10991/girls_will_be_boys/ /. Retrieved March 22, 2004.

Guenther, Katja M. *Making Their Place: Feminism After Socialism in Eastern Germany*. Palo Alto, CA: Stanford University Press, 2010.

Halcli, Abigail, and Jo Reger. "Strangers in a Strange Land: The Gendered Experiences of Women Politicians in Britain and the United States." In *Feminist Frontiers*, 4th ed., edited by Nancy Whittier, Verta Taylor, and Laurel Richardson, 457–471. New York: McGraw-Hill, 1996.

Hawkesworth, Mary. "The Semiotics of Premature Burial: Feminism in a Postfeminist Age." *Signs: Journal of Culture and Society* 29 (2004): 961–986.

Helmbold, Lois. "Classless and Clueless in NWSA: A History of the Poor and Working Class Caucus." *NWSA Journal* 14, 1(2002): 58–70.

Henry, Astrid. "Solitary Sisterhood: Individualism Meets Collectivity in Feminism's Third Wave." In *Different Wavelengths: Studies of the Contemporary Women's Movement*, edited by Jo Reger. New York: Routledge, 2005.

———. *Not My Mother's Sister: Generational Conflict and Third-Wave Feminism*. Bloomington: Indiana University Press, 2004.

———. "Feminism's Family Problem." In *Catching a Wave: Reclaiming Feminism for the 21st Century*, edited by Rory Dicker and Alison Piepmeier, 209–231. Boston: Northeastern University Press, 2003.

Hernandez, Daisy, and Bushra Rehman, eds. *Colonize This! Young Women of Color on Today's Feminism*. New York: Seal Press, 2002.

Hercus, Cheryl. *Stepping Out of Line: Becoming and Being Feminist*. New York: Routledge, 2005.

Herold, Stephanie. "Young Feminists to Old Feminists: If You Can't Find Us, It's Because We're Online." *Campus Progress,* July 19, 2010.http://www.campusprogress.org/opinions/5914/young-feminists-to-old-feminists-if-you-cant-find-us-its-because-were-online.Retrieved July 20, 2010.

Hewitt, Nancy, ed. *No Permanent Waves: Recasting Histories of U.S. Feminism*. New Brunswick, NJ: Rutgers University Press, 2010.

———. "From Seneca Falls to Suffrage: Reimagining a 'Master' Narrative in U.S. Women's History." In *No Permanent Waves: Recasting Histories of U.S. Feminism*, 15–38. New Brunswick, NJ: Rutgers University Press, 2010.

Heywood, Leslie, and Jennifer Drake, eds. *Third Wave Agenda: Being Feminist, Doing Feminism*. Minneapolis: University of Minnesota Press, 1997.

———. "Introduction." In *Third Wave Agenda: Being Feminist, Doing Feminism*, 1–20. Minneapolis: University of Minnesota Press, 1997.

Hines, Sally. "'I Am a Feminist but . . .,' Transgender Men and Women and Feminism." In *Different Wavelengths: Studies of the Contemporary Women's Movement*, edited by Jo Reger, 57–77. New York: Routledge, 2005.

hooks, bell. "Sisterhood: Political Solidarity Between Women." In *Feminism and Community*, edited by Penny A. Weiss and Marilyn Friedman, 293–316. Philadelphia: Temple University Press, 1995.

———. *Where We Stand: Class Matters*. New York, Routledge, 2000.

———. *Talking Back: Thinking Feminist, Thinking Black*. Boston: South End Press, 1989.

———. *Feminist Theory: From Margin to Center*. Cambridge: South End Press, 1984.

Hunt, Scott, Robert D. Benford, and David A. Snow. "Identity Fields: Framing Processes and the Social Construction of Movement Identities." In *New Social Movements: From Ideology to Identity*, edited by Enrique Larana, Hank Johnston, and *Joseph R. Gusfield*, 185–208. Philadelphia: Temple University Press, 1994.

Hurdis, Rebecca. "Heartbroken: Women of Color Feminism and the Third Wave." In *Colonize This! Young Women of Color on Today's Feminism*, edited by Daisy Hernandez and Bushra Rehman, 279–282. New York: Seal Press, 2002.

Isaac, Larry, and Lars Christiansen. "How the Civil Rights Movement Revitalized Labor Militancy." *American Sociological Review* 67 (2002): 722–46.

Jay, Karla. *Tales of the Lavender Menace: A Memoir of Liberation*. New York: Basic Books, 1999.

Jenkins, J. Craig. "Resource Mobilization Theory and the Study of Social Movements." *Annual Review of Sociology* 9 (1983): 527–553.

Jenkins, J. Craig, and Michael Wallace. "The Generalized Action Potential of Protest Movements: The New Class, Social Trends and Political Exclusion Explanations." *Sociological Forum* 11, 2(1996): 183–207.

Jolles, Majorie. "'Real Women' in Women's Studies: A Reflexive Look at the Theory/Practice Dilemma." *Feminist Teacher* 18, 1(2007): 74–85.

Johnson, Merri Lisa, ed. *Jane Sexes It Up: True Confessions of Feminist Desire*. New York: Four Walls Eight Windows, 2002.

———. "Jane Hocus, Jane Focus." In *Jane Sexes It Up: True Confessions of Feminist Desire*. New York: Four Walls Eight Windows, 2002.

Johnston, Hank. "Protest Cultures: Performances, Artifacts and Ideations." In *Culture, Social Movements and Protest*, edited by Hank Johnston, 3–29. Burlington, VT: Ashgate Publishing Limited, 2009.

Katzenstein, Mary Fainsod. "Feminism Within American Institutions: Unobtrusive Mobilization in the 1980s." *Signs: Journal of Culture and Society* 16, 11(1990): 27–54.

King, Deborah. "Multiple Jeopardy, Multiple Consciousness: The Context of a Black Feminist Ideology." *Signs: Journal of Culture and Society* 14, 1(1988): 42–72.

Kliff, Sarah. "Remember Roe! How Can the Next Generation Defend Abortion Rights When They Don't Think Abortion Rights Need Defending?" *Newsweek*, April 16, 2010. http://www.newsweek.com/2010/04/15/remember-roe.html/.

Koopmans, Ruud. "Protest in Time and Space: The Evolution of Waves of Contention." In *The Blackwell Companion to Social Movements*, edited by David Snow, Sarah A. Soule, and Hanspeter Kriesi, 19–46. Oxford, UK: Blackwell, 2004.

Koyama, Emi. "The Transfeminist Manifesto." In *Catching a Wave: Reclaiming Feminism for the 21st Century*, edited by Rory Dicker and Alison Piepmeier, 244–259. Boston: Northeastern University Press, 2003.

Lanpher, Katherine, moderator. "Are Younger Women Trying to Trash Feminism?" http://www.more.com/news/womens-issues/are-younger-women-trying-trash-feminism-0?page=5 Retrieved October 13, 2008.

Laughlin, Kathleen A., Julie Gallagher, Dorothy Sue Cobble, Eileen Boris, Premilla Nadasen, Stephanie Gilmore, and Leandra Zarnow. "Is It Time to Jump Ship? Historians Rethink the Waves Metaphor." *Feminist Formations* 22, 1(2010): 76–135.

Levy, Ariel. *Female Chauvinist Pigs: Women and the Rise of Raunch Culture.* New York: Free Press, 2005.

———. "The Prisoner of Sex." *New York Magazine*, May 29, 2005. http://nymag.com/nymetro/news/people/features/11907/.

Lorber, Judith. *Paradox of Gender.* New Haven: Yale University Press, 1994.

Mannheim, Karl. "The Problem with Generations." In *Essays on the Sociology of Knowledge*, edited by Paul Keckemeti and Paul Keegan, 276–320. London: Routledge, 1952.

Mansbridge, Jane J. *Why We Lost the ERA.* Chicago: University of Chicago Press, 1986.

Marcus, Sara. *Girls to the Front: The True Story of the Riot Grrrl Revolution.* New York: HarperCollins, 2010.

Martin, Courtney. "The End of the Women's Movement." *The American Prospect*, March 30, 2009. http://prospect.org/cs/articles?article=the_end_of_the_womens_movement/, retrieved March 31, 2009.

Marwell, Gerald, and Pamela Oliver. "Collective Action Theory and Social Movement Research." *Research in Social Movements, Conflicts and Change* 7, 1–27. Greenwich, CT: JAI Press, 1984.

McAdam, Doug. *Freedom Summer.* New York: Oxford University Press, 1990.

McAdam, Doug, John D. McCarthy, and Mayer N. Zald. "Social Movements." In *Handbook of Sociology*, edited by Neil Smelser, 695–737. Newbury Park, CA: Sage Publications, Inc., 1988.

McCammon, Holly J., Courtney Sanders Muse, Harmony D. Newman, and Teresa M. Terrell. "Movement Framing and Discursive Opportunity Structures: The Political Successes of the U.S. Women's Jury Movements." *American Sociological Review* 72, 5(2007): 725–749.

McCarthy, John, and Mayer Zald. "Resource Mobilization and Social Movements: A Partial Theory." *American Journal of Sociology* 82 (May 1977): 1212–1241.

———. "The Trend of Social Movements in America: Professionalization and Resource Mobilization." In *Social Movements in an Organizational Society: Collected Essays*, edited by Mayer Zald and John D. McCarthy, 337–391. New Brunswick, NJ: Transaction Books, 1987.

McCarthy, Kate. "Not Pretty Girls?: Sexuality, Spirituality, and Gender Construction in Women's Rock Music." *The Journal of Popular Culture* 39, 1(2006): 69–94. http://onlinelibrary.wiley.com/doi/10.1111/j.1540-5931.2006.00204.x/abstract/. Retrieved May 31, 2007.

McRobbie, Angela. *The Aftermath of Feminism: Gender, Culture and Social Change.* Los Angeles, CA: Sage Publications, 2009.

Melucci, Alberto. *Nomads of the Present: Social Movements and Individual Needs in Contemporary Society*. Philadelphia: Temple University Press, 1989.

Meltzer, Marisa. "Quiet Riot." *Bust*, June/July 2010, 69–72.

Messner, Michael. *Taking the Field: Women, Men and Sports*. Minneapolis: University of Minnesota Press, 2002.

Meyer, David S. "How Movements Matter." *Contexts* 2, 4 (2003): 30–35.

Meyer, David S. and Suzanne Staggenborg. "Thinking About Strategy." In *Making History: Movements, Strategy, and Social Change*, edited by Jeff Goodwin, Rachel Kutz-Flamenbaum, Gregory Maney, and Deana Rohlinger. Minneapolis: University of Minnesota Press, forthcoming.

Meyer, David S., and Nancy Whittier. "Social Movement Spillover." *Social Problems* 41, 2(1994): 277–298.

Moraga, Cherrie. "Foreword: The War Path of Greater Empowerment." In *Colonize This! Young Women of Color on Today's Feminism*, edited by Daisy Hernandez and Bushra Rehman, xiii. New York: Seal Press, 2002.

Moraga, Cherrie, and Gloria Anzaldua, eds. *This Bridge Called My Back: Writings by Radical Women of Color*. New York: Kitchen Table Women of Color Press, 1981.

———. Introduction to section "Entering the Lives of Others." In *This Bridge Called My Back: Writings by Radical Women of Color*, 23. New York: Kitchen Table Women of Color Press, 1983.

Muscio, Inga. *Cunt: A Declaration of Independence*. 2nd ed. Emeryville, CA: Seal Press, 2002.

Nadasen, Premilla. "Expanding the Boundaries of the Women's Movement: Black Feminism and the Struggle for Welfare Rights." *Feminist Studies* 28, 2(2002): 271–303.

Naples, Nancy, ed. *Community Activism and Feminist Politics: Organizing Across Race, Class and Gender*. New York: Routledge, 1998.

Naples, Nancy. "Confronting the Future, Learning from the Past: Feminist Praxis in the Twenty-First Century." In *Different Wavelengths: Studies of the Contemporary Women's Movement*, edited by Jo Reger, 215–236. New York: Routledge, 2005.

National Women's Studies Association. "NWSA/Ms. Magazine Guide to Women's Studies." 2009. http://www.nwsa.org/msmag/index.php/.

NYC Radical Cheerleaders. "No Justice." http://www.nycradicalcheerleaders.org/. Retrieved November 26, 2009. Web site no longer available.

Nyhoff, Norma. "NOW Conference Gives Young Feminists a Voice." *Say It, Sister, NOW's Blog for Equality*, July 13, 2010. http://www.now.org/news/blogs/index.php/sayit/The Onion. "Women Now Empowered by Everything a Woman Does," 39, 6(2003). http://www.theonion.com/articles/women-now-empowered-by-everything-a-woman-does,1398/. Retrieved February 25, 2003.

O'Reilly, Jane. "The Housewife's Moment of Truth." *Ms. Magazine*, Spring 1972, 54–59.

Orr, Catherine. "Charting the Currents of the Third Wave." *Hypatia: A Journal of Feminist Philosophy* 12, 3(1997): 29–45.

Piepzna-Samarasinha, Leah Lakshmi. "browngirlworld: queergirlofcolor organizing, sistahood, heartbreak." In *Catching a Wave: Reclaiming Feminism for the 21st Century*, edited by Rory Dicker and Alison Piepmeier, 3–16. Boston: Northeastern University Press, 2003.

Pollit, Katha. "Amber Waves of Blame." *The Nation*, May 27, 2009. http://www.the-nation.com/article/amber-waves-blame.

Quart, Alissa. "When Girls Will Be Boys." *New York Times*, March 16, 2008. http://www.nytimes.com/2008/03/16/magazine/16students-t.html/.

Ray, Raka. *Fields of Protest: Women's Movements in India*. Minneapolis: University of Minnesota Press, 1999.

Raymond, Janice. *The Transsexual Empire: The Making of the She-Male*. New York: Teachers College Press, 1979.

Reger, Jo. "Drawing Identity Boundaries: The Creation of Contemporary Feminism." In *Identity Work in Social Movements*, edited by Jo Reger, Daniel J. Myers, and Rachel L. Einwohner, 101–120. Minneapolis: University of Minnesota Press, 2008.

———. "Introduction." In *Different Wavelengths: Studies of the Contemporary Women's Movement*, edited by Jo Reger, xv-xxx. New York: Routledge, 2005.

———. "Organizational 'Emotion Work' Through Consciousness-Raising: An Analysis of a Feminist Organization." *Qualitative Sociology* 27, 2(2004): 205–222.

———. "More than One Feminism: Organizational Structure, Ideology and the Construction of Collective Identity." In *Social Movements: Identity, Culture and the State*, edited by David S. Meyer, Nancy Whittier, and Belinda Robnett, 171–184. New York: Oxford University Press, 2002.

Reger, Jo, and Suzanne Staggenborg. "Patterns of Mobilization in Local Movement Organizations: Leadership and Strategy in Four National Organization for Women Chapters." *Sociological Perspectives* 49, 3(2006): 297–323.

Reger, Jo, and Lacey Story. "Talking About My Vagina: Two College Campuses and the *Vagina Monologues*." In *Different Wavelengths: Studies of the Contemporary Women's Movement*, edited by Jo Reger, 139–160. New York: Routledge, 2005.

Reger, Jo, and Verta Taylor. "Women's Movement Research and Social Movement Theory: A Symbiotic Relationship." *Research in Political Sociology* 10 (2002): 85–121.

Rose, Fred. "Toward a Class-Cultural Theory of Social Movements: Reinterpreting New Social Movements." *Sociological Forum* 12, 3(1997): 461–494.

Roth, Benita. *Separate Roads to Feminism: Black Chicana and White Feminist Movements in America's Second Wave*. New York: Cambridge, 2002.

Roth, Silke. "Dealing with Diversity: The Coalition of Labor Union Women." In *Identity Work in Social Movements*, edited by Jo Reger, Daniel J. Myers, and Rachel L. Einwohner, 213–231. Minneapolis: University of Minnesota Press, 2008.

Rupp, Leila J. and Verta Taylor. "Foreword." In *Different Wavelengths: Studies of the Contemporary Women's Movement*, edited by Jo Reger, xi-xiv. New York: Routledge, 2005.

————. *Drag Queens at the 801 Cabaret*. Chicago: University of Chicago Press, 2003.

————. "Forging Feminist Identity in an International Movement: A Collective Identity Approach to Twentieth Century Feminism." *Signs: Journal of Culture and Society* 24, 2(1999): 363–386.

————. *Survival in the Doldrums: The American Women's Rights Movement, 1945 to 1960s*. New York: Oxford University Press, 1987.

Schneider, Beth. "Political Generations in the Contemporary Women's Movement." *Sociological Inquiry* 58 (1988): 4–21.

Scott, Linda. *Fresh Lipstick: Redressing Fashion and Feminism*. New York: Palgrave Macmillan, 2005.

Seidman, Steven. "Deconstructing Queer Theory, or the Under-theorization of the Social and the Ethical." In *Social Postmodernism: Beyond Identity Politics*, edited by Linda Nicholson and Steven Seidman, 116–141. Cambridge: Cambridge University Press, 1995.

Sherwin, Galen. "Girls Are to Be Seen, Heard, and Believed." *NOW NYC Newsletter*, May/June (1998).

Schilt, Kristin. *Just One of the Guys: Transgender Men and the Persistence of Gender Inequality*. Chicago: University of Chicago Press, 2010.

————. "'The Punk White Privilege Scene:' Riot Grrrl, White Privilege and Zines." In *Different Wavelengths: Studies of the Contemporary Women's Movement*, edited by Jo Reger, 39–56. New York: Routledge, 2005.

Shapiro, Eve. "Drag Kinging and the Transformation of Gender Identities." *Gender & Society* 21, 2(April 2007): 250–271.

Shechter, Therese. *I Was a Teen-age Feminist*. Women Make Movies, 2005.

Snitow, Ann, and Rachel Dupleissis. *The Feminist Memoir Project: Voices from Women's Liberation*. New York: Three Rivers Press, 1998.

Snow, David A., E. Burke Rochford, Jr., Steven K. Worden, and Robert D. Benford. "Frame Alignment, Micromobilization, and Movement Participation." *American Sociological Review* 51 (1986): 464–481.

Soule, Sarah. "The Student Divestment Movement in the United States and Tactical Diffusion: The Shanty Town Protest." *Social Forces* 75 (1997): 855–883.

Springer, Kimberly. "Strongblackwomen and Black Feminism: A Next Generation?" In *Different Wavelengths: Studies of the Contemporary Women's Movement*, edited by Jo Reger, 3–21. New York: Routledge, 2005.

Staggenborg, Suzanne. "Beyond Culture Versus Politics: A Case Study of a Local Women's Movement." *Gender & Society* 15 (2001): 507–530.

————. "Can Feminist Organizations Be Effective?" In *Feminist Organizations: Harvest of the New Women's Movement*, edited by Myra Marx Ferree and PatricaYancey Martin, 339–355. Philadelphia: Temple University Press, 1995.

Staggenborg, Suzanne, Donna Eder and Lori Sudderth. "Women's Culture and Social Change: Evidence from the National Women's Music Festival." *Berkeley Journal of Sociology* 38 (1993/4): 31–55.

Staggenborg, Suzanne, and Amy Lang. "Culture and Ritual in the Montreal Women's Movement." *Social Movement Studies* 6 (2007): 177–194.

Staggenborg, Suzanne, and Verta Taylor. "Whatever Happened to the Women's Movement?" *Mobilization: The International Journal of Research and Theory about Social Movements, Protest and Collective Behavior* 10, 1(2005): 37–52.

Steinem, Gloria. "Why Young Women Are More Conservative." In *Outrageous Acts and Everyday Rebellions*, 211–218. New York: Holt, Rinehart and Winston, 1983.

Straus, Tamara. "Is Feminism Dead?" Alternet, February 11, 2000, http://www.alternet.org/story/436/.

Sullivan, J. Courtney, and Courtney E. Martin, eds. *Click: When We Knew We Were Feminists*. New York: Avalon Publishing Group, 2010.

Tarrow, Sidney. *Struggle, Politics and Reform: Collective Action, Social Movements and Cycles of Protest*. Ithaca, NY: Cornell University Press, 1989.

Taylor, Judith. "The Problem of Women's Sociality in Contemporary North American Feminist Memoir." *Gender & Society* 22, 6(2008): 705–727.

Taylor, Verta. "Sources of Continuity in Social Movements: The Women's Movement in Abeyance." *American Sociological Review* 54 (1989): 761–775.

Taylor, Verta, Leila J. Rupp, and Joshua Gamson. "Performing Protest: Drag Shows as Tactical Repertoire of the Gay and Lesbian Movement." *Authority in Contention, Research in Social Movements, Conflict and Change* 25 (2004): 105–137.

Taylor, Verta, and Nancy Whittier. "The New Feminist Movement." In *Feminist Frontiers IV*, edited by Laurel Richardson, Verta Taylor, and Nancy Whittier, 544–561. New York: McGraw-Hill, 1997.

———. "Collective Identity in Social Movement Communities: Lesbian Feminist Mobilization." In *Frontiers in Social Movement Theory*, edited by Aldon D. Morris and Carol McClurg Mueller, 104–129. New Haven and London: Yale University Press, 1992.

Taylor, Verta, and Nella Van Dyke. "'Get Up, Stand Up': Tactical Repertoires of Social Movements." In *The Blackwell Companion to Social Movements*, edited by David Snow, Sarah Soule, and Hanspeter Kriesi, 262–293. Malden, MA: Blackwell Publishing, 2004.

Taylor, Verta, Nella Van Dyke, and Ellen Ann Andersen. "Culture and Mobilization: Tactical Repertoires, Same-Sex Weddings and the Impact on Gay Activism." *American Sociological Review* 74 (December 2009): 865–890.

Thom, Mary, ed. *Letters to Ms.: 1972–1987*. New York: Henry Holt Co., 1987.

Thompson, Becky. "Multiracial Feminism: Recasting the Chronology of Second Wave Feminism." *Feminist Studies* 28 (2002): 337–360.

Tilly, Charles. *Social Movements, 1768–2004*. Boulder, CO: Paradigm Publishers, 2004.

———. *From Mobilization to Revolution*. New York: Random House, 1978.

TransGender Michigan. *TransGender Michigan: Basic Terms and Definitions*. Detroit, MI: TransGender Michigan, 2004.

Van Dyke, Nella, Sarah A. Soule, and Verta A. Taylor. "The Targets of Social Movements: Beyond a Focus on the State." In *Authority in Contention, Research in Social Movements, Conflicts and Change* 25 (2004): 25–51. Edited by Daniel J. Myers and Daniel M. Cress.

Valenti, Jessica. *Full Frontal Feminism: A Young Woman's Guide to Why Feminism Matters*. Emeryville, CA: Seal Press, 2007.

Vogel, Traci. "Push Anywhere: An Interview with Nancy Hartsock." *The Stranger* 10 (March 29–April 4, 2001), 28. http://www.thestranger.com/seattle/push-anywhere/Content?oid=6882/.

Walker, Alice. *In Search of Our Mother's Gardens: Womanist Prose*. New York: HBJ Publishing, 1983.

Walker, Rebecca. "Foreword." In *The Fire This Time: Young Activists and the New Feminism*, edited by Viven Labaton and Dawn Lundy Martin, xiv. New York: Anchor Books, 2004.

———, ed. *To Be Real: Telling the Truth and Changing the Face of Feminism*. New York: Anchor Books, 1995.

Wallace, Michelle. "To Hell and Back: On the Road with Black Feminism in the 1960s & 1970s." In *Feminist Memoir Project: Voices from Women's Liberation*, edited by Rachel Blau DuPlessis and Ann Snitow, 426–442. (New York: Three Rivers Press, 1998.

Ward, Jane. "Diversity Discourse and Multi-identity Work in Lesbian and Gay Organizations." In *Identity Work in Social Movements*, edited by Jo Reger, Daniel J. Myers, and Rachel L. Einwohner, 233–255. Minneapolis: University of Minnesota Press, 2008.

Whittier, Nancy. *The Politics of Child Sexual Abuse: Emotions, Social Movements and the State*. New York: Oxford University Press, 2009.

———. "Political Generations, Micro-cohorts, and the Transformation of Social Movements." *American Sociological Review* 67 (1997): 760–778.

———. *Feminist Generations: The Persistence of the Radical Women's Movement*. Philadelphia: Temple University Press, 1995.

Winerip, Michael. "Where to Pass the Torch." *New York Times*, March 8, 2009. http://nytimes.com/2009/03/08/fashion/08generationb.html/.

Wolf, Naomi. "Who Won Feminism? Hint: She's the Diva Who Ran Cosmo." *Washington Post*, May 3, 2009. http://www.washingtonpost.com/wp-dyn/content/article/2009/05/01/AR2009050101859.html/.

Zald, Mayer. "Ideologically Structured Action: An Enlarged Agenda for Social Movement Research." *Mobilization: An International Journal* 5, 1(2000): 1–16.

Zarnow, Leandra. "From Sisterhood to Girlie Culture: Closing the Great Divide between Second and Third Wave Cultural Agenda." In *No Permanent Waves: Recasting Histories of U.S. Feminism*, edited by Nancy A. Hewitt, 273–302. (New Brunswick, NJ: Rutgers University Press, 2010.

Ziegler, Kathryn. "'Formidable-Femininity': Performing Gender and Third Wave Feminism in a Women's Self Defense Class." Doctoral dissertation, Southern Illinois University—Carbondale, 2008.

Index

Muscio, Inga, 34, 208n8
Myers, Dan, 20

N

Nadasen, Premilla, 21
names, 178
Naples, Nancy, 86
NARAL (National Abortion Rights
    Action League), 13, 26, 42, 48,
    95, 118, 130
National American Woman Suffrage
    Association, 19
National Black Feminist Organization,
    21
National Conference on Women (1977),
    12
National Woman Suffrage Association
    (NWSA), 10, 11
National Woman's Party, 11, 18
National Women's Political Caucus, 12
networks, 10, 12, 40
    personal networks, 40–41
New Left, 11, 19, 59
New York Radical Women, 12, 15
New York Times
    "Feminists Find Unity Is Elusive," 85
    "Where to Pass the Torch?", 4
Newsweek magazine
    "Remember Roe!", 20
Nineteenth Amendment, 11
Northwest feminist communities, 6, 23,
    24, 32. *See also* Green City
NOW (National Organization of
    Women), 7, 12, 13, 15, 33, 34, 42,
    48, 95, 118, 122, 130, 155, 190, 193
    conferences, 191–193
    lesbians in organization of, 22
    president candidates 2009, 20, 205n84
    Women's Strike for Equality, 15–16
nowhere, concept of, 4–5, 8, 24, 32, 56,
    185–186

O

O'Neill, Terry, 20, 192
Onion, The, 186
oppression, movements against, 59, 69,
    132–158 *passim*
O'Reilly, Jane, 55
Organization of Pan Asian
    American Women, 21
organizations
    change and, 95, 117–123
    fund raising, 96
Orr, Catherine, 87
"others," 19
outcomes, 24

P

Pappas, Marcia, 85
Paul, Alice, 11, 19
pay equity, 14
performance, 109
"personal is political," 55, 93
Piepzna-Samarasinha, Leah Lakshmi,
    159
place, dimensions of, 32, 207n1
Planned Parenthood, 13, 26,
    95, 118
political fields, 6
political generations, 6, 17–18, 20
political opportunity theories, 6
politics of location, 207n1
Pollit, Katha, 85–86
post-feminist era, 13
President's Commission on the
    Status of Women, 12
privilege, 132–158. *See also* movements
    against oppression
    appropriation and, 146–147, 156
    masculine, 176, 180, 181
Pro-Choice America, 42
protagonists, 18
protest movements, 31